Award-winning producer D for producing the high musical special in television history, *Michael Jackson: 30th Anniversary Celebration, The Solo Years,* which was seen by more than ninety million people worldwide. David also produced the critically acclaimed comeback of Liza Minelli in *Liza's Back,* which had a triumphant five-day run at the Royal Albert Hall.

In addition to this, he produced the American Cinema Awards show for eleven years and the International Achievement in Arts Awards for four years. To date, he has produced more than one hundred shows globally, including specials for Whitney Houston, Frank Sinatra, Ginger Rogers, the Four Tops and Elizabeth Taylor. He has raised millions of dollars for various charities throughout the world.

He became an international star on *I'm a Celebrity . . . Get me Out of Here!,* and, as Angie Dickinson says, 'the world got to see what I already knew'.

Simply the Gest

The Autobiography

David Gest

with Garry Jenkins

headline
review

First published in 2007 by
HEADLINE PUBLISHING GROUP

First published in paperback in 2007 by HEADLINE REVIEW
An imprint of HEADLINE PUBLISHING GROUP

1

Cataloguing in Publication Data is available from the British Library

ISBN 978 0 7553 1697 7

Typeset in Bell MT by Avon DataSet Ltd,
Bidford-on-Avon, Warwickshire

Printed and bound in Great Britain by Clays Ltd, St Ives plc

HEADLINE PUBLISHING GROUP
An Hachette Livre UK Company
338 Euston Road
London NW1 3BH

www.headline.co.uk
www.hodderheadline.com

Contents

Acknowledgements

This book is dedicated to my ITV family for their belief
in me as a human being and entertainer:

Paul Jackson
Layla Smith
Natalka Znak
Emma Ford
Marty Benson
Craig Blackhurst
Andy Burgess
Matt Smith
Ben Bradley

My two closest friends in London who
changed my life forever:

Jason Donovan
&
Matt Willis

My best friends of a lifetime:

Michael Jackson
Tito Jackson
Willie Green

Imad Handi

Tristan Rogers

Irwin Lehrhoff

James Ingram

Bruce Cohn

Freda Payne

Angie Dickinson

Tom Cuddy

Leigh Shockey

Larry & Judy Moss

Deborah Cox & Lascelles Stephens

Candi Staton

Joanne Lichtenstein

Vittorio Manya & Manuela Bettarello

Joey Melotti

Michael Bolton

Chuck Imhof

Tom Gleason

Deniece Williams

David & Christie Weild

Aaron Sheldon

Edward Bearman

Petula Clark

My second mum:

Jane Russell

But most importantly to:

The People Of The UK

for all the love you have shown me.

'There are no second acts in American life.'

F. Scott Fitzgerald

'Bullshit.'

David Gest

A Different Beat

Rice paddies and sardines. That's all I can see, rice paddies and sardines.

Some people can remember all sorts of details about their early childhood: the toys they had, the pets, the happy, loving moments they shared with their parents. I can't. My first five years are a blank. The only things I can recall vividly are being surrounded by paddy fields full of workers and eating sardines. Lots and lots of sardines. I was born in May 1953, somewhere in Taiwan.

When they met, my mother was training to be a

nun and my father was a fisherman. They were immediately attracted to each other because he only had a right leg and she only had a left leg. I think men and women are always looking for partners who complement them, and my mother and father really did find the other half of the jigsaw. They made a perfect couple: together they had a working pair of legs.

When I was born they were going to call me Hoppity. It was a joke I think. But for some reason, I really don't know why, they changed their minds and christened me David. I was one of seven children, six boys and a girl. My sister was called Ting Ling and one of my brothers was called Ying Ling.

Apart from the paddy fields of rice and the endless meals of sardines, I can't remember anything about those early years until we moved to Hungary when I was five. I don't know why we went there. I think it might have had something to do with my mother's nunnery. Anyhow, it was while we were in Hungary that my sister, five brothers and I were adopted by a family from California and my life started all over again.

I don't know why my real parents gave us up for adoption, or how my adopted parents came to find us in Hungary. All I remember is moving into a nice big house with a garden and a giant fridge full of American food. Not a single sardine in sight.

I took to life there pretty well. I started playing Little League baseball and watching television. My brothers didn't all settle down so easily however. Ying Ling and Sing Ling ran away from home. My adopted parents tried to find them but they had just disappeared off the face of the earth. Perhaps they were missing the sardines.

I have tried to trace them over the years but with no luck. I don't know what happened to them, or to my parents back in Hungary or Taiwan or wherever they ended up. My other three brothers, whose names were Dick Ling, Ring Ling and little Ding Ling, also disappeared within a few months of our move to the States. I remember my sister would always play with that little Ding Ling, and I think she misses him the most. She has searched all over the world for that Ding Ling, who I am sure is now much bigger!

My connections with that part of my life are non-existent. I don't own a photograph of any of them and I have not seen them or heard anything about them since. I doubt very much I'll ever get to see them now. Too much time has passed.

People often shake their heads when they hear me recall my childhood. Some tell me they find it so moving and sad. Some cry uncontrollably. When they do, I always tell them the same thing: please don't shed any tears for me. Whatever the difficulties and deprivations of my early life, I have gone on to have a rich and rewarding career. I have met some of the most interesting and famous people in the world, had some unforgettable experiences. Really, I have had a great life. And besides, it's not as if the story is true . . .

The truth is there wasn't a lot of love in my real childhood either. A friend once told me that he thought my entire life had been driven by a need to find the love I didn't have back then. He was absolutely right.

I was born in Los Angeles on 11 May 1953. My parents, Jesse and Eleanor (or Ellie) Gest, were Jewish, although I believed in Christianity at an early age. I felt both religions had great things to offer. People say I got my looks from my mother, who was dark-haired like me. My younger sister, Barbara, had lighter hair like our father. Until I was in my early teens, we all lived in Van Nuys, a middle-class suburb of the San Fernando Valley in Los Angeles. The house, on a street called Sunnyslope, was nothing too exciting, just three bedrooms with a garden; pretty much like most of the other houses in that area, on the outside at least.

My parents were pretty well off. My father had a firm that became huge and invested millions of dollars for his clients. I think it was just called Jesse Gest Investments. He was very good at what he did and made very wise investments but that meant he was always wrapped up in his work. My mother worked too, as a substitute teacher, even though she didn't need to. She was quite a serious person. Like my father, she had been university educated and lived in a very intellectual world. They both enjoyed reading and history. My mother wasn't a woman who just liked to go out and shop or go to luncheons with other women. That wasn't her cup of tea.

They weren't the loving parents that so many of my friends had who had this bonding with their parents. With me, there was no bond. I think the problem was that my parents never had the time to give me much attention or show me a lot of love. It wasn't that they didn't care for me, it was just that they were so involved in their own lives and careers.

What made it even harder for me was the fact that, as well as being distant, my parents were kind of tough and miserly people. They didn't believe in giving me much other than the basic necessities, although I believe it was different with my sister. Their philosophy was, 'We are here to put a roof over your heads and give you some meals, the rest is down to you.'

My father drove around in a big, black Lincoln Continental but my parents gave me an allowance of $3 a week. When I was at Erwin Street Elementary School it was enough to pay for five school meals at 35 cents each, leaving $1.25 for other things. If I wanted to see a movie, that was 75 cents; if I had popcorn and a drink, there went the other 50 cents. If I didn't get popcorn and a drink, I could spend it on a record or play one round of miniature golf or go bowling. They wouldn't give me more. If I wanted anything else they would say, 'Go out and earn it.' I was only around seven years old so there wasn't much I could do about that.

At one stage, I knew my parents had become millionaires but somehow I felt like I was growing up in the poorest ghetto in the world. I don't resent it now, but I did resent it then.

My father believed in beating me for the stupidest of reasons. He seemed to get a joyful satisfaction out of hitting me with a strap. At the tender age of seven, I got caught for buying a whole bag of candy bars, which I had hidden under my bed. Somehow he found them, and I was beaten unmercifully for what is normal for most kids of that age: simple defiance and a love of sugar.

When most children would have received a reprimand, I was always beaten. I think I built up a tolerance to pain at a very early age, as I have always been strong. And whether it's being bitten by an alligator or a snake, or hit by someone in a fight, I have never been afraid.

Being beaten constantly is not something a child should have to endure. When he was frustrated with my mother or with his business or just in a bad mood, my father's anger seemed to be taken out on me. Even though I was very angry, I actually felt sorry for him early on, as I knew he was not a happy man. I have always been so jealous of people that were close to their parents. My strong-willed character was formed at an early age, and by the time I was ten I already felt I was on my own. Oddly enough, my sister was the apple of their eye and she was treated completely differently.

Looking back on it now, I can see that being raised in this way had a big impact on me. I was left to fend for myself, and that made me go out and find friends, something I have done ever since.

People were not as crazy in the early 1960s, so, in a community like Van Nuys, you could just walk into people's houses because the doors were not locked. When I started elementary school I made a lot of friends. I would usually come home from school to find my house empty, so I would go round to friends' places and hang out with them.

Van Nuys was a really middle-class area, mostly white, with kids from backgrounds that seemed so much more interesting than mine. Among my friends in elementary school was Ed Homeier, the son of a former child actor named Skip Homeier and Mitch Factor, whose family was related to the Max Factor company. There was also Mike Holtzer, Kevin Wolf, Nico March, Dick Gumpert, Sheldon Draiman, Jeff Croke, Amy Raff, John Grossman and a girl called Dee Dee Caplan, who went on to become an attorney in the entertainment business. A girl called Laurie Chait was my first girlfriend in school. I was around ten. She was my sweetheart, and we would hold hands and kiss.

We were a very tight-knit group. We all lived in the same area and we had a lot of fun. We used to play Little League baseball together. I was a second baseman and I could hit. I hit a grand slam home run in the 8th inning once. The opposition team struck out in the next inning and we won the game. That was the best moment of my early child-hood. I enjoyed competing and liked to win.

The other useful thing my upbringing did was to make me into an entrepreneur. At home there wasn't an abundance of anything. I had two pairs of shoes, not ten or twenty pairs like the other kids around me. I had three or four pairs of pants. My parents' attitude was, 'Here are your school clothes. You want more, go earn them.' So I knew that if I wanted to have money, I would have to earn it myself. That's exactly what I did.

When I was in the fourth grade, my cousin Bob Rosenthal and I decided to launch our own newspaper, *The Dennis the Menace News*. Dennis the Menace (the American version, not the British one) was huge then.

Bob and I spent three days producing a four-page newspaper filled with drawings and stories. We then hand-copied 400 of them and headed out into the neighbourhood, selling subscriptions for $1 each.

At first we thought we must have been pretty good salesmen because we sold all 400 copies. Bob and I were thinking, 'We're rich!' When we sat down and counted our money however, we realised what we had done. That $1 investment had bought people a year's worth of editions. We would have to produce another 365 newspapers, hand-writing every edition and then copying them, for no extra money.

We were only nine years old, but even we could work out we would be bankrupt before we started. Somehow we just hadn't figured that out in advance. Our business acumen was sorely lacking.

When we realised what we had done, Bob said we should just keep the money but when I told my parents they said we had to return every single dollar. So we went back to every single one of the 400 houses and gave each person back their money. In hindsight, I can see it was a valuable lesson.

That's when I learned that you had better think things through when you go into business.

The next venture I started was much more successful. Right next to my house was a lot of land, a twenty-square-foot patch of dirt. I built a miniature golf course with the help of a friend. I got hold of some grass and pieces of old wood, then dug some holes in the ground and came up with different designs for each hole. Kids would come around to play after school and we would charge them 50 cents a go. We also sold lemonade, which we made ourselves, and charged 5 cents a glass.

It was only five holes, but the kids used to love coming to my miniature golf course. I had that running for two years while I was in the fifth and sixth grades, and this time I didn't have to give anyone their money back.

The other thing about my childhood was that it hardened me up. My parents were tough, so I learned to be tough too. When I was in fifth grade, there was this one kid, Kevin, who was already six feet tall. I remember getting into a fist fight with him.

What happened was, one day he called a girl a 'fat pig'. I told him he had to take it back because it was unkind, but he wouldn't. I knew that if I fought him I would lose, so I decided to break his nose before he beat the shit out of me. I took one great swing and broke his nose. I will never forget it; that kid was bleeding everywhere.

He beat the hell out of me, of course. I was black and blue and I had a sprained arm, sprained knee and tons of bruises but I was so proud to have broken his nose that it didn't matter. Kevin always stayed away from me after that, and he never mistreated that girl again.

It wasn't surprising, I suppose, that the other thing my parents' treatment made me do was rebel, and boy did I rebel.

Until I was ten years old or so, I had been a pretty well-behaved kid. It was around the time I was in sixth grade that my wild side started to come out. From then on I started drumming to a different beat. I've never stopped.

There was a teacher at school who had always been mean to everybody. I thought it was so unjust. Students had to stand in the corner when they were bad. One day I got in five minutes late after physical education because I had to pick up all the baseball mitts and bats and turn them in. This teacher was always picking on me and made me stand in the corner for not being at my desk on time.

One day I got to class three or four minutes early. I had found this firecracker and my friends and I attached a longer fuse to it and put it in the closet where the teacher's purse was. We thought it would just make a little bit of a noise that would scare her. It blew the closet to pieces. Fortunately, the closet was at the other end of the classroom from where she was sitting. When that thing exploded, the teacher went crazy.

She saw that it was a firecracker and tried over and over to get somebody to confess. She lined us up and started interrogating us. It was now a matter of survival. I knew that if she found out it was me, I was going to be in big trouble, so I spun some line or other. That was when I learned to lie really well, to come up with a story and deliver it with a deadpan face. It was far from the last time I would use that particular skill.

Three things immediately spring to mind about my extended family. First, it was huge. My mother was one of 14 children, so I had 284 cousins on her side of the family alone, with another 148 on my father's side. Second, it was a family who loved to tell stories, something I think I might have inherited. The thing I remember most about them, however, is that they were really weird.

When I was a kid, for instance, I used to go to visit my cousins who lived outside Philadelphia. They were cousins on my mother's side of the family: Robert and his wife Honey and their two children Dickie and Lollie, who we all used to call Lollipop. I visited them every year from about the age of eight until I was fourteen. Then I had to stop going there. Forever.

Robert and Honey were always fighting. They used to have these stand-up rows, usually because she had caught him cheating on her. When he was drunk, Robert used to tell stories. He would brag that he was a real ladies' man. Once he told me that he had had eight women in one night. Not only that, he had brought them all to multiple orgasms. He then explained to me what an orgasm was! He also told me that every boy grows a third leg between his regular two legs and the more it grows, the happier you are in life. He told me he was very very happy because his had grown into a large tree branch! He was very funny when he was drunk.

What happened was, one day, when I was around fourteen or fifteen, Honey caught Robert in bed with three women. Honey was a very sensual woman. She had huge breasts and used to say to me, 'Some women milk cows but I was meant to milk men.' So she didn't take kindly to Robert fooling around.

She went nuts and chopped both Robert's testicles off. She then shot him and the three women in the bed. She then killed herself.

The effect on the kids was pretty bad. Dickie became a drug addict and died at nineteen. Their daughter, Lollie, joined a nunnery and has been cloistered ever since.

Every now and again I think about Robert and how weird it was that they buried him minus his testicles and with just a large tree branch.

What happened to Robert taught me to be very careful what you do because you never know what kind of nuts are out there. It also taught me that you never know who's missing nuts!

On the subject of nuts, I also had a cousin, Caroline, who lived in Chicago. She was another headcase. She knocked out all her husband's teeth with a hammer.

She did it when they were having dinner one night. He must have said something she didn't like because she smashed his mouth in and then said, 'That'll teach you to talk.' Obviously it did. He was in so much pain, he didn't speak much again after that.

Caroline ran away after that happened and they got divorced. He sued her on the grounds that he had no teeth and he won. He never had them replaced, but he sleeps with all his broken teeth under his pillow, a superstition that obviously brings him comfort.

When I was eleven, I went to Milliken Junior High in Sherman Oaks. I picked up where I left off at elementary school. Soon after we started there, my friends and I made these cherry bombs, which we put inside the toilet. We took off the cistern lid and stuck them in there on a timer, and – bam! – they exploded. There was water everywhere and the water department had to be called in. The staff were livid but I kept the straightest face when they questioned me.

I still drummed to a different beat. The main difference now was that I took more of an interest in girls. My first real girlfriend was called Lisa. She was in the same class as I was. She was really wild, and she taught me a lot.

Lisa had a real reputation at school, mainly because of a story everyone had heard about her and a guy called Ron, who was in the year ahead of us. Ron had wanted to have sex with Lisa and she had agreed to give him a blow job. The only problem was that she had never given a blow job before. She understood that you had to put the guy's penis in your mouth but thought you were supposed to bite. When Ron took off his pants and lay down, she started chomping on his penis. Ron started screaming. Naturally, Lisa thought she was doing well, so the louder Ron screamed the more she chomped.

By the time Lisa realised something was wrong there was blood all over the place. She had almost bitten his penis off. I heard she had to run a mile to a phone booth to call for an ambulance. They took Ron to hospital and he had to have seventeen stitches in his penis. She was a hero after that at school. People thought it was the funniest thing ever. It must have been odd for his parents to visit him in the hospital with his little penis in a splint.

In about 1983 or 1984, I went out to eat at a place on Ventura Boulevard called the Hot Dog Show with Michael McDonald from the Doobie Brothers. It was a cold day and Michael and I were having split pea soup. In walked this guy Ron. He looked very effeminate but I knew it was the same guy who had had the run-in with Lisa. I told the story to Michael and he spat his pea soup all over my new shirt. He was dying laughing and said he didn't believe me. So I went up to the guy and asked him if he remembered me. He said no. I asked him whether he remembered this girl Lisa at Milliken Junior High School. He started laughing. He told me he had been gay ever since then.

Anyhow, the good news for me was that Lisa had learned a lot since her experience with Ron. I used to sneak into her bedroom at night so I could sleep with her. Her bedroom was on the first floor of a two-storey house; there was a little alleyway and she would open the window. It was pretty risky, with her father there. He used to beat her with a strap on her breasts. How weird is that?

Lisa was very funny. She used to give me hickeys, or love bites, and had this great sense of humour. Even better, she was into the thing that, by the age of eleven, started to become more important to me than anything else: music.

Music came into my life in September 1964, when I enrolled at the Ted Raden Dancing School. The big dance at the time was the Slauson. ('One, two, three, step, kick.')

When you did well in the class, you got to pick a free 45 record. I did pretty well, so I got to pick some records. The first one I ever chose was Jan & Dean's 'Ride the Wild Surf'. And from then on, music was like a new world opening up to me.

I remember hearing all these songs, hits like Shirley Ellis's 'The Name Game' and Gary Lewis and the Playboys' 'This Diamond Ring' and 'Save Your Heart for Me'. I thought it was the coolest music I'd ever heard. I was like a kid in a candy store.

At Christmas that year, my parents took me to the May Company, a department store in North Hollywood, to get a Christmas gift. I chose my first record album, naturally: *Downtown* by Petula Clark, who I was in love with. It was the first album I ever bought. While Dusty Springfield was the biggest female vocalist in England in the sixties, Petula Clark was up there with The Beatles and The

Supremes in America. She was it, she was our Madonna. I used to have her picture on my wall.

If I inherited my love of music and entertainment from anyone in my family, it was from my maternal grandmother, Bess Berneger. She was the most fantastic woman I had ever met. She was so dignified and elegant. She had real class.

She had worked as a ticket-taker in a movie theatre in New York during the silent era and ever since then Bess had loved the cinema and music. I used to go and stay with her and my grandfather, Herman, at their home in Los Angeles. I would go with her to see double bills at the Fairfax and Beverly cinemas. I remember watching films like *The Carpetbaggers* with Carroll Baker, *The Singing Nun* with Debbie Reynolds and *Taras Bulba* with Yul Brynner. I loved it.

My grandmother understood early on that I had a real love for the arts. It wasn't something my parents ever noticed but then they didn't notice anything much about me. When she heard me talking about music, my grandmother began to give me money to go and buy 45s at a record store called The Frigate, on the corner of Third and Beverly Boulevard.

She was an incredible woman. I really dug her a lot and I wish she had been alive to see my success. She had died by the time I really made it in the music business.

Lisa and I used to ride our bikes or hitchhike all the way from Van Nuys to North Hollywood, where the best record stores were. We would go to the record section at the May Company department store. There was also another record store there called ATV, where they used to get all these promotional copies of records from the record companies. The albums back then cost $3.98 (mono) and $4.98 (stereo) for the bestsellers. They would sell these promotional copies for $1.98.

If Lisa and I didn't have the money, we'd steal the records. Lisa had a technique where she would pick up all these 45s and stuff them into her jacket. I remember one time we went to Sears, one of the biggest department stores in the city. Lisa had put on a new big, baggy coat that day, with the intention of clearing out the racks in their record department.

When we arrived, however, a security lady spotted Lisa straight away. She knew what Lisa was planning to do and she wasn't going to let her do it.

So Lisa and this guard had a standoff. It went on for about an hour or so, with Lisa pretending to browse and the guard pretending not to be watching Lisa.

At that point, Lisa turned to me and said, 'Run!' She then started grabbing all these Beatles albums and putting them in her jacket. She did it right in front of this lady and then ran down the stairs and out the door. We ran like the wind and I was laughing all the way. Lisa always made me laugh. She had balls, perhaps more than I did.

Soon after she stole all that stuff from Sears, I tried the same thing at a place called Thrifty Drugs, right down the street on Laurel Canyon in North Hollywood. The store was a part of a chain and they sold records. I went in there and stuck nine albums under my jacket.

As I was walking out, this security guy came up to me. 'Excuse me, young man, what's under your jacket?' he asked me.

'Nothing,' I said.

'Let me see,' he said, tugging open my jacket. 'Wait right here, I'm calling the police.'

He went off to make the call and I just ran out the door, leaving the records in the store. I rode my bike the five miles back home faster than I had ever cycled in my life. I took a different route. If I had been caught my parents would have sent me away. I stopped shoplifting there and then.

Back then I didn't really know what a concert was until Lisa started taking me to places where bands played live. We used to hitchhike from the Valley, or take the RTD bus. When we didn't have money, we would take some from our parents' wallets. We did what we had to do. Music was everything to us. I knew that the worst that could happen was that my father would beat me. His beatings no longer scared me and I didn't cry anymore, which made him more furious.

One of my first experiences of speaking to a genuine singing star was when The Four Tops played at the Whisky a Go Go. I called the Whisky one night in 1965 and the operator actually put me through to the dressing room. Oddly enough, Duke Fakir of The Four Tops answered the phone! I asked him to send me an autographed picture and he did. Ironically, years later, we became really good friends. The Four Tops played at an evening honouring me and I did a show honouring them in London. They became an important part of my life. Levi Stubbs, their lead singer, is one of my all-time favourites and a smile still comes to my face every time I hear 'I Can't Help Myself (Sugar Pie, Honey Bunch)' or 'Reach Out, I'll Be There'.

During my childhood, acts would perform at places like the Whisky, the Troubadour, PJ's, the Greek Theatre and the Hollywood Bowl. The Greek Theatre was where I experienced my first concert. I saw The Association there, along with 2,500 other people. It was mind-boggling. I heard them perform 'Along Comes Mary', 'Cherish' and 'Windy', their current big hit. It was the coolest thing. The real highlight of the year 1966 was the Teenage Fair, held at the Hollywood Palladium. People like Sonny & Cher played there and it was incredible. Sonny & Cher still remain my favourite duo next to Marvin Gaye and Tammi Terrell, and I collect all their memorabilia. I even have the original gold record presented to them for 'I Got You Babe'.

My parents weren't impressed by show business but that didn't mean there was nobody at home who shared my love of music. At that time, we had an African-American cleaning woman called Geneva. She was a big, heavy-set woman who must have weighed about 390 pounds. Geneva put mountains of mayonnaise on everything. I started doing it too, putting tons of mayonnaise on my bacon and lettuce like it was going out of style. Like Geneva, I could eat a bottle of mayonnaise without even flinching.

Geneva got me into soul music. I remember her bringing over Aretha Franklin's first record on Atlantic, 'I Never Loved a Man the Way I Love You'. She played it for me and I thought it was the coolest sound I had ever heard. I started really getting into black records. She would go to a store called Dolphins of Hollywood and I would give her extra money to buy records for me.

Geneva taught me to appreciate music that normal white kids where I lived were not into. Most kids were into The Beatles and The Rolling Stones. I liked them too but I was now really into The Supremes, The Isley Brothers, Marvin Gaye, Gladys Knight & the Pips, The Temptations, Percy Sledge, Aretha, Deon Jackson, J.J. Jackson, Booker T. & the MGs, Carla Thomas, Otis Redding, Linda Jones, Brenda and the Tabulations, Intruders, Jackie Wilson and Wilson Pickett. When I heard James & Bobby Purify doing 'I'm Your Puppet', I went crazy.

The more I learned about soul music, the more I

loved it. If I was at home at night, I would watch the music shows on television. I loved two shows hosted by Sam Riddle: *Ninth Street West* on Channel 9 and *Hollywood a Go Go*, a show that took place on the Sunset Strip. Then there was *Shindig, Hullabaloo, The Ed Sullivan Show* and *Where the Action Is* and *American Bandstand*, both with Dick Clark.

From the moment I discovered music, that was my life. It was embedded in me and I knew I wanted to have something to do with it. I just didn't know how at that point.

One thing I knew at that time was that I wanted to meet more of the people who were making all this great music. Lisa and I would go down to Sunset Boulevard, where all the record companies were based. Liberty Records was there, which also had the Imperial label and recorded Cher, Johnny Rivers, The Sunshine Company, Vikki Carr and Canned Heat. We worked out that there was a room in a shed at the back of the offices where they kept all the promotional copies of 45s and LPs. We used to go there and get ourselves free records by making friends with the workers.

We were two cute little kids and they would give us ten or more copies of each new record. We would take them to school and sell them for 35 cents each. It was a great way to make extra money.

Lisa and I would also hang around the recording studios. For a while we hung around a place called TT&G which was owned by a man named Ami Hadani. There was this one particular guy there who would often come up to me and ask to look at my records. I remember one time I had with me Iron Butterfly's first album *Heavy*, *Gris-Gris* by Dr. John and the first album by Cream, *Fresh Cream*. He was really interested in them.

After a while, he started talking to me about music in more detail. Then one day he invited me to his recording sessions. His name was Jim Morrison. One of my earliest recollections of listening to live music was sitting in on a session with Jim Morrison and The Doors when they recorded 'Touch Me'.

All in all, I saw Jim Morrison in the recording studio maybe 10 to 20 times. He always treated me as if I was his age. He was really sweet but he always looked sad to me. It would give me great pleasure when I could make him smile. Even then, I liked to make people smile.

After getting in to listen to The Doors, I was invited to all sorts of different recording sessions. I remember seeing Vikki Carr record her song 'Your Heart Is Free Just Like the Wind'. Another time, I watched Eric Burdon and The Animals record. It was a new adventure every time I went there and I loved it.

Musically, it was a real period of change. I liked all kinds of music. Around that time, I remember that The Electric Prunes had a great song called 'I Had Too Much to Dream (Last Night)' that summed up the way I felt at that time in my life. I was already dreaming of living and working in the music world.

I Want Candy

Lisa and I had been like Sonny & Cher, Bonnie and Clyde and, just like them, our time together didn't last.

She was always getting into trouble at Milliken, even more than I was. One day Lisa set all the trash cans on fire, which caused a huge commotion involving the fire brigade. The final straw came when she called one of the PE teachers a lesbian to her face. She got expelled and sent to another school. I didn't see her much after that. I had to get used to heading to the studios and concerts without Lisa. It was sad.

It didn't take me too long to find another girlfriend though. Linda came from a real hippyish family that was really into free love.

Once I was watching television in Linda's room, which was next to her parents' room. They hadn't closed the door all the way and started making love. It was the first time I had ever seen two people have full-on sex in every position. I watched them take off all their clothes, then start doing everything imaginable to each other. Linda's mother was screaming at one point, they were going at it so hard. When they both began yelling so loudly, I was tempted to go in there because I thought they needed help. Thank God I didn't.

It was probably the best sex education I had ever received. Linda's parents answered all my questions about how to do everything. They didn't know I was watching but I don't think they would have cared. Linda was there with me. I asked if this happened a lot and she said, 'All the time.'

Her whole family had that kind of attitude. Everybody would walk around pretty much naked. It was totally different from what went on in my house.

Not surprisingly, Linda was really relaxed about sex. She gave the best blow jobs in the whole school. She would give me one every other day. It became a ritual with us. She also taught me how to taste her pleasures and make her really enjoy it. She was advanced well beyond her years. She was also really, really sweet.

At junior high, I continued the rebellion I had started at the end of elementary school. I got up to all sorts of things. I did things by my rules and didn't care too much about what anybody else said.

I wasn't an academic kid; I couldn't be bothered. When there were tests, my friends and I would steal the papers in advance. The only problem was that we once stole the wrong test. When we handed in the answers they were the right ones – but to another class's paper.

They lined us up in the principal's office and started asking us all these equations. We didn't have a clue, so we all spent four weeks in detention. I was always in detention or doing paper pick-up.

There was a girl in my math class who knew everything but wouldn't let me cheat off her paper. One time, I remember thinking I had had enough of her. So I excused myself for a bathroom break and went to get a giant frog that I had smuggled into school and kept hidden in my locker. This girl was looking down at her paper with her legs spread wide open. As I walked past her I threw the frog on to her chair and it went right up her dress. She never saw me do it. All of a sudden she started screaming and the frog was right there between her legs. She put her hand on this thing and she fainted there and then in the class. While everyone went nuts, I could see her test and copied every answer. I proudly showed my parents the 'A' I got for that paper.

The smart kids were often my targets. On one occasion, we were told that a doctor was coming to school and that everyone would have to provide urine samples for him to analyse. I put lemon juice and prune juice in a test tube and labelled it with the name of the real smart guy in the class. He was always too good to talk to us. They called him in to the principal and almost expelled him for giving fake urine.

By now, the school knew I was the ringleader of most of the mischief that went on. The vice principal called me in and asked whether I had any idea how someone had managed to pass lemon juice and prune juice as urine. I acted affronted. I said I had no idea what he was talking about.

'Mr Gest, did you put that fake urine in a jar and put someone else's name on it?' he asked me. 'Absolutely not. This is disgusting and you should be ashamed of yourself for even asking me! I am leaving,' I said.

I just walked out. I could always keep a straight face.

The most outrageous thing I did was to a teacher who was anti-Semitic and also didn't like African-Americans. A friend and I decided to teach her a lesson.

She always used to go to the cafeteria and get a piece of hot meatloaf, which she would then eat at her desk in the classroom. Sometimes she would have the cafeteria deliver it to her room as she liked to work during lunch. We decided we would make her a different kind of meatloaf. We went back home and pooped, then took the poop and mixed it with ground beef. Then we added hash to it. We put it in a blender and then baked it. Wow, did it stink! The next day we went to the cafeteria and said it was for this teacher. They heated it up and brought it to her with potatoes. We followed her back to her room and sat outside.

I will never forget watching her start to eat that meatloaf. She ate one piece and made this face, as if to say, 'What's this?' Then she took another bite. After the third bite she just spat that shit out. She kept on smelling it. I think she heard us laughing and we ran and ran. We thought it was the funniest thing.

Given all this, I tried to spend as little time as possible in school. Instead, I cut out and went to the beach, a place called POP (Pacific Ocean Park), which Southern Californian kids all loved.

I was constantly writing fake notes saying that I had streptococcus or whatever. One time, I wrote a note because it was coming up to the time of the Teenage Fair and I didn't want to miss one single day of it.

The note said, 'Please excuse David, as he is having his tonsils removed this week.' About two months after that, this doctor came to school and looked at me. He was just a bit surprised to find I still had tonsils, so the school rang my home.

I knew my mother was going to be out, so I got my girlfriend Linda to slip into my house and answer the phone. She told the school that the truth was that I had a huge wart on my penis and they had decided not to tell the school about it so other children wouldn't tease me. They didn't want me embarrassed. Linda told them she thought I might have got it from a frog. The most amazing thing about that was that they actually bought it!

I was not the easiest kid to deal with. Nobody could stop my rebelliousness from getting more and more extreme.

I always liked girls. At that point, I never felt ugly. I did later in life but not then. I never went out with anyone at school for more than a year or so. Like all kids of that age, I wanted a taste of something new all the time.

The girl I went out with after Linda was called Jenny. I think I was in love with her. We used to go and have sex in the bathroom. One day, when we should have been in class, I took her there and was giving her cunnilingus. I had her legs stretched out so that she was against the wall with her feet against the door and I was between her legs, holding her up. Suddenly someone came in. It was a teacher. All she could see were my legs on the floor, so we had to be very quiet.

Unfortunately, I accidentally dropped Jenny.

Before I knew it, she was lying on the floor with no skirt, no nothing. I tried to get away by jumping over the top of the cubicles but the teacher was too quick for me.

She marched us straight off to the principal and explained what had happened. I've always been able to think on my feet, so I said Jenny had an itch on her back and I was trying to scratch it.

'In the girls' bathroom?'

'Yeah, she was very concerned about it. She didn't want anybody else to see it. She thought she might have scurvy.'

'Scurvy! Mr Gest, you're suspended for a week.'

My parents weren't happy. The girl's parents were even more pissed off because their daughter had been discovered lying on the floor, flashing her beaver in front of this teacher.

The other thing I used to do then was imitate voices. I had a knack for it. In the mornings they used to make announcements over the Tannoy system. They would announce the after-school activities for that day, all that kind of stuff. One morning, my friends and I sent the teacher who made the announcements to the other end of the school, saying there was an emergency, and I got into the announcements office. I put on a phony voice and made an announcement.

'Good morning, boys and girls. This morning there will be a sex education class where all children will be able to take off all their clothes. If you have any questions, please come to the principal's office. Thank you.'

Within minutes, there was a horde of teachers crowding around the principal's office. They were all thinking, 'I'm not going to have my kids stripping. I'm not going to have a bunch of penises and vaginas being shown in my class.' I think the principal suspected me but he had no way of proving it.

As far as school was concerned, the final straw came towards the end of ninth grade. There was a male teacher, a very gay guy, who didn't like me because I was disruptive and rebellious. He always used to give candy bars to the students who did well, as if to rub it in the faces of those of us who weren't A students. So one day, at the end of class, I got a girlfriend of mine to distract him by talking to him about something or other. The moment she started talking to him, I went over to his desk where he kept the candy bars. I found about a hundred of them in his drawer and just grabbed them all, stuffing them into my pockets and school bag. As soon as I got out, I started throwing them to kids around the school and dropping them on the lawn.

It didn't take him long to realise what I had done and he was soon chasing after me. I saw him coming down the corridor and just ran. He couldn't keep up with me because I was a pretty fast runner.

All the time he was chasing me I was laughing and singing songs like 'We Can Work It Out' by The Beatles or 'I Want Candy' by The Strange-loves. In the end, he gave up.

It wasn't long before I was being called to the principal's office. I was told that they were going to speak to my parents and that, in all likelihood, I was going to be expelled. I knew this was going to be bad news. So I told the office that my parents would be in between 10 and 12 the following morning and that they should call them then.

That evening I briefed Linda on what was going on, and gave her a key to my house. When the school called the following morning, Linda was there. She put on a grown-up voice. When the principal said I had been a real bad boy, Linda said she had been having problems with me too.

'David has been so difficult, my husband and I are thinking of shipping him overseas so he can get military training.'

The school had been keeping count of my absenteeism and filled Linda in on it.

'Mrs Gest, did you know that he has missed seventy-one out of one hundred and sixty days this year?'

'Yes, we know. David has a terrible throat disorder from his tonsils and he is going through a lot of itching with puberty.'

'Itching?'

'Yes, his glands are always swollen,' Linda said, dying to burst out laughing. They didn't want to discuss that and just said, 'Oh.'

Linda played it perfectly, just as I had coached her. She ended up asking whether I could finish the semester while she and my father worked out how they were going to discipline me. The school agreed.

I was called in afterwards and they said they had spoken to my mother and I had lost all my privileges. I couldn't go to the movies or bowling for five years or something. I thought, 'Yeah right!'

They must have been so glad when I moved to Encino.

My mother grew up in California and there was some Spanish blood in the family, which produced some more strange relatives.

My cousin Jorge lived in Tijuana with my cousin Christianna. Jorge loved archery and used to spend a lot of time shooting arrows. One day Christianna got so mad at Jorge for spending all his time doing archery rather than being with her that she took the bow and arrow and shot him right in the ass. She told him that next time it wouldn't be the tush, it would be the coccyx.

He never talked back to her again. In fact, he always talked real low so she couldn't hear. He was scared of her.

Christianna ran the family. She turned out to be a lesbian and had a girlfriend but Jorge was still in love with her so he ended up sharing her. He was also worried about leaving her in case she cut off his balls or something. That's what he told me, anyway.

Those Mexican cousins were wild. Another one became a huge drug dealer. Then he got his head run over by a tyre. A car went right over his head. That taught him not to mess around with drugs.

My parents had been making so much money that they wanted to live in a more affluent area. Truthfully, I don't think Van Nuys was ever really meant for them. When I was around fourteen, we left the old house and moved to the more upscale area of Encino, about 12 miles away.

Originally, we were going to move across the street from Sonny and Cher, on Escalon Road I think it was. The duo were huge at that time, so I was pretty excited by the prospect of being their neighbour. They lived in a corner house with a giant 'S&C' on the gates. I went there a couple of times to check the house out and once I found Sonny in the garage playing music.

I got talking to him and he gave me a copy of their new single, 'What Now My Love', before it was released. He even sang it for me.

As it turned out, we didn't buy that house because it was reckoned not to be stable, although it's still there. Instead, we moved to a house near the corner of Louise and Rancho. It was a mansion, with four bedrooms and huge grounds. Our property connected to the songwriter Jimmy Webb's, the guy behind hits like 'Up, Up and Away' and 'MacArthur Park' and some of Glen Campbell's songs – 'By the Time I Get to Phoenix' and 'Galveston'. Oddly enough, we would become friends many years later.

As I got to know the area, I realised he was typical of the type of person that lived there. It was a real show-business area. On one corner was Aretha Franklin; on another was Patty Andrews, lead singer of The Andrews Sisters, who also became a friend later on. On another corner lived the actor Mike Connors, who played Mannix on television. Other famous actors like Michael Landon, Tab Hunter and Efrem Zimbalist Jr lived down the street. We even had Walt Disney's daughter in the neighbourhood.

I enjoyed the fact that we were living around show-business people, but in every other sense I was unhappy. In Van Nuys, I had had a really tight-knit group of friends. We had grown up together. Now I had to leave Milliken and go to a new school, Portola Junior High School, for my final year. That was really hard. The kids were different there; they were a lot snobbier. The only person I knew was a girl named Sandi Berg, whose mother had grown up with my mother.

I started to grow my hair long, so that it was

almost down to my shoulders. My parents kept telling me to get it cut but I refused. One day I was at Sandi's house and her father Ted got hold of me and gave me a haircut there and then. If it had been my father, I would have fought back but I really liked and respected Ted and I didn't resist.

Rather than trying to fit in, I got depressed and decided to drop out. I had already started smoking weed but around the time we moved to Encino I also got into pills. Pills were big then, uppers and downers in particular. I would take one to get high and then the other to come back down again. I don't remember how I got hold of them, but I did. I just wanted to get through the day, and when I had done that go to sleep.

It did not take long for me to get into trouble at my new school. One of the female teachers there had a moustache. One day I took too many uppers and, during the break, snuck out to a market to buy some shaving cream and a razor. I must have been as high as a kite because when I got back to class I walked straight up to her with the shaving kit and said, 'Can I shave your moustache because it's bugging the hell out of me?'

She went ballistic.

'Mr Gest, you are going straight to the principal's office,' she said.

'Why the principal's office? Do you want me to shave you there?' I said.

That was it, she just marched me off. They must have thought I was nuts.

Not long after that, I had been taking downers and fell asleep in a French class. I woke up to the sound of the French teacher rapping her ruler on the desk.

'Excusez moi, Monsieur Gest,' she said. 'And what is wrong with you?' I just looked up at her and said, 'Fuck you.' I had a real 'nobody tells me what to do attitude' then. I got detention, of course.

I was so unhappy at school. I didn't know that many people and I missed my old friends. I wasn't doing that well in class and I wanted to be somewhere else. I cut class as much as I could and went surfing.

When school was out, I was still riding my bike or hitchhiking to Hollywood. I wanted to be in the recording studios, I wanted to be with Morrison, I wanted to be where the music was happening. I was just drifting. Things soon got worse.

When I was fifteen, my friend Jay Clark and I

decided that we had had enough of school and all
the bullshit that went with it. We decided to steal
his sister's car.

Neither of us had driver's licences because we
weren't yet sixteen, so we stole Jay's father's
licence along with some money, and I also took
some cash from my dad's wallet. We had about
$400 in all. We then spray-painted the car pink
with blue stripes and polka dots and went to Las
Vegas. Just like that.

We got stopped on the way. At that point, the
police weren't looking for us so our licence-plate
number didn't show up. Amazingly, when they
looked at Jay's father's licence, they thought it was
him. His father was forty-seven or something and
Jay was fifteen!

We took turns driving. We stayed in this cheap
little hotel and there was a prostitute there. (*She was
called Twatta Givemealot. No bull! That was her name:
Twatta Givemealot.*)

She told us that because we were so young she'd
do it for free. She also had a friend who was even
younger and told us we could have sex with her as
well. And we did! We did it both with her and her
friend. We were in heaven. We also went to see

Phyllis Diller at the Riviera Hotel. That was our big splurge.

Then, somehow, we found out that the police had been notified. When we drove back, I had to go to the police station. I was put on some kind of probation at the Sybil Brand Reform Detention Center.

Needless to say, our parents weren't happy. Jay's mother and father slaughtered him. My parents weren't pleased about it either. My father and I got in a fist fight over that one. It was the last time he ever hit me because I hit him very hard and it scared the hell out of him.

It didn't bother me though. By that time, I don't think my parents could have changed who I was or the direction I was headed. I think I knew what I wanted and that was it. Nothing else mattered.

By the time I was fifteen or so, my parents had become very rich. But they still wouldn't give me any money. I had done all sorts of weekend jobs since I was twelve. I had worked as a busboy and waiter. I had even worked at the May Company department store, the place in North Hollywood where I had bought my first records years earlier. I had never made any real money though. I was getting tired of this, so I decided to start my own business.

It was the hippy era and everyone was wearing what were known then as love beads. They were beads made out of glass or wood, threaded on to pieces of leather or string.

I decided to form a company making love beads and all sorts of other jewellery. My girlfriend at the time was called Ellen. She was pretty and blonde, with buck teeth. We joined forces and got things moving.

Once we had a small amount of stock, Ellen and I went to one of the big department stores, Ohrbach's. We had made an appointment with their jewellery buyer over the phone and she said she would be interested in buying our stuff.

I don't know what she must have thought when she saw these two fifteen-year-old kids walk in with their chokers and chains but she must have liked what she saw because she placed an order for $10,000 worth of stock there and then. It was just incredible.

I got all these kids at school to work for me. I was paying them minimum wage. A girl named Gay Meyler ran the business for me. Somehow we made the order and delivered it. It sold out and soon the buyer placed an order for another $30,000 worth of jewellery.

When the business was really flying, I had ten kids at school working for me. They would come over after school, smoke a joint and put the beads together in all these different designs while listening to The Doors and Jimi Hendrix.

This was something my parents could approve of, making money. They were kind of stunned that I was making as much as I was. They took out the tax money to make sure it was paid. My mother even turned a blind eye to my pot-smoking.

To be fair to my mother, she had had that attitude for a while. She preferred that we do it in the house, rather than going out and doing it somewhere else where we may not be quite so safe. She'd say, 'Go to your room and smoke a joint, and while you're at it, here's a packet of cigarettes. Go and smoke those too. Cough till you drop.'

Of course, it was smart. I think that's why I got turned off it early on. Because my mother did let us do it, it lost its charm.

Within a year or so of starting the bead business, I was doing really well. I opened up a 'head shop' on

Ventura Boulevard. Head shops were psychedelic shops where you could buy love beads, bongs, pipes and all the paraphernalia you needed for smoking. We also sold Ravi Shankar records and we laid out mats so that people could sit down and listen to the music.

By the time I was sixteen, I was making thousands of dollars, and spending all of it. At that age, the word 'savings' is not in your vocabulary. The world is your oyster and you think everything's going to be like that forever.

When I took girls out on dates, I would hire limousines for the night. I would have a friend buy Courvoisier brandy and champagne. I was spending money as fast as I was making it.

Of course it came to an end. For about a year and a half the business did really well but then people didn't want those things any more. I didn't mind when it came to an end. I'd had a ball.

One of the reasons why we had so many relatives was all the divorces in the family. They were always getting married and having offspring with different people. My cousin Eunice was married nine times and had 14 boys, all of whom she gave a name starting with the letter M. There was Mark, Mel, Murray, Morgan, Mario, Michael, Marty, Merigo, Manuel, Mele, Manny, Maurice, Marcus and Maury. To be honest, every one of them looked like a monkey. Basically, she had 14 monkeys. Eunice was another sensual woman. Her famous line was, 'There's not one dish that I cannot put seasoning on.'

It was a weird family. There were times when we would get together and everybody would fight. I will never forget the time one cousin, little Junior, married this girl in Arizona somewhere. She was a real slut; everybody hated her. The wedding turned into a fiasco.

When I arrived for the wedding rehearsal with my mother and father, we found two cousins, Phil and Sally, fighting with each other and two other cousins, Lamarr and Tushy (we called her that because she always smelled). Two of them were telling the others that they were illegitimate. Two of the girls were arguing over who was better in bed. The men were arguing over who was a better lover. One said he had a bigger penis than the other. What was really weird was when they pulled them out and you saw that Big Dick really had a little dick and that

Little Dick really had a big dick. It just goes to show you. Anyway, it got crazy and turned into a huge free-for-all.

At one point they started grabbing food off the tables and throwing it at each other, wrecking the flowers. Before we knew it, people were hitting each other with bottles, people were being knifed. One cousin got taken away in a straitjacket.

Everybody left in the end. Nobody stayed for the wedding itself. There was too much friction. I believe it was at their wedding that my cousin Eunice got knocked up for the fifteenth time. She does not remember who it was, but she named the baby Monster because she felt only a monster would do that to her at the party. And it starts with an M.

When I think back on it, most of my family were mental and that starts with an M.

Soul Man

By 1970 music had become my life. Two or three nights a week I would hitchhike or take the bus to LA's hottest venues, clubs like the Troubadour, PJ's and the Whisky. When I wasn't going to live shows, I would hang around the recording studios and record companies, picking up all the new singles and albums I could get my hands on. It really didn't matter what it was; I was really into everything. I liked psychedelic stuff like Jimi Hendrix, Buffalo Springfield and The Seeds. I loved soul music and bands like The Supremes, The Four

Tops, Smokey Robinson and the Miracles and The Temptations.

At that time, I also had a kind of photographic memory and knew everything there was to know about all these bands: the names of the bass guitarist and drummer, where they recorded, on what label, the b-sides of each record, everything. I loved the music business and had made my mind up that I wanted to be a part of it.

So, soon after starting at Birmingham High School, I went to the offices of the local newspaper, the *Valley News & Green Sheet* in Van Nuys, asking for a job. It was a good newspaper, long established in the area. Today it's the *Daily News*, which is owned by the Tribune Group and has the second highest circulation in Los Angeles.

Oddly enough, the publisher agreed to see me. I went in full of confidence – and with a plan.

I told him that Ray Charles was about to play at the Century Plaza Hotel, in a place called the Westside Room, and I wanted to go and review the concert for them. Not only that, I wanted a regular music column.

It was ridiculous, really. I was sixteen or so. Legally speaking, I wasn't even allowed into most of the places my job would take me. Under Californian law, you needed to be twenty-one, old enough to drink or to be allowed into a club that sold alcohol. Luckily, I had two things going for me: confidence and mature looks. By now my hair had grown back again and I had an Afro that was down to my tush. It was huge. I had also grown a beard and moustache, so I could easily pass for someone in his early twenties.

Even I knew deep down that what I was asking for was plain crazy but nothing had ever deterred me in the past and it wasn't going to now. I wanted this job really badly.

This guy sat in his chair, listening to me make my pitch. I thought it went really well. I felt like I had given it my best shot. But in the end, the publisher just shrugged his shoulders and sighed.

'I'm sorry, David, but we already have a music critic,' he said. 'We will keep your details in our files and if something comes up we'll be in touch.'

If I've learned anything in life, it's to never take no for an answer. I certainly wasn't going to accept this. I knew this was my chance to get my foot in the door of the music business and I wasn't in the mood to have someone slam it in my face.

I told him that I wasn't going to let him make the mistake of letting me slip through his fingers.

'I'll wait outside,' I said. 'I'm not leaving here until you hire me.'

I sat there for seven hours. He hired me.

A few days later, I turned up at the Westside Room and introduced myself at the door as the critic from the *Valley News*. I walked into a new career, and a new world.

I turned in my review of the concert and the paper ran it. I started writing every week. I became the music writer and critic. I don't know what happened to the old one.

I was pretty good at it. I always turned my copy in on time and I knew what I was talking about. I started going to all the concerts I could and this helped me to get closer and closer to the stars that I had always wanted to meet.

I remember going to see Dusty Springfield perform. At the party afterwards she was a distant figure, surrounded by her friends and handlers. I noticed one of the guests there was a singer called Norma Tanega, who sang one of my favourite songs in 1966. It was called 'Walkin' My Cat Named Dog' and had been released on the New

Voice label in America. The song was also a huge hit in England. She was a one-hit wonder and very few of the other guests at the party knew who she was but I did. I also knew that Norma and Dusty had been very close friends.

I went up to Norma and told her she just had to sing 'Walkin' My Cat Named Dog' for me. I told her how much I loved that song. She was so flattered that some kid had remembered her record that she dragged Dusty over to meet me.

'Darling, he remembers me, he remembers me,' she said as she introduced us. I was soon being invited to have a drink with Dusty. Even better, Norma performed the song right there and then, with Dusty smiling on. Since then, whenever I meet artists whose music moves me, I invariably ask them to perform live on the spot. They must think I am very weird but they all do it.

The *Valley News* gave me a great start but I was hungry to grow and knew it wasn't the big platform I needed to really get into the music business. I wanted to write for a more serious music paper. Encino hadn't been a happy place for me until now. Living next door to so many show-business figures was finally about to pay off.

I had become friends with a guy named Eddie Eckstine, who lived near me. His father was Billy Eckstine, one of the great figures of American jazz. As well as being a great jazz singer and trumpet player, Billy Eckstine had run a band that at various times had contained some of the greatest names in the history of jazz, from Miles Davis and Dizzy Gillespie to Lena Horne and Eckstine's protégée, Sarah Vaughan.

Billy was still working like crazy, especially touring the UK, where he had had massive hits with 'Gigi' and 'Passing Strangers', the latter a duet with Sarah Vaughan. Eddie smoothed the way for me to talk to his father. Billy also had connections at *Soul*, a black newspaper with a high circulation that came out every two weeks all over America. He arranged for me to write an article on him and they agreed to run it.

The article on Billy Eckstine proved a breakthrough. After *Soul*, I got into *Black Stars Magazine*, a subsidiary of *Jet*. Within a year or so of writing my first piece for the *Valley News*, I was writing for more publications, some of them really influential magazines, like the record trade's *Record World* and *Cashbox* and *Blues & Soul*, another big soul magazine. The more I wrote, the more people seemed to want my writing.

Pretty soon I was going to every concert and interviewing every star coming into Los Angeles. And there were a lot of them there at that time.

I met R.B. Greaves, who had had a big hit with 'Take a Letter Maria'. I met the songwriting team behind the Philly sound, Gamble and Huff as well as Thom Bell (when I was flown to Philadelphia) and singers like Carla Thomas and Freda Payne. I began writing articles for additional newspapers, including the *LA Free Press*.

Soul, in particular, was a very influential paper. Once I interviewed Stevie Wonder. He was on tour promoting his new album, *Talking Book*, and had just released 'Superstition' as a single.

Stevie was at the big crossroads in his career. He had really changed his style. Everything was very techno-ish, with a lot of electronic keyboard effects. When he performed live, he even did his old songs, the classics like 'I Was Made to Love Her' and 'My Cherie Amour', in this modern, more techno style.

I remember we talked about the old songs in his songbook. I loved them all. I had also just picked up a collection of *Oldies but Goodies* albums that I received free from my friend Art Laboe of Original Sound Records. He specialised in putting together collections of 12 classic hits on one album, getting the rights from the original labels, long before these collections were sold on television and became big chart-toppers.

Stevie didn't seem to know about these albums and said he'd like a set of them himself. So I said, 'I tell you what, Stevie, I'll get you a set of these old records if you do all your old hits the original way tonight.'

'Deal,' he said.

That night I went to the show with another singer I had made friends with and started to date named Martha Reeves, who with The Vandellas had scored a string of huge worldwide hits with songs like 'Dancing in the Street' and 'Nowhere to Run'. True to his word, Stevie introduced the oldies section by saying, 'This is for David.'

He did all the oldies the original way. I don't know if that was me being persuasive or the power of *Soul* magazine. Perhaps it was a bit of both. He knew I loved those songs.

Hanging out with the music crowd was great,

although it brought its risks too, with drugs in particular.

By now I was back smoking weed with a vengeance. It was making me a bit loony.

I was still seeing Ellen, and would go out with her to a market called Ralph's, which was set on a hill near the hippy area of Franklin and Hollywood Boulevard where Joni Mitchell and all that crowd were living. I would put her in a shopping trolley, then let her go rolling down the hill as I chased after her. She would be screaming and I would be screaming and once or twice I nearly killed her, I'm sure. Weed made me do weird crap like that.

Another night, when I was really high, I met two girls at Ralph's. I wasn't with Ellen that night so these two girls took me home. It was the first time I had sex with two women. After I finished, they had sex with each other. It was the time of free love in LA. It was fun. It was fascinating to see that they could get so much pleasure from each other just by licking!

The other crazy thing I got into back then was driving around as high as a kite. I had my licence by then and borrowed my parents' cars as often as I could get away with it. When they were away on their frequent holidays, I used to take my dad's Lincoln Continental out for a spin. I would smoke a joint or two then head down the hill and pick up some friends.

I remember once I took my friend Sandi Berg and a friend of hers called Lynn out for a cruise in the Lincoln. We went into Encino and drove down the high street. If I saw any guys checking the girls out, I would slow down to usher them over and say, 'Looking for a good time? These two work for me and I can do you a good deal.'

At one point, one guy got real interested and started waving some cash around. I could see from the girls' faces that if I had taken it any further they would have killed me, so I hit the gas and got the hell out of there.

Sandi and Lynn weren't impressed. Thankfully, Sandi knew me well enough not to hold a grudge, which was good news given what happened not long afterwards.

I was driving down the hill in another car, a Datsun, the first car I ever owned, when suddenly I saw a police car in my rear-view mirror. For some reason I panicked, hit the accelerator and raced away from them. They switched on their sirens and started chasing me. It was like a scene out of a TV cop show.

I knew Sandi's house was nearby, so I made a dash for it. I pulled up there and was about to make a run for her porch when two officers grabbed me.

Sandi appeared just as the cops were handcuffing me and bundling me into the car. I was taken away to Encino police station and banged up for an hour. Fortunately, Sandi and her father Ted turned up to bail me out. They had to borrow the $50 bail from Sandi's sister, which hadn't pleased her too much. I was far from her favourite person.

Even more fortunately, my parents were away and the police decided against pressing charges. By a minor miracle, I hadn't been smoking that day. If I had, they would probably have done what Sandi's sister had apparently said they should do: thrown away the key.

It was while I was hanging out with one major recording artist that I realised that the whole drug thing was getting out of control.

One night, I went with a group of my cohorts to a friend's house for a smoke. This friend lived in a condo, a dozen storeys up. Instead of pot, she gave us angel dust. I had never done anything heavy before, so this stuff took me completely by surprise. It literally blew my mind.

I will never forget it. It was nine hours of true hell. At different stages I was watching myself coming out of my body and seeing things in triplicate. At one point I looked at a car and saw eight of them. It was such a bad trip I wanted to jump off the building. It was a long way down and if I had done it, that would have been the end of me. It was really scary.

It took a while for me to straighten out afterwards but once I did I thought, 'This is not for me.' It was a real turning point. It was so bad that I knew I had to get away from that scene. From then on, I was really careful about drugs and gave them a wide berth most of the time.

By far the most famous people in my neighbour-hood in Encino were the Jacksons. At the beginning of the seventies, The Jackson Five were one of the world's biggest acts. In the United States they had just had their fourth gold single with 'I'll Be There'. They had moved into a huge, ten-bedroom mansion on Hayvenhurst, a short drive away from my parents' house.

From the moment they moved in, in the spring of 1971, I had really wanted to meet them. Everyone knew they were tightly controlled by their father, Joseph. Luckily, I had a connection. Through my friend Eddie Eckstine, I got to know a guy called Mike Merkow, who was a good friend of the family. I told Mike I'd love to meet The Jackson Five, and one day he arranged to take me over to the private school they attended, Walton in Panorama City.

Two of The Jackson Five happened to be there that day: eighteen-year-old Tito, who was just six months younger than me, and Michael, who was then around thirteen. Tito seemed a nice, quiet guy and I suggested we get together some time. They were relatively new to the Encino area, so I offered to show him around. He didn't seem too keen, though. Michael was engrossed in an art class. He seemed lost in his own world as he made a papier mâché giraffe.

Shortly afterwards, I ran into Tito again at McDonald's in Encino. This time he was with his girlfriend, Dee Dee, who he had met at Fairfax High School in LA.

Dee Dee was a really sweet girl. She was Spanish

Puerto Rican, with a bit of black in her too. She was very small and outgoing. When I went over to say hi to Tito, she just leaned over and introduced herself. We got on pretty well. Tito seemed much more relaxed when he was on his own, away from the family.

Quite soon afterwards, I heard through the grapevine that Tito and Dee Dee were planning to get married. I thought to myself, 'I really want to go to that wedding.' So from then on I kept going to McDonald's, hoping to meet up with them again. I went there just about every day for seven weeks or so. About three days before the wedding, I was ready to give up when my luck changed.

I was sitting there eating my thousandth cheeseburger in two months when both Tito and Dee Dee walked in. Dee Dee immediately came over and we were soon talking away.

Sure enough, they asked me if I wanted to come to the wedding. I pretended to be unsure and said something about checking my diary but the truth was that there was no way on earth I was going to miss out on this. It was really exciting, not least because until that time I had never attended a wedding of any kind.

The wedding and reception took place at the Ivy House in Torrance. Dee Dee looked beautiful in white and the service was really nice. I spent most of the time observing one of the most famous families in the world. I found them fascinating.

For a start, there were so many of them. As well as Tito, Marlon, Jackie and Jermaine, there was Michael and the youngest brother, little Randy, who was then around ten. I knew there were two sisters, the baby of the family, little Janet, who was five or so, and the older La Toya but I didn't know there was another one, Maureen, who was called Rebbie, the oldest child of all.

The dominant figure was their father, Joseph or Joe. Everyone had heard the stories about Joe. Back in their home town of Gary, Indiana, he had originally formed a three-piece band with the three oldest boys, Jackie, Tito and Jermaine, before creating The Jackson Five, which included their younger brothers Marlon and Michael. He was known as a tough disciplinarian who drove his kids hard and wasn't afraid to intimidate them to get what he wanted.

Joe's hard work had paid off, no one could question that. Seeing him in person for the first time, he seemed very stern. You could never make him smile. By contrast, their mother, Katherine, was wonderful. She was a very warm person, even towards me, a complete stranger to her at that point. She was eventually to become like a mother to me.

Tito and Dee Dee set up home in an apartment near the McDonald's in Encino. After the wedding, I dropped by with a gift. Dee Dee was very welcoming and invited me in. I was soon dropping by on a regular basis, and started getting together with them two or three times a week. Tito and I really hit it off. Within nine months, we were doing everything together. We became like brothers. It was to prove to be the closest friendship of my life. Oddly enough, Tito can just look at me now and he knows what I am thinking.

I began to go round to the Jackson family house too. My parents' house was pretty big but it was nothing compared to the Jackson mansion, which had a pool and large grounds. There was even a separate building that they had converted into a recording studio. Despite the size of the place, it felt like a family home.

Joe was a distant figure. You could sense that

they all kind of dreaded him and they tended to steer clear of him. On the other hand, Katherine was a saint. She always treated me like I was her own son. She would ask me if I was hungry and would make food for me. She was wonderful.

Joe's mother visited them quite often. She was this really ballsy woman, and very, very funny too! She was the complete opposite of Joe and had a great personality. The more I got to know them, the more I could see that there was a bond there that was missing with my own mother and father. This made me even more attracted to them. I suppose in many ways they were a surrogate family. They felt more like a family to me than my own did.

As a teenager, there were many times when I had to pinch myself to believe that I was doing what I was doing. This was never more the case than one night in 1972.

After more than a decade at the top, Smokey Robinson, the artist widely regarded as America's greatest modern songwriter, had decided to quit performing to concentrate on his family and his job as vice president of Motown Records. Smokey was conducting a six-month farewell tour of America with his band, The Miracles, and they had come to Los Angeles to play the Forum, an 18,000-seat hall which they had packed to capacity.

It was a big bill, with many supporting acts, including The Whispers and Honey Cone. The act that really caught my imagination, however, was a young singer from Memphis named Al Green, who was the special guest star on the bill. I went to the show with a big star at the time, Freda Payne, who had been very hot with 'Band of Gold' and 'Bring the Boys Home'. She is still my closest female friend. I think of her as the sister I never really had as Barbara and I were just too many years apart to be close.

Al had a great voice, really smooth and soulful. He also had the most amazing rapport with the audience, especially with the women. He could work them into a frenzy one minute and have them sitting there dewy-eyed the next. He was a great natural performer and clearly had a big, big future.

I wrote as much in my piece, which ran under the headline 'Smokey's Goodbye, Al Green's Hello'. That summed it up pretty well, I thought. The King was dead, long live the King.

The piece went down well, particularly at Hi, the

label at London Records that was being run by the Memphis-based producer Willie Mitchell, who was recording Al Green. Not long after my piece ran, I got a phone call thanking me for my story and sounding me about something else. I was told that London/Hi Records were on the lookout for someone to open up a West Coast publicity office. The company was based in New York, on the opposite coast, but felt they needed a presence in LA. They wondered whether this was something that might interest me.

I was excited. I knew that if I really wanted to get into the music business, journalism wasn't the route. This was a big opportunity. So, once more, I applied for a job that I was way too young to do.

I was nineteen or so, still not even legally allowed to drink. After finally leaving high school, I had started a degree course at the University of Northridge. I was in my first semester, studying psychology and journalism, although I couldn't have been less interested.

Two top executives, Ray Caviano and Bob Small, flew out from New York to conduct the interviews. When I met them, I made out that I was in my early twenties. Again, I put up a pretty convincing act.

To be fair, I did have a small amount of PR experience.

A few months earlier, I had worked for promoter and former band leader Art Laboe, who put together 'oldies' shows, featuring stars of yesteryear. They were pretty popular in LA at the time. He would get together a bunch of fifties and early sixties icons and put them together on one bill. It wasn't my style of music at the time but I was eager to learn from any kind of experience I could get.

Art had read my reviews in various papers and asked me to help him out. He really knew me as the kid who used to come by his office for free records since I was thirteen or fourteen. It had been a real eye-opener to see some of these older acts. One day, I had to go to LA airport to pick up Clyde McPhatter, the former lead singer of The Drifters, whose solo hits included 'Lover Please' and 'A Lover's Question'. I had become used to seeing artists on the upslopes of their careers. Seeing Clyde showed me that there was a downside to the business as well, that success could be a fleeting thing.

Clyde had had all these great hits but now he was really down and out. I think he was an alcoholic too. When I picked him up at the airport he was shaking. He was in a real mess. I had to buy him a bottle of booze to ease his shakes.

I got an even starker reminder of just how quickly the world can forget you when we started rehearsing the show at the Hollywood Palladium, the same place they had held the Teenage Fair I went to as a kid. While we were rehearsing there one day, this guy came up to me and asked me, 'Do you know who I am?'

I thought I knew everything about music but I had to admit 'no'. He didn't even look vaguely familiar.

It was Gene Vincent, the famous rock 'n' roll singer, the man behind 'Be-Bop-A-Lula' and other hits.

I told the story at the London Records interview and got a laugh. Again, against the odds, I got the job. It was a moment that transformed my life.

When I was hired by London Records I felt as if all my dreams had come true. I quit college and at last moved into my own apartment on Balboa Boulevard in Encino. All of a sudden I was getting $850 a week, a lot in those days, and had also been given a Lincoln Continental. Even my father had to admit he was impressed. I felt on top of the world.

I worked really hard. I realised that I had lucked out and had to act mature. I had to act older than my age, since I was still basically a kid.

London Records had been known for some of the world's greatest rock bands, like The Rolling Stones and The Moody Blues. They had big international names, like the British singers Tom Jones, Engelbert Humperdinck and Gilbert O'Sullivan, and they also had up-and-coming bands like ZZ Top. Part of my job was to break the smaller acts. I worked with bands like Savoy Brown and 10cc, the British band whose single 'Rubber Bullets' I helped make a hit in America.

For my initiation, London Records sent me to New York to meet all the top brass before I started work in Los Angeles. The first thing that hit me was how totally different New York was to Los Angeles and not just in the obvious ways. The company put me up at a hotel on the Avenue of the Americas. I checked in, rested and got ready to get stuck into work.

On my first day, I arrived at London Records' New York office at 8.30 a.m. for my initiation only to find the offices empty apart from the secretaries.

I had expected to meet Bob Small and Ray Caviano at 9 a.m. Ten o'clock came, then noon. Lunchtime passed, and so did 3 p.m. It was 4 p.m. when they arrived. My first lesson about life in New York was that it moved to a different clock.

At that time, the club scene in New York was really on fire. Places like CBGB were just starting up, and a revolution in music was beginning to bubble away. The music industry was totally connected to it. Every night, Bob and Ray went to the discos and clubs, and that is why they didn't start work until early afternoon.

This went on for four days, so towards the end of that first week I arranged to meet Ray at his home. I was about to get my second wake-up call about life in the music business New York style.

I must have been so naïve then. I turned up at Ray's house and he was there with another guy who also lived there. I noticed that there was only one bedroom. I just thought it was another example of New York's cramped living conditions, so I said, 'God, you have to share one bed? How unfortunate.' They both looked at me and laughed.

Later, I was speaking to Jack Ross on the phone and he explained to me that Ray was gay. I said,

'What's that?' He said, 'Guys sleeping with guys' and he went on to explain this concept to me in a lot of detail! I had no bloody clue. Yes, I was that naïve.

They asked me if I wanted to go to a club with them one night. I made an excuse and declined.

For every act that succeeded, though, there were many that didn't. We were often asked to listen to new artists who were trying to get record deals. I would sit in a studio with a colleague, Jack Ross, and listen to these hopefuls. I was always straight with them.

I have never believed in bullshitting people. It's hard to get a break in this business and it is pointless to keep people dangling. If I didn't think somebody had a chance, I just told it like it was. I said, 'Get yourself a day job and keep it.' I haven't changed in that way. I have always been true to who and what I am.

The other thing I had going for me was an eye for detail. Some people would call it anal retentive-ness but I have always been that way, always looking after the smallest detail. When I gave a party, I would always make sure everything was just right, from the flowers and the napkins to the wines and the food. It was just my way.

You need a lot of things to break an artist. They need to have talent, obviously, and good songs and good production, of course. The way I see it, you also need some other things. You have to pay attention to detail. You have to get some kind of word of mouth working for your artist. You need to make friends with people in the business who can help you out with favours. Finally, you need luck, lots and lots of luck.

I don't think all these ingredients ever came together so well as they did when I worked with a singer called Ann Peebles. I was given responsibility for handling a number of emerging artists, including Ann. She was this Memphis girl, an incredible vocalist with a beautiful face and a great look. The one unfortunate thing that let her down was that she didn't know how to perform.

Sitting in the studio with Jack Ross one day, we had heard a track called 'I Can't Stand the Rain'. I thought it had real potential and was a song around which I could start a campaign that might bring Ann national prominence. I really believed in the record.

I started spreading the word by having Ann do

lots of pop interviews, positioning her as an unsung hero of R&B, a new star on the horizon. I then booked her to perform at the Troubadour on Santa Monica Boulevard, which at that time was the hottest place in LA for breaking new acts.

I knew that Ann was going to struggle performing, so when we were doing the rehearsal I went through some signals I was going to give her from the audience, where I would be sitting in the front row. I told her, 'When I point in this direction, I want you to walk to this side of the stage, and when I point you in that direction, I want you to walk to that side.' She was so lacking in stage skills I had to be that basic with her.

The night of the show came and there was a full house, including some huge stars. One of them was Carole King, who was then the biggest singer in the world with her album *Tapestry*. I told Ann she needed to acknowledge this superstar in the audience. Unfortunately, Ann didn't know who Carole King was, so the introduction went like this: 'Ladies and gentlemen, in the audience tonight is Carole . . .' and she waited about three minutes . . . 'King.' Everybody was laughing because it was obvious that Ann didn't know who Carole was.

When Ann started singing, people started taking notice. She really could sing and she had a great repertoire. The night went well but it really took off when John Lennon turned up. He was with Harry Nilsson and Jesse Ed Davis. John was as high as a kite. For some reason which I still don't understand, he had a Kotex sanitary towel on his forehead.

He was in a feisty mood. At one stage a waitress came up to him to take his order. He asked her if she knew who he was and she replied, 'Yeah, I do. An asshole with a Kotex on your forehead.' That became a very famous story that hit every paper in America and beyond. Most importantly, they all mentioned the fact that he had been watching a new artist called Ann Peebles, who sang this fantastic song called 'I Can't Stand the Rain'.

In the end, Lennon got kicked out for being so drunk but he wasn't ejected until after he had heard Ann sing. He, like everyone else, loved her. During the show he was shouting out: 'Annie, baby, I want to fuck you.' He later went on to say that 'I Can't Stand the Rain' was his favourite record of the year.

The Lennon incident was a dream for a publicist. You could never buy publicity like that. In the wake of that night at the Troubadour, 'I Can't Stand the Rain' started to get serious air play across the country's radio stations. We got a hit and a Grammy nomination on the back of my publicity campaign and the album is now considered a classic.

It really was the era of sex, drugs and rock 'n' roll. I remember one afternoon I organised a party for the band Savoy Brown at a restaurant called Benihana's on La Cienega.

The waitresses were serving hot dog appetisers. One of the guests was talking to a female music journalist. When the hot dogs came around, he saw her looking rather disinterestedly at them, so he grabbed a bun, unzipped himself and put his penis in the bun.

'How'd you like that one?' he said.

That thing was at least eleven inches long! It went right from the top of the bun to the end. People were speechless. Obviously, that thing did not need warming up!

I worked hard but I partied hard too. I moved to a new rented apartment at 100 South Doheny, on the outskirts of Beverly Hills. My neighbours there included John Travolta, Marilu Henner, Jackie Jackson, George Foreman, Melvyn Franklin of The Temptations and a ton of others. It was a very happening building.

I got in with a group of people who became my close friends. A lot of them were singers or musicians. There were the soul singers Billy Paul, Eddie Kendricks of The Temptations, who was starting a solo career, Martha Reeves, Freda Payne, Louis Gossett, Jr (who later became the first African-American to win an Academy Award for Best Supporting Actor for his role in *An Officer and a Gentleman*) and Carla Thomas. I was also friendly with Lamonte McLemore, a member of the vocal group The Fifth Dimension that made my old neighbour Jimmy Webb's song 'Up, Up and Away' a worldwide hit. Lamonte introduced me to many other singers, including Harry Elston and Floyd Butler from The Friends of Distinction, who had two huge hits called 'Grazing In The Grass' and 'Going In Circles'. I also got to know other music journalists, like Michael Walton, who became one of my closest buddies. We were all living near each other and partying very hard.

At that time I was still going out with Ellen. We

used to double date with Jackie Jackson and his girlfriend who, many years later, became known as Paula Abdul. We would go out with them three times a week to the Luau on Rodeo Drive, where we would have traditional Hawaiian 'Pupus' (hors d'oeuvres) and drinks. I drank a lot in those days.

I would give big parties at my place and we would smoke the weed, toot the toot and drink the drink. We would play music and sing. We were pretty loud and pretty outrageous at times.

I'll never forget one night when Martha Reeves's neighbour, a middle-aged woman, was complaining because the music was too loud. She had called the cops many times on Martha to turn down the music. So at three in the morning, Martha, who was pretty high, called a funeral home and told them the lady had died. Martha asked them to send a casket to the neighbour's house immediately.

Well, within a couple of hours a truck pulled up and some guys started unloading a coffin. They went to this lady's door and asked her to confirm the name of the family living there. When she did, they told her the casket had her name engraved on it.

She started screaming, 'I'm not dead, I'm not dead.'

They just said, 'Well, according to this paperwork you are.'

The woman was freaked out. Martha was watching from a distance, wetting herself.

No one in my family ever liked my cousin Spookie.

Spookie was absolutely one of the craziest women in the world. Not only did she have no sense of humour, she was also really kookie. In fact, they used to call her Kookie Spookie.

Kookie worked in a funeral parlour in Detroit. The parlour was called Dark's Funeral Parlour.

Well, one day, the mother of a friend of Kookie's died, so the men with the casket were sent to pick up the body. When they came back to Dark's, they didn't see Kookie because she was so short. She was only 4'4". They hit her with the casket by accident, right in the head. The blow was so severe that she died on the spot.

Nobody knew what to do with Kookie. There was no one to call because she wasn't married. So, from what I have been told, they just threw her into the casket with her dead friend's mother and buried them together. They then called the police and told them where Spookie was. At least Spookie had company in death.

Now that is one Spookie story!

As I worked to establish myself in the music business, I started to get involved with African-American women. Maybe this was because I loved soul music so much. It really didn't matter to me that they were African-American. In fact, I have always felt that the darker your skin, the more attractive you are.

I had my mother to thank for that. That was one thing about my mother; she taught us that the colour of someone's skin made no difference. Tito Jackson used to come round to our house and she would always greet him with a kiss. Tito said that of all the white mothers he knew, mine was the only one who used to kiss him hello on the lips.

Despite moving to Beverly Hills, I still visited the Jacksons regularly, and since Jackie Jackson lived in my building, at least one of the brothers would be there every day.

As I got to know the family better, I couldn't help noticing La Toya, who was a few years younger than I was. She was so beautiful and had this pudgy nose. This was before she had her surgery.

I knew La Toya was quite withdrawn and naïve but I couldn't help myself falling for her. In fact, I was soon totally, I mean totally, in love with her. La Toya had gone to school with my sister Barbara and they were friends. She really liked Barbara. As I tried to build up the courage to ask her out, I was encouraged by her grandmother.

Joe's mother used to make me laugh. She was a really jovial woman and she would say to me in front of La Toya, 'What La Toya needs is to get laid. She needs a man. She's just too stuck in her ways.' La Toya would turn red. Michael and Randy would burst out laughing hysterically, as would Katherine and little Janet.

I acted on my gut feeling and started dating her. I was really attracted to her. We became closer and closer. I remember the first time I kissed her. She had the softest lips.

One night, I turned up at the Jackson house to take La Toya out on a date. When I got there, Katherine told me she was sick and would have to cancel. As I was about to leave, Michael appeared.

'Hi, David,' he said. 'How'd you like to go to a memorabilia show?'

'What's memorabilia?' I asked.

'Memorabilia is old stuff from the movies and music industry. I collect Three Stooges and Gene Kelly stuff, and other movie things,' Michael said, bouncing around excitedly.

'Why would you want that old junk?' I asked him.

'It's not junk. Come on, you'll see.'

I drove Michael to his show, where he bought all sorts of stuff, from posters to autographs and other bits and pieces. I had to admit I found it fascinating.

It was the first day I really spent any time with Michael. Everyone in the family knew that he had something special. He was magical as a performer. He had a special personality. He always made you feel like a million dollars. From then on, we started spending more and more time together. We would usually hang out at least three days a week, at his house or mine.

Michael was five years younger than me but I soon discovered he was much smarter than his years. His passion for the movies, in particular, was endless. We would sit up all night in sleeping bags watching old Gene Kelly, Fred Astaire and Three Stooges movies. At other times, he would call me up and ask me to drive him somewhere or other. I didn't mind.

One of his – and my – favourites was a place called Dupars Pancake House. We would go there late at night, and sometimes just for lunch.

Occasionally Mrs Jackson would make us take Janet along, which we didn't want to do. By now she was eight or nine years old and she was a pain in the ass. She had this little attitude. I used to call her 'the heifer'. Sometimes we would take Randy, whom I loved.

Some afternoons, Michael, Tito, Jackie, Marlon and I would play basketball at the park or at the house. We used to play it a lot, and they were all really good at it.

They also had to work hard too. The group would always be in the recording studio, working on songs or perfecting their dance routines. I loved to watch them dance. Michael used to come up with these routines. He would practise his turnaround spins in the mirror. Marlon was also brilliant at creating many of the Jackson Five new routines.

I used to think at times that they were a bit

repetitive. One day I said, 'Oh, the same old step. Why don't you try something new?' It wasn't too long afterwards that he came up with his new moves. No one ever said they were boring!

Fish out
of Water

There is one thing you can always expect in the music business: the totally unexpected. The unexpected came nine months into my first year with London Records.

One day, all the New York staff were gathered together to be told an executive in the company had been canned. The senior management tried to kid them with the usual smokescreen about him 'seeking new challenges' but everyone knew the reason he had been fired. No one could have kept a lid on the real story; it was too incredible. The details soon filtered down to me and Jack Ross in the West Coast office.

What had happened was this. Even by record industry standards, this guy had had a serious drug habit. He was not just on dope but acid and other things like that. A month or so earlier, he was so high on acid he had gone out and bought every member of staff thousands of dollars worth of gifts. Everybody had willingly accepted the gifts and who could blame them? It's not every day that someone in the typing pool is given a Cartier necklace. Everyone was happy. Until, that is, the bills came in at the end of the month. It turned out the guy had put all the gifts on the company credit card while he was high. The total bill ran to a quarter of a million dollars. Everybody had to return the gifts and they fired him.

The news left me in an interesting position because it opened up a spot as national public relations director at the company's head office in New York. It was one that I, in theory, might be eligible for. Also, the pay was around 50 per cent more than I was making, which at twenty years old was incredible.

When I spoke to my boss, Bob Small, he

confirmed that I was a candidate for the job. 'Let's both think about it first, David,' he said. 'You're still pretty young.'

He was right, of course, but things weren't quite that simple. It wasn't the only job offer I was weighing up.

A lot had happened in my first year in the record industry. I had done a good job working with established and new artists. I had proven wrong those who thought I was too young to have been given such a senior position. People had clearly heard good things about me.

Al Bell, who owned Stax Records, the black music label in Memphis, had spoken to me about plans he had to divide his PR into white and black divisions. He had me in mind to look after one half of the company, although which one he wasn't sure. I had done well with both white and black artists and press. At the same time, Motown in Los Angeles had come to me with an offer to work in their press department. I had heard that Stax could be in big financial trouble and might even go bankrupt, so it didn't take me long to work out that that wasn't a good move. The Motown offer, while flattering, didn't amount to a real step up. Bob

Small didn't know what I knew though, so when he inevitably got wind of the other two offers he was bounced into making a decision.

Soon he was offering me the job in New York. It wasn't a real tough decision to make. I was twenty years old and, apart from my friends and my social life, there wasn't anything keeping me in Los Angeles.

I was still seeing La Toya but, truth be told, things were fizzling out. We had been seeing each other for about a year but it hadn't really blossomed into anything serious, on her part at least. I was in love with her but she could not commit to anything. She was in many ways still a child. When I stood back and thought about it, it was kind of a puppy love. I really cared about her and I was going to miss her and all my friends in LA but I knew the move was a great opportunity. It was a big jump in responsibility as well as money. I was climbing up the ladder fast. I said yes.

As I got ready to head east, the Jacksons organised a small send-off for me at a little bar in Santa Monica. I didn't know how long it would be before I would see them all again. Boarding the plane to New York, I really was heading into the unknown.

I had an aunt who grew up in New York. Her name was Adele and she was a little off the rock. Well, maybe not just a little!

Adele had been to school in a rough section of the Bronx but had left there to live in Torrance, California. One day, around 40 years later, she decided to have a school reunion back in the Bronx. Just like that.

She flew to New York with me and my cousin Bobby and immediately went to look for her best friend, who used to be the most beautiful girl in the school. When my aunt had last seen her friend, everyone had expected this girl to go into modelling or perhaps become an actress. When Adele found her, she weighed 350lbs and could hardly fit through the door of my Uncle Irving's house, where the three of us were staying.

From her schooldays, Adele remembered an old warehouse in the Bronx that had an Italian restaurant on the ninth floor. She wanted to have the reunion there but everyone told her to look for somewhere else. The building was condemned and was about to be flattened. Adele never took no for an answer, however, and got the place for free.

Adele wanted to round up all 400 kids who had

gone to school with her but in the end she only found 50, since many had died. She got a guy to set up some hotplates and heaters inside the warehouse but the electrics were so old they shorted and started a fire. Adele, her fat friend and five others tried to get out in the lift but it got stuck and they were trapped inside for seven hours. Eventually the fire brigade got there and broke them out. No one died.

Adele's dead now though. She was a certifiable nutcase but a truly loveable one!

Being away from LA unsettled me more than I had expected. I had grown up in California, under clear blue skies, with tons of open space and mountains and the beach always a short drive away. Now I was living in the most intense, cramped city on the planet, sharing my life with people who were leading a lifestyle that was unlike anything I was used to.

I really felt like I was a fish out of water. I even looked different from other guys there. They were all smooth, clean-cut characters, while I still had my big Afro and my beard and moustache. I probably did stick out in the crowd there.

As I struggled to settle down, I began to become unstable. One night, I was smoking a joint in my hotel room, where I was staying temporarily until I found an apartment, when I suddenly saw this huge rat coming out from under the bed. I freaked and ran out into the hall in my underwear. I was shouting like a lunatic. 'There's a rat in my room!'

Someone came up to have a look but they couldn't find anything. I think they thought I was a wacko. So I had another joint and sat nervously on the bed. About an hour had gone by when I saw the rat again. It looked even bigger this time, probably because I was high!

Again someone came and looked, and again they couldn't find anything. Then, just as they were leaving, it appeared. By now it looked four or five feet long to me. I was so stoned. They put me in another room but the incident left me feeling even more on edge.

I might not have survived in New York if it hadn't been for a couple of girls that I really got on with. By a coincidence, the girl who answered the phones at London Records had grown up with my good friend, the singer Freda Payne. In fact, she had taken her first trip to New York with Freda.

Her name was Joanne and we became pals. I also struck up a friendship with Jean, a beautiful black girl in the accounts department. She was just the sort of girl I had been used to back in LA. We were soon dating and moved in together, renting a small apartment with a kitchen in the East Village, the hippest part of the city back then.

Work wasn't quite what I expected at times. I was not only national public relations director but also artist relations director, overseeing everybody's careers. I worked with people I had known from LA, Al Green in particular. I also got some odd artists to look after. At one stage, I found myself working with, of all people, the legendary Broadway actress and singer Ethel Merman, who had just put out a disco album. Every day she would be on the phone booming, 'Helloooow.' It was bizarre.

Throughout all this, I was seeing my boss maybe twice a week for five minutes. He was always clubbing and doing his own thing. Looking back on it, I think he hired me because he knew I was so inexperienced. He had things set up in a way that suited him, and if he had hired somebody who was experienced it would have cramped his style. He guessed I wouldn't be a problem, and I wasn't, but I was so unhappy.

As time went by, my disillusionment became pretty obvious. I didn't exactly hit it off with the rest of the staff. I didn't much care.

There was this girl in the classical department. She had huge breasts. She wouldn't acknowledge anyone else in the company except for those in the classical department. She would walk around with her nose up in the air. One morning, I was running along the hallway with some coffee and I ran straight into her. The coffee poured all over her breasts. They had to take her to hospital because her breasts were steaming. She never spoke to me after that, and who can blame her? I thought it was pretty funny. She wasn't that badly burned and her boobs quickly recovered.

Relations with a guy in another department were, if anything, even worse. This guy had been brought over from Europe, and my Californian sense of humour went down like a lead balloon with him. I remember introducing my girlfriend Jean as one of The Supremes. He, for some reason, immediately assumed it was Mary Wilson and got really excited.

'Oh, Miss Wilson, it's so wonderful to meet you,' he said, kissing her hand and going crazy. When he found out she worked in the accounting department he never spoke to me again. He was so pissed off.

What made this even funnier was the fact that he lived in the same building as I did. It turned out that he was a transvestite. By day he was this uptight European executive, by night he was a woman. One night, I ran into him in the elevator with Jean and he was in a dress. He acted as if he didn't know me. He said hello in a very effeminate voice, then tottered off on his heels into the night.

I knew a lot of people thought California was strange but we were so dull compared to New Yorkers. The place was weird.

It was Al Green who rescued me. Twice, in fact.

By 1973, Al had become one of the biggest recording artists in America. The previous year he had had his first number one hit with 'Let's Stay Together'. Since then he had had another five top ten hits. He was on a hot streak.

So that year the record company decided to have him perform in Central Park, as part of a big open-air concert. He would be the first black performer to play there. The concert drew an amazing crowd.

There were something like 100,000 people packed into Central Park.

Al was the most natural performer I ever saw – bar none. Michael Jackson was the most exciting but Al had an ability to work an audience that I have never seen the likes of, before or since. He didn't always display it. When he wasn't up for it, he could be so disinterested that he would let the audience sing his songs for him. When he was 'on' he was unbelievable. It was partly his vocal ability – Al could have sung the Yellow Pages and made it sound soulful – but he also had this incredible ability to drive an audience, the female part of it in particular, absolutely wild. Just how wild, I discovered that day.

The problems started after he had played three songs. Suddenly people started tearing down the safety barriers and heading for the stage. They were mostly women, determined to get to Al. He was such a sex symbol.

The security people didn't like the look of this and alerted us to the problem quickly. We made a snap decision. We had to get him off and out of there lest the crowd break the stage apart, injuring many. So we cut short the show after three songs and rushed him to a waiting helicopter. I got into the helicopter with him and two girls. Al was in the front with the pilot and I was in the back with the two girls, sitting next to the door.

We were climbing high above Manhattan when suddenly the door next to me flew open. I had been leaning against it, so I was sent lurching outwards. I didn't exactly react calmly. I started screaming. We were hundreds, if not thousands, of feet above Central Park and I could see the ground far beneath me. For a split second my life flashed in front of me.

In the chaos, the two girls grabbed me. But it was Al who saved the situation. He coolly turned around, reached back, grabbed the door and managed to pull it shut. It was the most frightening moment of my life. I really thought I was going to fall out of the helicopter.

It wasn't long after that that Al saved me a second time.

After about a year in New York, I'd really had enough. I didn't like living there. I missed LA and my friends. I was still so young.

One day, Al called me and said he was so busy, he just couldn't cope with all that was happening around him. He needed someone to look after him full-time.

I sensed an opportunity and went for it. 'OK, Al. I'll leave London Records, set up my own company and look after you myself,' I said. 'You sign a two-year contract with me and I'll move back to California and do it.'

He was keen immediately, so I set about organising things. A few weeks later, I sent him a contract, which he initially got his secretary to sign. I was already too wise to fall for something as stupid as that.

'No, Al, *you* sign it,' I told him.

Soon I had a contract signed by Al Green, right on top of the secretary's signature. I still have it in fact.

I immediately headed back to LA and opened up my own PR firm, David Gest Public Relations. Al Green was my first client. He was so compassionate to me; we had a couple of great years together.

Al opened my eyes to a whole new world of music, particularly black music. To get on black radio stations back then, you had to tour round the so-called 'Chitlin' Circuit', a network of clubs around the southern United States and in the ghettos of big cities. We would play at clubs through the night, doing three shows, at 9 p.m., 1 a.m. and 5 a.m. I saw Al perform live more than 1,000 times and I never got bored watching him. He introduced me to some great venues and some great black music. Often I would be the only white guy there but I always felt at home. I learned so much from Al; he was my mentor.

Women loved Al Green and Al Green loved them back; as many of them as he possibly could. He was a phenomenal ladies' man. Oddly enough, for a guy who was so handsome, he really wasn't bothered by how good-looking the girls he went with were.

He had gone out with a girl called Cheryl, for a while. She had bad acne but was really sweet. She had noticed Al did not always go for the most beautiful women. I asked her once why she thought that was and she replied with a line I will never forget.

'Because,' she replied, 'he told me his dick don't know no better.'

Al's appetite for women was huge, as I discovered one night when we went to Philadelphia together.

I had brought with me a white girl from LA

called Jackie, who Al had met weeks before. She loved Al and they wanted to jump each other's bones. I introduced them and just let things take their natural course.

I had also brought along a girl for myself and went to collect her. Her name was Beth. When I arrived at the hotel, I discovered Al had three women on the go.

I found Al in bed with a beautiful and very successful young singer from a group. Then I discovered that in another room was a girl named Mary Woodson. She was a long-standing girlfriend of Al who we, rather cruelly, called Cockeye because she wasn't very pretty and had this eye that rolled around. He was even more excited when he saw Jackie, so he set her up in another part of his suite. I left him to it and went back to my room with Beth.

I hadn't been there long when the phone rang. It was Al. He had already slept with Mary, the singer and Jackie that evening. He wanted me to go talk to Jackie, I think to reassure her that everything was OK.

I did as he asked. Jackie had, after all, flown over from LA with me. I spent around an hour talking to her, then headed back to my room. When I walked in I couldn't believe my eyes.

Al was on the bed, talking to my girlfriend Beth, clearly trying to persuade her to become the fourth member of his harem that night.

I was furious. I told him to go and screw the three girls he already had, as well as himself. He was the only guy I ever met who could go ten hours straight and still keep going. Eventually, it was to cause him mayhem.

In October 1974, I met Al in Memphis. The next day was meant to be Al Green Day in the city, a huge honour. There was a string of events planned.

At the time, Al was recording as well. He was about to release his eighth album, *Al Green Explores Your Mind*, which featured some of his best songs yet, including 'Take Me to the River'. He was working at his studios in Memphis, where he was locked away into the small hours most nights.

As was his habit, Al was coping with the pressure of it all by having affairs with two women at the same time. That night, he was with a beauty queen from Arizona, but he had also been with Mary the week before.

I knew from first-hand experience that the

relationship between Al and Mary was a volatile one. Earlier that week, they had been arguing again and Al had had enough. He had given her a plane ticket and told her to take a flight out of town. He even dropped her off at the airport.

It turned out that Mary hadn't caught the plane and she appeared at the studio a week later, the night before Al Green Day. Al recorded a couple of songs that night, 'Mimi' and 'Strong As Death Sweet As Love', but there was a tension in the air. I could tell he was pissed off that these two girls were meeting. Also, he must have been wondering where he was going to put Mary.

I left him to it. We finally all left the studio around 12.15 a.m. I had booked myself into the Holiday Inn Rivermont, a big hotel by the river. I headed back there and got ready for the big celebrations the following day. As it turned out, there would be none.

Exactly what happened that night has long been the subject of speculation. What is clear is that Al took both girls back to his home. He put them in separate rooms and went to the bathroom.

No one seems clear on what sparked the subsequent chain of events. Some claim Mary asked

Al to marry him and he refused. Others think they had a row about the other girl. I don't know exactly what started Mary Woodson off. I wasn't there. No one disputes what happened next, though.

Mary went downstairs to make grits, a traditional Southern dish in which dried corn is heated up and turned into a red-hot paste. The paste has to cool before you eat it or it will literally burn off your tongue. Mary came into the bathroom with a pot of the baking-hot grits and flung it at Al. The grits were so hot they scalded him badly. He ended up with second-degree burns all over his back. As Al was screaming in agony, Mary ran back to her room.

Al was desperate to cool himself down but the bathtub was full of hot water. Before he could do anything else he heard a single gunshot.

When she heard the shot, the beauty queen ran into the bathroom and she and Al locked themselves in. They didn't know where the shot had come from. When they emerged an hour later, they found Mary lying dead on the floor of her room. She had shot herself in the head. Al grabbed the gun out of her hand to make sure she wasn't playing dead, or possum as they called it.

When Al called me at my hotel, he was already at the hospital. His voice was shaking. All he kept saying was, 'I didn't kill her, I didn't kill her. David, you have to believe me. Get over here quick, I really need you.'

As his PR manager, this was a nightmare. I had to get there as fast as I could. I remember that I was suffering from acne at the time and had Clearasil all over my face. I had to wash it all off before I went running down to the lobby.

When I got to the hospital, I found Al lying on his stomach in a hospital bed. It was a really gruesome sight. He had all these grits sticking to his back. I tried to pull some off, and that pulled his skin off all the way to the bone. I pushed it back in and said, 'Oh my God.'

The next few weeks were the toughest of my life so far. The story was front-page news everywhere. For a while I think the finger of suspicion hung over Al. Throughout that time, though, I defended him. In the end, it was accepted that Mary had committed suicide.

As Al's PR man, I did as good a job as I could under the circumstances. Things could have been much, much worse for Al. Despite my best attempts, though, the impact on his career was huge, and from the grits incident onwards his record sales dipped. To make matters worse, a week after he got out of the hospital it was reported in the papers that a girlfriend claimed she was hurt by him. Years later, his wife Shirley did a whole Oprah Winfrey Show on her life with Al. It was clear Oprah was not a fan of Al. Shirley's appearance more than anything else hurt Al's career.

Mary's death hit Al really hard emotionally too. He immediately converted to Christianity and became an ordained pastor of the Full Gospel Tabernacle in Memphis. He became known as the Reverend Al Green. He continued making music for a year after that but then went totally gospel. By the end of the seventies, he was concentrating almost completely on his church.

It would take many years for Al to re-emerge into the mainstream of pop music.

His Shelby farm burned down in the 1990s and I remember his girlfriend went back to Chicago immediately after. I think Marshall Resnick, his booking agent at William Morris, is one of the most insecure men I have ever met in the record business. In my view he never guided Al on a real, huge comeback to bring him back to his seventies status. The funny thing about this business is how many insecure people there are in it. It never ceases to amaze me.

I had a cousin, Prunetta, who was very close to my age. Her mother, my Aunt Bumba (pronounced Boom-ba), loved prunes so much that she decided to name Prunetta after them.

Prunetta had the worst case of acne I have ever seen. She used to get all these pimples with big white heads on them. They made her face look so unappetising that nobody would take any notice of her, especially boys. And it was very sad because she was one of the smartest and nicest women I have ever known. She had an IQ of 184 and she also had a photographic memory. Unfortunately, those pimples just came up everywhere: around her nose, around her eyes and around her mouth. According to my Aunt Bumba, Prunetta even had acne on her breasts and stomach. I felt so sorry for Prunetta.

One day, Prunetta decided to try to make herself look more appealing so she could attract a guy. She went out and found a new acne medication. She was so excited she bought eight bottles of it. She thought the way to get rid of all the puss and pimples was to put it all on at once, before she went to sleep at night.

So Prunetta put eight bottles of acne medication all over her face and her face got stuck to the pillow. She couldn't breathe. She was trying to scream for my Aunt Bumba but nobody could hear her. She suffocated and died in her own bed.

My Aunt Bumba was really upset because she had just bought new sheets two days earlier at Bloomingdale's, and they were 500-thread-count Egyptian cotton. Prunetta was stuck to these brand-new sheets.

Everyone wanted to give Prunetta a great burial, so they left her in those Egyptian cotton sheets. My Aunt Bumba even went out and bought a really unique Egyptian-looking coffin to match the sheets. It had mummies all over it. This was the only time I have ever attended an Egyptian burial.

In memory of Prunetta, my Aunt Bumba wanted to help people with bad acne. She decided to go to cosmetology school and now she gives people facials and uses only 500-thread-count cotton sheets to wipe their faces afterwards!

That Ain't
No Reverend

In 1975, I was still looking after Al Green but had also picked up a few other acts. Among them was a pop group, Captain & Tennille, who had a Grammy-winning hit with a version of Neil Sedaka's song 'Love Will Keep Us Together'. I also represented the band LTD, led by a brilliant vocalist named Jeffrey Osborne, the legendary Freddy Cannon, instrumentalist Tim Weisberg and a band called Pablo Cruise.

Still, I was looking around for another major name to build the business up. One day, Al called me from Memphis and asked me if I wanted to work with The Doobie Brothers.

'Al, you've gotta be kidding?'

At that time, The Doobie Brothers were the biggest group in the United States. They had just had a no. 1 hit with 'Black Water' and prior to that had had hits with 'Listen to the Music', 'Long Train Running' and 'China Grove'. The band was huge.

Al told me The Doobie Brothers were putting out a new album, *Takin' It to the Streets*, with a brand-new lead singer named Michael McDonald. They wanted to have a party in Memphis and make a big splash. Al said he had recommended me to their manager, Bruce Cohn.

Al set up a meeting with Bruce in Memphis and I flew out a couple of days later. Bruce eventually became one of my four greatest friends. He was one of my groomsmen. When I first met him, however, he was cold and a bit wary of me. The first thing he asked me was what I would charge for handling the party.

I wasn't going to undersell myself, so I aimed high.

'Seven thousand five hundred dollars,' I said.

Bruce gave me a look and said, 'Talk is cheap. Show me what you can do.'

I showed him that talk is, in fact, very expensive. The party was so successful, generating tons of publicity and positive feedback for the new album, Bruce asked me to handle the band full-time. He paid me a lot more than $7,500.

The money aside, I was ecstatic when I got the call. From then on, I put everything I had into driving the Doobies.

At times I think I drove them crazy. Bruce once called me a superstar of intimidation. He was right. When I wanted something, I made sure I got it.

The Doobies were a huge act but I felt they could become even bigger. I was positive they could stretch the envelope even further. When *Takin' It to the Streets* came out in 1976, I suggested they do just that. I suggested they start doing the sort of mainstream television shows that no other bands had done before.

They really didn't want to do a lot of national television shows at first but I talked, or maybe intimidated, them into it. Soon they were appearing on things like Dinah Shore's prime-time summer variety show, as well as her daytime talk show. On her prime-time show, they played the seven dwarves and Dinah played Snow White. It was actually quite funny.

With Bruce Cohn's help, I then got them to do a half-hour comedy show called *What's Happening?* It was huge at the time, a black comedy that pulled in a big audience across America. No band had ever done a sitcom before, so I went to the producers, Bernie Orenstein and Saul Turtletaub, and played hardball. They thought it would only work if it was a two-parter but they still weren't convinced they wanted to do it at all. I sat there until I had persuaded them to do the two-parter, which was a half hour longer than I had originally planned.

The two-episode story was built around the premise that someone had been selling a bootleg edition of the new Doobies album before it had been released. It had the guys running around trying to find the bootlegger and save the day. There was one line which they kept repeating and which really caught on with the public: 'Which Doobie you be?' When the Doobies saw it, they couldn't stand it.

Those two episodes really did the trick. It made them a household name and the show is still being repeated thirty years later. Mothers and grandmothers got to hear about The Doobie Brothers. Their record sales went through the roof, the album went platinum and the single of the same name made the top ten. It also helped to create a star of their new lead singer, Michael McDonald, who had never met a person like me in his life.

I was as weird then as I am now. I drove my clients nuts, especially the Doobies.

One time, Bruce, Michael and the other lead singer, Pat Simmons, came by the apartment I was renting in Santa Monica to pick me up for a flight from Los Angeles. Time was tight when they arrived but I was nowhere near ready. I was in the bathroom trying to fix my hair and face and Bruce kept shouting, 'David, come on, we're going to miss the flight.'

I kept saying, 'Two minutes, two minutes', which quickly turned into half an hour.

After waiting 20 minutes, the three of them had had enough. So they just went. Bruce shouted, 'See you at the car park at the airport,' and they drove off.

Somehow I got myself together, threw a bag into my Mercedes and drove to LAX as fast as I have ever driven in my life.

When I got there, I saw the guys on the tarmac, unloading all their stuff. I swung into one of the car parks and they followed me there to give me a ride back. They waited while I parked. No sooner had I done so, than I realised that it was the wrong one. This car park was not for long stays and we were going to be away for weeks. I immediately stuck the Mercedes into reverse and tried to get out.

Unfortunately, the road had these spikes which were designed to stop people going back out through the entrance. I tried to drive over them and blew all four tyres out.

The car just flopped down to the ground. I got out, took one look at the situation and picked up my case.

I figured, 'I don't have time to deal with this now. Someone else will deal with it. Someone will have to move the Mercedes.' Bruce and the Doobies were just standing there, dying from laughter. Apparently, the car blocked the entrance for more than two days and I got a hefty fine when I returned!

When we were on the road, I was a little choosy about hotel rooms. While the rest of the band and management were happy to take what was going in the main, I wasn't quite so easy to please. I had always been a bit of a neat freak. I didn't like dusty or smoky rooms. I didn't like air conditioning if it was possible to have fresh air instead. My list of requirements went on and on. (To put it bluntly, I am kind of a nutcase, with lots of superstitions. I also used to clean everything with rubbing spirit but I finally let go of this ridiculous habit when I left *I'm A Celebrity* . . . To put it bluntly, it took me more than 30 years to become sane!)

My superstitions usually meant that I would have to view a few rooms before I found the right one. Once, in New Haven, Connecticut, we stayed in a hotel which was a blend of old and new. The new rooms had windows, while the older ones often had no windows, just air conditioning. When I was shown the room allocated to me it was an old one. I couldn't stay there, as it had too much dust, and asked to see another. That wasn't right either, so I asked to see a different one again. This went on until I had seen 16 rooms and finally found one that I was happy with: large windows, no dust and no hairs on the sheets or pillows.

The funny thing was, we went back there six months later to play another concert in the area.

When we checked in, the manager was there waiting for me. He had 16 keys laid out on the counter and a bottle of spirits in case the floors weren't clean enough.

'Mr Gest,' he said, picking up the first of them, 'start here and work your way through them. Somewhere here is your dream room!' We both laughed. By the 14th room I think I had found one that was OK.

Of course, it wasn't always possible for me to get the room I wanted. When that happened I had to resort to other measures.

On a European tour we visited Sweden and were booked into the Grand Hotel Saltsjöbaden near Stockholm. As the new star lead singer of the band, Michael McDonald, like the original lead singer Tommy Johnston, had been given a great big, airy room. As their PR man, I had been given a small, dusty room.

Michael didn't know this, luckily. So I went to his room and came up with a bullshit story.

'Michael, I'm really sorry but there's something wrong with your room. They want you to move. It's a health thing. They found lice in the bed and on the sheets and you could catch it. If you caught the lice, they would have to quarantine you here in a detention hospital for a month.' He got scared and immediately moved. He came to see me in that room later on and couldn't believe I was so brave.

'That's OK, Michael,' I said, using the same poker face I had perfected back in elementary school. 'The important thing is your health, not mine.'

When we left the hotel, Michael asked the manager, when I was not around, if I should see a doctor because he was worried. The manager told him that my room was their most expensive suite and the only disease I could get was complete relaxation. Michael didn't speak to me for two days.

Things were going so well with Bruce Cohn and the Doobies that Bruce and I agreed to share an office. We got a place above Scoops, an ice-cream parlour in Sherman Oaks. The band helped us move in.

We had a great time there. The only problem we had was finding the right staff. I fired three secretaries in a row. Then we hired this Mexican girl (*Juanatta Loveshack, no bull!*). I would give her work and she would never do it, so pretty soon I wanted to fire her too.

Bruce always trusted people. He said, 'No, she's real honest. We're keeping this one. I'm sorry, David, but this time she stays.'

Bruce would give her cheques to deposit and things to file. I kept saying, 'I natta believe in her.' He would say, 'You're wrong.'

Six months or so after she had started, Juanatta left early one day. Bruce was there and he needed something, so he went into her drawer to look for it. There he found everything he had ever given her over the last six months: all the cheques, all the letters he had dictated to her, everything. She hadn't done a thing.

Bruce got rid of Juanatta in five minutes and she left that night for her birthplace, Tijuana, Mexico.

I was close to all the Doobies, especially Patrick Simmons (who wrote and sang 'Black Water'), Tommy Johnston (who wrote and sang 'Listen to the Music', 'China Grove', 'Long Train Running' and my favourite, 'Another Park, Another Sunday'). I was even closer to Michael McDonald, as we were nearly the same age. Around 1977, when the album *Minute by Minute* came out, Michael and I started working even more closely together. We had a ball.

The Doobies had two massive hits off the album,

the title track and the Grammy Award-winning Record of the Year, 'What a Fool Believes'. When the third single, 'Here to Love You', came out, however, their record label, Warner Brothers, wouldn't give Bruce and Michael any more money to go out on the road to promote it. Michael had written the song and he wanted to have a third hit single off the album.

Michael asked me, as their PR director, to go with him to Nashville. From there we would drive all the way up to Memphis, going to all the radio stations on the way to promote the song and get a buzz going. In those days that's how you did it. A music promotion man could do the job but by far the best way to do it was for the musicians to do the hard slog themselves.

On Michael's own money, he and I flew to Nashville and rented a car. He drove. I soon set about driving him mad, just totally bonkers.

In Nashville, we were booked into a really nice hotel, Spence Manor. We pulled up alongside an intercom system you had to get past to go through the main gates.

Michael didn't know Nashville, so I sensed an opportunity to have some fun.

I told him that because we were in the self-styled 'Music City', he had to abide by one of the local traditions.

'Michael, you have to sing into the intercom,' I said.

'Sing what?'

'You have to sing, "It's Music City and I am here. I'm Mike McDonald so let's raise a cheer." Otherwise they won't let you in. You have to do it,' I told him.

He gave me a puzzled look but went along with it. The guy on the other end of the intercom came on and said in his southern accent, 'How can I help you?'

Michael began to sing and the voice on the intercom replied, 'Sorry, we don't let weirdos in here.'

They wouldn't open the gates. I was laughing so hard I was on the floor. Michael didn't quite get it for a minute but as soon as he did he nearly peed in his pants too. He couldn't believe that he had been such an idiot as to do that.

Over the following days, we went to radio stations and had a lot of fun. I must have been on some kind of natural high at the time because I couldn't stop playing jokes on Michael – and other people too.

When we arrived in Memphis, I wanted to go to Al Green's church. We arranged to visit him one Sunday but the night before we were invited to a party, a church-related charity function, at the house of his long-time producer, Willie Mitchell. Willie is one of the best-dressed and classiest men I have ever met, and we are friends to this day. He has two lovely daughters, Lorraine and Yvonne. They are like my sisters. He produced all of Al's great records, as well as Ann Peebles' 'I Can't Stand the Rain', one of my first PR successes back at London Records.

When it came time to head for the party, Michael cried off. He had the worst case of crotch-rot from wearing his underwear too tight. He couldn't move. The sides of his legs were all sore and had broken out in a rash.

I had to go this alone. Everybody was black except for me, and they were all from different southern churches, and they were either middle-class or poor. I didn't exactly fit in, so I thought, 'Oh well, let's have some fun.'

I had barely walked into the place when this lady

came up to me. She looked like Butterfly McQueen when she played Prissy in *Gone With the Wind*, except she was six foot four inches tall. I had to really, really look up to talk to her.

'Hi, and what's your name?' she said.

'Reverend Gest,' I replied.

'Reverend, such a pleasure to meet you. What denomination are you?'

At first, I thought, 'What the hell does denomination mean?' but I figured it out.

'Why, I'm a Baptist, of course,' I said.

'Oh Reverend, I am too. So good to meet you. And what book are you reading from?'

I thought to myself, 'Book?'

'Why, the *Book of Life*,' I stated. 'We as people should all come together, no matter what race, colour or creed, for the glory of thine spirit, loving us as we are and not as who we are not. I ordain you to join me in God's blessing of our meeting.'

She said, 'Oh Reverend, you are an inspiration. Where is your parish located?'

In my best Southern accent, I said, 'In North Hollywood, California.'

'How many in your parish?'

'One thousand, five hundred and twelve.'

'Oh Reverend, I would love to come and visit you there.'

'Please, I would love to have you there. My door leads to God's pathway and you are always welcome in our parking lot o' life,' I exclaimed.

'Reverend, let me get you some food. I do not want you to wear out your weary feet,' she said and headed off to the kitchen, where Willie's wife Ann was. Ann was beautiful but feisty.

The lady told her about me and said how lovely I was. 'What a pleasure it is to meet this true man of God,' she said.

Ann just looked at her in amazement and said, 'That ain't no reverend, that's a damn fool if I ever did meet one.'

She was laughing so hard her bridge fell out.

The lady never brought me any food, and after that nobody in the room would speak to me. There must have been 200 people there. I had to leave because they were all ignoring me. When I told Michael he was on the floor laughing.

We went to Al Green's church the next day, even though Michael was still in a lot of pain. The rash had spread all over his legs and he couldn't walk properly.

When we arrived, Al was singing the Curtis Mayfield classic 'People Get Ready'. He still had the most amazing effect on people, only now it was a more religious thing.

This woman who was sitting next to us suddenly started hyperventilating, like a lot of Southern African-American women do when they go to church. She started speaking in tongues and was jumping up and down. Then she fell right into Michael's crotch.

I will never forget the look on Michael's face. It was pure horror.

He just sat there, frozen, obviously in terrible pain, whispering, 'Help me, help me.'

I just smiled at him and said, 'What am I going to do? I'm not getting her off your penis. You will have to play with your own organ today!'

That woman lay there for ten minutes. It was only when Al Green ushered Michael up to sing with him that we were able to remove her from Michael's lap.

Michael and I used to have so much fun playing jokes on each other. My favourite prank was to put on another voice and pretend to be someone else – I loved to do voices. In the early days of working together, Michael went to stay at a hotel in Little Rock, Arkansas. He loved to eat. He had just arrived and I knew the first thing he would do was order food from room service. So I beat him to the punch. As soon as he got to his room, I rang him up, putting on a woman's voice, and said, 'Honey, do you want to order room service?'

'Oh yes, baby, I'll have a hamburger,' he said. He always called people 'sweetheart' or 'baby'.

'OK, darling,' I replied.

'I would like some mustard and ketchup.'

'Baby, we have no mustard or ketchup.'

'None?' he asked.

'None. We just ran out and our shipment is two days late,' I replied.

'OK, I will have some relish.'

'Honey, we're all out of relish. We just got rid of the last of it.'

'OK, I'll have mayonnaise.'

'No mayonnaise.'

'Cheese and lettuce?'

'No cheese or lettuce.'

'Fries?'

'No fries.'

'Well, just put some butter and tomato in the bun.'

'Honey, we have no buns, just toast.'

By this point Michael had had enough, so he started screaming, 'You have no mustard, you have no ketchup, you have no fries, you have no buns. What kind of restaurant is this?'

I started cracking up. It was then that he realised I had had him. I did exactly the same thing to him 25 years later. We weren't working together then but I knew where he was staying.

To his credit, Michael learned to pull practical jokes too.

I was doing a lot of business at that time with Gail Davis, a really smart A&R executive at A&M Records. She would come over to the office I shared with Bruce and we would always have fun.

I loved playing jokes on Gail. I would do things like call her up and pretend to be ringing from the White House. Gail and I used to disagree on things every now and again. She could be tough to break down, so on one occasion I tracked down her mother. I got her to call Gail and give her a talking to.

'Now, Gail, why are you being so mean to that nice Mr Gest?' she told her. 'You really shouldn't be so unkind to such a lovely man.' When we were in

Baltimore one night, I sent a limousine to pick up Gail's mother as a thank you.

I loved making up names for people too, and when I got the opportunity to combine that with a practical joke, I couldn't resist it.

Once we were at a major party in Los Angeles and Gail was, as usual, schmoozing a group of important executives. I went over to the group and started pointing at her, as if she was a long-lost relative.

'Poolitta?' I said. 'Poolitta Barffman, is that you?'

She looked at me as if she wanted to shoot me. One guy corrected me and said, 'No, I think this is Gail Davis.' I ignored that. By the end of the night everyone was calling her Poolitta. I still use that name when I speak to her today, 30 years on.

It was Michael McDonald who really left Gail speechless, however.

One night, late in the seventies, she had brought a bunch of important people to see the Doobies. Halfway through the show, Michael McDonald said he wanted to dedicate the next song to someone special in the audience, Gail Davis.

'We're so glad Gail can be with us tonight,' Michael said, straight-faced. 'She's just recovering from a very serious social disease and we wish her well with her recuperation.'

Afterwards, backstage, she threatened to kill me. 'I know it was you, I know it was you,' she said, pummelling my chest. I was hysterical. I nearly died laughing.

Back when I was a kid, I learned to treat others with respect. I was never mean to anyone and hated it when I saw other people behaving that way. (It is only when someone is rude, out of control or really mean that my temper begins to show. When my temper shows, I can promise you you do not want to mess with me. If you do not believe me, ask anyone I have gotten into an argument with.)

It was the story of my cousin Björn that really brought home to me the dangers of having a mean streak.

Björn lived in Sweden, with my Aunt Uraprik, (pronounced your-a-prick) and was born with magical good-looks. He was so handsome. Unfortunately, he was vain with it. Björn believed that because he was better looking than most people, he was superior to them in every other way too. When he was growing up, he would pick on other children who looked wimpy or ugly or were heavy-set. Björn was a bully and picked on everyone.

He was always very mean to my acne-ridden cousin Prunetta whenever she came to Sweden. Prunetta, as you know, was named after my Aunt Bumba's favourite fruit, the prune. The love of prunes must have run in the family, as my cousin Björn also loved them. Aunt Uraprik would prepare prunes for him every single day, removing the pits (or pips, as you call them in the UK).

Apart from prunes, Björn had two great loves in life: himself and acting. His favourite movie was Grease and he always imagined meeting a girl like Olivia Newton-John and moving to a home in Visby, where they would live happily together for the rest of their lives.

So Björn started acting, and in the early eighties his dream came true and he landed the leading role of Danny in a theatre production of Grease. It was a role he had always wanted and I think I can honestly say he was meant to play the part. A neighbour of Björn's, Agnetha, got the role of Sandy.

Björn did not like Agnetha because she was very overweight. She weighed exactly 247lbs but had the voice of an angel and the sweetest smile in the world. She also had a very dark moustache, which was probably genetic. Björn hated the fact that an overweight twenty-three-year-old girl with a moustache was hired to play his Sandy.

Needless to say, the two leads didn't always get along very well, so the day before they opened at the concert house in Stockholm, at the rehearsal, Agnetha brought a peace-offering for Björn. It was a glass jar filled with his favourite fruit:

prunes.

She knew Björn loved prunes and thought this might change his attitude towards her. The truth was that nothing could elevate Agnetha in Björn's eyes but he did love prunes. So he opened the jar and shoved a few down his throat.

Because my Aunt Uraprik had always prepared the prunes specially for him, Björn did not realise that there were pits in the middle. Björn was not the brightest guy in the world. The pits got stuck in his throat and he choked to death, right there on the stage where he was meant to be opening the very next day.

The odd thing was that Björn's last words to Agnetha, right before she gave him the gift, were: 'You are the pits.' I guess, in the end, he was.

Agnetha went to the funeral and, in honour of Björn, shaved off her moustache with a special grease.

(I recently told this story to David Ian, the producer of a new stage version of *Grease*, who I am currently working with on the ITV1 series, *Grease is the Word*. I have a funny feeling that he thinks all my relatives are idiots. I do not understand where he would get an idea like that from.)

The Doobies' career was in overdrive, and my job was to push them on to even greater heights. Not all my acts were in such a great position, however. Most needed handling differently and I faced a real mix of challenges, some of which I could handle and some I couldn't.

When I was asked to briefly look after The Jackson Five, my job was just to stabilise their career. They came to me at a tricky time, when they had decided to leave Motown Records and were about to join Epic Records. At that time, they were at a virtual standstill. It was sad. Here was a group that had been so big but now they were faltering because Motown, which had written a lot of their earlier material, had not come up with good new songs for them. The Jackson Five had had a recent big hit with 'Dancing Machine', their first major smash in a number of years, which was a gold record but they were still single-sellers when the music business was dominated by albums.

I was only with The Jackson Five for about six to eight months. It was fun to work with them because we were such good friends.

I was hired by Joe Jackson, only for their upcoming tour of the US. I would set up interviews but it was the wrong point in their career. Interest in them was low. It was a bad time for them. They played in Oakland, near San Francisco, and failed to sell out the Coliseum for the first time. That was unheard-of for The Jackson Five. I got Tommy Johnston from the Doobies to be a surprise guest star on one of their shows, singing with Michael. This didn't have any real impact. The Jacksons – and Michael, in particular – were moving inexorably towards another phase in their careers.

At that time, Michael used to come over to my office a lot. I knew that he had his eye on a solo career. That was still a couple of years away but I knew he was planning his next move. He would

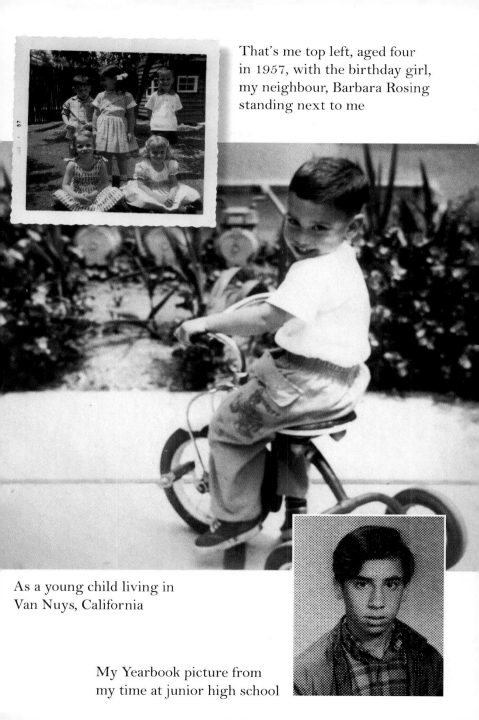

That's me top left, aged four in 1957, with the birthday girl, my neighbour, Barbara Rosing standing next to me

As a young child living in Van Nuys, California

My Yearbook picture from my time at junior high school

In a photo booth at the time of *Off the Wall*. I wish now I would have kept my old nose

Hanging out with Michael in the early 1980s at my office in Studio City, California. Michael always loved waffles!

Michael and my plastic surgeon, Steven Hoefflin

A note from Michael after a face peel

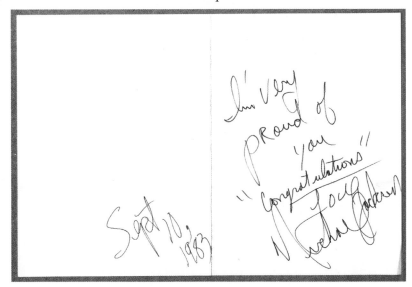

I'm very
PROUD of
you
"Congratulations"
love
Michael Jackson

Sept 10,
1983

I can't remember what
Al Green did to his arm but
looks like he doesn't care.
My associate at London
Records, Jack Ross, is in the
background

With Carla Thomas and
Dee Dee Jackson, my best
friend until the day she died

With (*clockwise from top right*)
Ann 'I Can't Stand the Rain'
Peebles, Ray Caviano, Don
Bryant and Bob Small

ROBERT FOOTHORAP

Tito and Dee Dee with their
first two sons, Taj and Taryll

Savoy Brown with Kim Simmonds (*far left*) and Stan Webb (*centre*). In the background are all my London Records associates

With the legendary film producer Frank Capra around 1982

I must have been contemplating a big deal because I look very serious!

The 1970s with that hair and beard!

My sunglasses phase . . . I no longer hide behind them. If I learned anything from the British public, it is do not wear sunglasses at night!

The 1994 International Achievement In Arts Awards poster –
my first major production in England at London's Dominion Theatre.
What an amazing line-up

hang out at the office, listening and talking to people, picking up all the advice and all the knowledge he could. He soaked it up like a sponge. Michael and I were so close at this point, we were like brothers. He understood me better than anybody else; still does.

Bruce and the other people in the office didn't quite understand the relationship I had with the Jacksons. To them they were superstars, to me they were friends I treated the same way I treated everyone else.

Bruce was amazed one day when Michael asked whether someone could give him a lift home to Encino.

I was tied up with something. Without looking up, I just said, 'Someone tell him to shut up and sit there until I have finished.' Bruce couldn't believe I talked to Michael that way.

Some acts were beyond help, of course.

Towards the mid-seventies, I was asked to handle Harold Melvin & the Blue Notes. With Gamble and Huff at Philadelphia International guiding them, they had had a string of inter-national hits between 1972 and 1975. Songs like 'If

You Don't Know Me By Now', 'Don't Leave Me This Way' and 'The Love I Lost' became classics but there had been tensions both inside and outside the band.

When I met them I heard alarm bells straight away. At our first meeting, Harold Melvin was stoned. I discovered he had a real drink and drugs problem. I did like their lead singer, Teddy Pendergrass, who was very shy.

I was wary of getting involved so I said I would work with them for three months and review things after that. It was soon clear that it wasn't going to work. Whenever I turned up to see Harold, he was drunk or stoned. It was sad to see a figure I had admired so much in such a bad way. I remember once meeting him and talking about our contract, which he had just signed. He didn't even know he had signed it. I realised pretty quickly that there was little point in me carrying on. You could never do anything for Harold because he was always so out there.

The hardest thing to do in my job was to revive careers. It was hard enough to get an artist one bite of the cherry; a second one was almost impossible. That was the challenge I faced when I was asked to breathe some new life into the career of the legendary songwriter Burt Bacharach.

Burt had been introduced to me by his then wife Angie Dickinson, the legendary actress who starred in TV's *Police Woman* and numerous hit Hollywood movies, including *Ocean's Eleven*, *Dressed to Kill*, *Point Blank* and *Rio Bravo*, among others. I had become friendly with her after she had attended a Doobies concert as a guest in 1975. I loved Angie. She is an amazingly warm and funny woman and is still one of my best friends today. (The loss of her daughter Nikki in 2007 really took its toll on her. I loved Nikki and Angie is by far one of the greatest ladies I have ever met and was a wonderful and dedicated mother.)

Burt's career had nosedived by 1981, after he and his long-time collaborator Hal David had worked on a remake of the classic movie *Lost Horizon* in the mid-seventies. The film had been a critical and commercial disaster and had hit Burt's career hard. He and Hal David had fallen out afterwards and stopped working together. Burt had produced a couple of albums but nothing had really happened.

I knew Burt wasn't the easiest guy to get close

to – like many great artists he was something of a loner – but I always wanted to meet my heroes and he had always been one to me because I loved the songs he wrote. I felt that the more people you know, the more interesting your life.

So I threw a party to mark Burt becoming one of my clients. I didn't want to overdo it, so it was a really intimate party at a sushi restaurant in Studio City. There were about 40 people there. Michael and Tito came, the former a huge admirer of Burt. Also attending were Eddie van Halen, with his then girlfriend Valeri Bertinelli, and Dusty Springfield, for whom Burt had written 'The Look of Love' back in the sixties.

I had also invited the composer Marvin Hamlisch and his then girlfriend, the talented lyricist Carole Bayer Sager. Burt told me he had once tried to work with her and it had not worked out but I thought they would still make a good writing team. I put Burt and Carole together with Michael McDonald and they wrote some songs. Burt and Carole's talents really shone when they wrote the theme song for the movie *Arthur*, starring Dudley Moore and a girl named Liza Minnelli. This song, 'Arthur's Theme (The Best That You

Can Do)', won Burt and Carole the Oscar and set his career flying again. It made me realise that I had a knack for helping people's careers out of the doldrums. It was something I would do a lot in the years to come.

I had helped to get Burt back to the top, where he belongs, but the irony was that within a year and a half he had left Angie and married Carole. I had revived a career and killed a marriage. My working relationship with Burt didn't last long either. After Burt left Angie, I was let go by both Burt and Carole, who I also handled for a short time. Welcome to showbusiness, baby! Nothing lasts forever.

Men in
the Mirror

One of my favourite cousins was called Ida. She was a teacher in Chicago. Ida was married to a guy called Cosmo, who was a dentist. They had three children: two sons, Dexter and Billy, and a daughter, Dilly. All three children worked in the food industry. Dexter worked for Godiva chocolates, packaging the sweets. Billy worked as a manager for McDonald's. He put all the cheese on the cheeseburgers. Dilly worked for McDonald's too. She put the dill pickles on the burgers. It was very odd but whenever I went to Chicago I got free burgers, with lots of pickles, and free chocolates.

What happened to Ida was pretty sad. She was a diabetic and had put on a lot of weight. I went to visit her once and she was 425 pounds.

Anyhow, the day before Christmas one year, she ate a chocolate caramel that had grown really hard and she died. They thought at first it was diabetes but it wasn't. She couldn't breathe. The caramel had stuck her teeth together.

It was odd, as Cosmo was a dentist. They buried her with the caramel still stuck to her teeth. Somehow they couldn't get it out. I used to visit them a lot, but when Ida died it took all the excitement out of the visits.

At the funeral wake there were lots of McDonald's cheeseburgers with extra pickles and Godiva chocolates. I avoided the chocolate-covered caramels. Ida kept that family together; she was a really sweet woman. Whenever I get overweight I think about her.

One day, in 1977, I organised a lunch meeting with Burt Bacharach, who I had just signed, and Jerry Moss, the 'M' of the hugely successful A&M Records label he ran with Herb Alpert. We went to

La Scala, one of the best Italian restaurants in Beverly Hills.

It was a good, productive lunch, discussing promotion for Burt's new A&M album *Woman*, but as we sat and talked something suddenly hit me. Both Jerry and Burt were 15 to 18 years older than me. I was twenty-four and they were both in their forties. The thing was, they both looked younger, healthier and much more handsome than I did. I suddenly felt very ugly sitting next to them.

My time in New York with London Records and the troubles I had been through with Al Green had really taken their toll on me physically. I am the type of person who, when unhappy, really puts on weight. I had come back from New York weighing about 220lbs. I had a triple chin and a huge nose and I compared myself to these two guys in this meeting and thought how ugly I looked.

I remember going to the bathroom that day and looking in the mirror properly for the first time in ages and realising what I had become. I knew exactly what I needed to do. I also knew exactly who was going to help me do it.

Over the years, Michael Jackson and I had become the best of friends. We were truly brothers.

Even though we came from very different backgrounds, in many ways we had a lot in common. An awful lot.

We never talked about it much but we had both had a hard time at the hands of our fathers. Perhaps as a result of that, we were both very driven people. We both had a real need to make it.

From an early age, Michael's goal was to be the biggest star in the world. He was so intense, so intent on beating every Beatles record, every Elvis Presley record. He wanted to be the king of it all. It meant more to him than anything else. Having split from The Jackson Five by now, he was at work on his first big solo album, *Off the Wall*, and was determined that this was going to be the record that got that process going.

Another of the things we had in common was that we were both deeply insecure about our looks. At the time, we both had huge Afros and bad skin. Michael's Afro was enormous and he used to treat it with oil that kept it in good condition. Unfortunately, it would also make his forehead break out in spots. He used to stay at my apartment on Doheny often. When he did, he used to go to bed with a pair of underpants around his hair, so the oil wouldn't get on his forehead during the night. What a sight that was.

We both used to put bottles and bottles of Clearasil on our faces. At times, I'm sure we must have looked like we were from a different planet. We used to laugh hysterically sometimes, as we both stared into the mirror, smearing this stuff on.

A couple of days after my lunch with Burt and Jerry, I went to see Michael. I could talk to him about this. Also, I knew that he had a plastic surgeon, a guy named Steven Hoefflin, who had done some work to thin out Michael's nose a little.

'When you did that thing to your nose,' I asked him, 'did it make you feel better?'

'Yeah, it did,' he said. 'Why?'

'Because I think I would like to change the way I look.'

Michael put me in touch with Steven and I went to meet him at his office in Santa Monica. He immediately put me at ease. He was a brilliant, sympathetic man.

As a kid, I never worried about my looks. I had always been able to attract girls and it hadn't really been something I had thought about. Now it was different. There were a lot of things I wasn't happy with. I had a very hooked nose and I didn't like my chin. It didn't look strong enough, I felt.

Steven showed me some drawings of what he thought he could do for me. He suggested taking the hook out of my nose and putting in a chin implant. He also suggested I have some implants put in to make my cheekbones look higher and a face-lift to get rid of my triple chin.

Soon afterwards, I went into his surgery to start the process. The first thing that happened was my nose job. I felt weird going in for the surgery. I really wasn't sure how it was going to turn out.

I was still living on Doheny and Michael came over to look after me during my recuperation. He was great. He stayed with me for a week. Very soon afterwards, I had the second procedure, the chin implant, and he nursed me through that too.

All in all, Michael stayed with me for three weeks. He was fantastic company. We loved to just hang out. We used to stay in and listen to LP after LP. We would also watch murder mysteries and comedies, both of which Michael loved.

It may seem odd to some people but Michael waited on me hand and foot. He nursed me back to health.

His mother and La Toya would come over to check up on us and bring us food. I will never forget one day when they brought some containers full of food over to the apartment. I have never exactly been good around the kitchen. In fact, I didn't even know how to work a microwave. Neither did La Toya. So when she stuck the Styrofoam containers of food in the microwave later that day, the whole meal just disappeared. All that was left was a little ball of Styrofoam. Mrs Jackson hadn't explained to La Toya that you had to take the food out of the Styrofoam before cooking it. Michael had been out that day. When he came back he was on the floor for an hour, laughing at her.

One of the best things about being with Michael was that he didn't judge me for what I was doing and he wasn't fazed by the way I looked in the immediate aftermath of the surgery. I remember my old school friend Sandi Berg came over to see me. I had rung her and asked her to bring over some movies for Michael and me to watch. I wanted to surprise her, so I told her I wasn't feeling well because I had just had my tonsils removed.

I will never forget the look on her face when she opened the door and saw my face, looking black and blue as if I had just been in a car crash. She looked stunned. She told me later that she thought she was going to die.

Michael was having more work done too, in particular on his nose. So, a few weeks later, when he went in for his operation, I returned the favour and looked after him.

Again, Michael stayed at my place on Doheny. We used to play a game where we would have to guess the exact year of a record release. If I won, I would get something like his costume from *The Wiz*, the film he had starred in opposite Diana Ross. If he won, he would take one of my albums or rare books. We were always trading things and playing games.

Our experience during that period brought me and Michael even closer. We started spending more and more time together. When we went out, we didn't like to take security. We would always go alone.

We used to sing together in the car. I'm totally off-key and Michael would always turn to me and say, 'I have no idea what you are singing.' Al Green and Whitney Houston used to say the same. I would tease Michael about his singing too. One day, we heard one of his old singles, 'Ben', on the radio and I said, 'You'll never hit those notes again.' He cracked up.

Within a year or so of that time, Michael's life had been transformed. *Off the Wall* had come out and he had been elevated to the status of a true global superstar. His innovative dance moves were also becoming legendary.

What always amazed people was that I would get Michael to do stuff for me. When we needed to get gas, I would always make Michael go out and pump the gas. I have never learned to do it. To this day, I don't know how to connect the pump to the gas tank. Michael would get out and complain, 'But I'm the star!' He would be standing there, filling the car up with petrol, and people would ask for autographs.

Often, we would go out to buy records and antiques. We would go to Tower Records at midnight, after it had closed to the public. Sometimes Michael would pick out 1,500 CDs and the bill would be like $8,000 or $10,000 or $12,000. Often, he would give me a large chunk of what he had bought. He was always very generous, and I had learned from that. I tried to become generous too. The key lesson to learn in life is that it is much more important to give than to take. I still believe that.

Aside from all this, the thing that really made us close was the fact that we shared the same sense of humour. I think that, for whatever reasons, both of us were still kids at heart. We were both incurable practical jokers. We were always playing jokes on people.

Michael used to love calling people up. He would do it when he came over to my house. He would just pick up the phone, dial a random number and start horsing around.

The person at the other end would pick up the phone and Michael would say, 'Who's this?'

They would reply something like, 'It's Lenore.'

He would go, 'Oh, Lenore, listen, we're going to have to get a divorce. I can't carry on like this.'

She would go, 'No, no, you have the wrong . . .'

Michael would interrupt and say, 'No, Lenore, don't even try that on me. I've just had it with you. We'll divide the property evenly and everything but it's got to be this way.'

Then he would hang up, leaving the person at the other end of the line wondering what the hell had just happened.

When we went out to restaurants together he would love to mess around with the waitresses. If a waitress was walking through the restaurant carrying a plate with a BLT and french fries, we would steal all the french fries off it while she was walking. When she gave the customers their meals, they would say, 'Where are the fries?' She would turn around in a panic, muttering to herself, 'I know I put them on there.'

We would go to Disneyland. We both loved rollercoasters. Sometimes we would go on them 20 times in a row.

Often, Michael would wear disguises. Once, he was a sheikh and I was his translator. We would go into a place called Carnation Restaurant in Disneyland where they served great tuna salad and sandwiches. Michael was eating organic food only, although, at that time, he had a rather strange idea of what organic was. We would go to Kentucky Fried Chicken. Michael reckoned that if you took off the skin it became organic.

Anyhow, at Carnation on this particular day, there were two elderly women and a gentleman in their eighties from Croydon. We started talking in our mock Arabic to each other.

When the two ladies looked over, I turned to one of them and explained, 'The Sheikh Majolini wanted me to tell you that you are a beautiful woman and so is your friend,' I said.

These two ladies probably hadn't been paid a compliment in the last couple of decades, so they started smiling. We then got talking. They asked what the sheikh was doing here and I said he had just got divorced from his 97th wife and was here to see his 154th child.

'He has 154 children?' they asked, looking shocked.

'That he knows of,' I said. 'He has had 97 wives . . .' and I started naming them, 'Jada, Jami, Shakira, Vera . . .' with Michael saying them in mock Arabic.

There was nothing malicious in it. In fact, Michael picked up their bill. He was like that, always pulling practical jokes on people.

Sometimes, though, the joke would be on us. The funniest thing that ever happened to us was when we went for pancakes one night. It was after 1 a.m. and our regular haunt, Dupars, was closed, so we went to another pancake house that we knew on Ventura Boulevard. There was only one couple in there; normally it held 150 people.

The waitress who served us was in her late sixties or early seventies. This was around 1979, when *Off the Wall* had come out. Michael was the no. 1 artist in the world. She didn't recognise him at all.

We got to the table and she came over and asked us what we wanted to order. I put on a Saudi accent and went, 'Yamaka fallesh.'

Michael started laughing. The waitress slapped Michael across the face with the back of her hand. She said, 'This is not funny. Your friend is from a foreign country and you have respect for people from foreign countries.'

Michael got nervous. He wasn't used to being treated like that in public. He slid further inside the booth so he couldn't get slapped again.

I asked, 'What is pancake? Explain please.'

The waitress started miming a pressing motion. She said, 'It's like a cake that you press down.'

Michael started to laugh again and she started to put her hand up again, so he slid further away.

She then said, 'OK, I'm going to take you back to the kitchen.' She and the cook showed us how to make pancakes. I ordered some.

When the pancakes came to our table, I took the

syrup bottle and emptied the whole bottle all over the pancakes. She immediately slapped me across the face. It hurt.

'Not funny,' she said. Michael was laughing again.

She brought me a new batch and I ate them. When we left, Michael left her a $200 tip.

We were in the car park, heading back to Michael's Rolls Royce, when the waitress came running after us.

'I'm not taking this. You boys are probably working your way through college and you need this money,' she said, not even noticing the car that he was driving.

Michael insisted but she said, 'No, I'm not taking it.' We couldn't believe it.

In November 1980, my father died suddenly. He was fifty-eight. The distance that had opened between us when I was a kid had remained in place ever since.

We would see each other now and again. He respected the fact that I had made it in the record business on my own, without any help from him. He had been to a couple of my concerts over the years. He saw Al Green and the Doobies when they played in Los Angeles. There just had never been a real connection between us.

Truthfully, when I heard the news that he had passed on, the loss didn't have any effect on me. What upset me most were the circumstances surrounding his death. My father had died cheating on my mother. He had dropped dead of a heart attack while leaving the home of his long-time lover. He died on her doorstep. She must have been one great lay.

Nobody wants to hear that their father is being unfaithful to their mother. To hear that this was the last thing he had done was even harder to take. I wasn't angry. As far as I was concerned, it was his life. I never get involved with what other people do. Ultimately, people have to take responsibility for themselves and their actions.

My friends supported me at the funeral. I remember Randy and Tito Jackson came, as did many of my friends from the music industry in Los Angeles and my father's greatest friend, Aaron, who was also a good friend to me. I was also really touched to see Michael at the house in Encino, where my mother was still living. He was, by then, the biggest star in the entire world and in demand everywhere. He knew that my father and I were never close, that there was no love lost there. That Michael Jackson took the time to come and pay his respects meant a great deal to me.

I regarded my clients as an extended family and would frequently get them together. Michael McDonald and Michael Jackson and I would often go out together. I was the leader of the gang at that point. The three of us went to see Diana Ross at the Forum in Los Angeles, and other times we would just go to the Dairy Queen, an ice-cream parlour near my office. We'd always have a lot of fun.

One night, Michael Jackson and I went to the Roxy to see The Four Tops, who had just left Motown Records for ABC/Dunhill Records and were having hits again. Stevie Wonder was also there in the audience.

Afterwards, Michael and I went backstage to meet the group's lead singer, Levi Stubbs, whom we both knew. I gave him a big congratulatory hug. 'Levi, you are the greatest singer. I think you are just incredible,' I said.

Michael said the same thing. 'Levi, I learned everything from you. You are the greatest.'

Before he knew what had hit him, Michael was being picked up by Stevie Wonder, who had been standing behind him. He threw him up against the wall and started shaking him.

'Who is the greatest?' he said. 'Who did you learn everything from?'

Michael soon changed his tune. 'You, Stevie, you,' he said. 'Put me down.'

We all laughed. We knew Stevie was joking.

Another time, I got Michael together with Burt Bacharach and Carole Bayer Sager. It was a memorable evening, mainly because it was the first time Michael had drunk wine.

We went out to dinner at a place called Dominic's, a hole in the wall across the road from Cedars Sinai Hospital on Beverly Boulevard in Los Angeles. Burt used to like to go there. Carole was recording her second album for Elektra and wanted to see Michael.

Michael was staying at my place on Doheny and was happy to come along. He really respected Burt but wondered, as we all did, what made him tick.

Burt had ordered a bottle of expensive French red wine, which he, Carole and I were drinking. Michael never drank but that night he got interested in wine. Unbelievably, he didn't even know what wine was.

'What's it made of?' he asked me.

'Grapes,' I said.

'I like grapes,' Michael said. 'I think I'll try some.'

So we poured Michael a glass and he drank it. He obviously liked it because he drank another one. We were drinking a 1982 Pomerol that tasted like candy, so he was bound to like it.

By this time, we had all had a glass or two and the bottle was finished. So Burt ordered a second bottle. This time, Michael drank virtually the whole bottle. He had really acquired a taste for wine, fine wine at that, and was guzzling the stuff down. So we ordered a third bottle and Michael drank most of that as well. That's when I knew we were going to have a problem that night.

The evening came to an end and I drove Michael back to my place. He was, understandably, happy. In fact, he was flying high, very high. In the car he was talking and laughing. He was singing 'I Want to Be Where You Are' and 'Never Can Say Goodbye'. Then he started singing more of his hits, songs like 'Ben'. He was giggling away all the time.

'You're going to be in trouble,' he said. 'I'm going to tell Joseph what you did.'

I wasn't taking the bait. 'I didn't do it, you did,' I said.

It took us a few minutes to get back to my place. The minute I parked the car and opened the door for him, Michael leaned out and threw up all over the place. He spent the rest of the night hanging over the toilet. He was as sick as a dog. I was up all night with him.

He kept saying, 'I'm going to tell Joe you corrupted me.' I was kinda worried he would but he never did.

It was his first taste of wine, something he would come to love a little too much in later years. I always felt bad about that night but it sure was funny!

All in all, I spent three years or so having plastic surgery. It came to an end at the beginning of the eighties. I was pretty happy with what Steven Hoefflin had done for me. He elongated my face by putting in the chin implant, then added a cleft chin and gave my face some dimension with cheekbones. This made me feel really different about myself. On top of this, I had lost a lot of weight by dieting. I had gone down from 240lbs to 150lbs. I had really got myself together.

I didn't feel like I needed any more work done on my face. Michael wasn't so sure. We were hanging out together one day and Michael started looking me up and down. 'Are you sure you don't want to make your nose even thinner?' he said.

I looked long and hard in the mirror and said, 'No, it's fine. I'm happy with it now.' Unfortunately, I wasn't so strong-willed a few months later when I went through the experience that finally persuaded me to stop having plastic surgery.

What happened was that I met another plastic surgeon at a function. He could see that I had had some work done and we got talking. He was very complimentary about what Steven had achieved for me.

'You look great,' he said, but surgeons, like entertainers, have egos and he couldn't resist a little boasting.

'I reckon I can make you look even better,' he smiled at me. He reckoned I should have bigger cheekbones inserted. Even better, he said he would do it for free. I would be his walking advertisement.

So once again I went into surgery and had cheek

implants inserted on top of my already large cheek implants. What a mistake.

It was around five months later that I realised what the doctor had done to me, or rather what I had done to me. I'll never forget looking in the mirror as I was getting into an elevator and thinking to myself, 'I look like a Martian.' It suddenly dawned on me that the cheekbones he had put in made it look like an American football player's helmet was stuck on the inside of my face.

Michael wasn't in town at the time so I called my close friend Freda Payne and asked her straight what she thought.

'Freda, have you noticed that my new cheekbones look excessively high?' I asked. 'You can be honest with me.'

There was a moment's silence and then she started laughing. 'David, they are the worst thing you could possibly have done. They look utterly ridiculous.'

So I went back to Steven Hoefflin and he took them out. That's when I realised that this was the end of my little romance with plastic surgery. It was 1981. Contrary to what many tabloids have written, I haven't had anything else done since.

The only other thing I have done since then is to have some hair transplants put in at the end of the eighties. My hair was really going by then. It helped but it didn't work on the crown, which carried on thinning.

I still fill in the thin spots on my head with black eye shadow by MAC. What the hell, we are all entitled to be vain in some way.

Apart from that, my philosophy has been simple. This is me, this is who I am. Take me or leave me.

New Day

I've always been someone who makes changes in
my life. I get to a point when I say, 'Hey, that's it,
New Day.' I will just make the change and go with
the flow. That's exactly what happened in 1981.

In the seven years or so since setting up my PR
firm, I had built it into a thriving business. I had
handled some of the world's most successful acts,
from The Jacksons and Al Green, to The Doobie
Brothers and Burt Bacharach. I had done everything
from creating careers to reviving them.

When I was approached by another company

that year with a view to selling off my firm and client list, however, I had to think about it seriously. As I did so, I started to wonder whether the time was right to bring down the curtain on this part of my life.

If I was honest, I had an ego myself and rather than building stars, I had ambitions to do something more creative. Producing, in particular, was something I felt I could do well and I had all sorts of ideas in that direction. So when I got a formal offer of a couple of million dollars for my company, I knew pretty much immediately what to say. New Day.

It was an incredible amount of money at the time. I was twenty-seven years old and I was a millionaire. I had a house on the beach in Santa Monica, which I had purchased for over $1.2 million, and another house in Palm Springs, where I liked to spend the winters. I was made for life, or so I thought.

My cousin Elmo Gluk was a very clever guy. He was a plumber. When he was in his thirties, he fell in love with an Eskimo, a girl named Yakacheenah. They got married and went to live in an igloo in the snowy wastes of Alaska. Now what not a lot of people know is that there are 50,000 Eskimos in Alaska, and some of their igloos melt because there is no plumbing to keep them cool all through the year.

So Elmo came up with a technique to stop the ice from melting. He would install piping that kept the ice and snow on the outside chilled throughout the year, even when the sun was shining.

It was a great idea and lots of Eskimos wanted to take it up. So he gave up plumbing regular homes and started dealing strictly with igloos. He made a lot of money out of it. He and Yakacheenah live in one of the biggest igloos in Alaska now. You can look him up in the phone book. Under Gluck Igloo Plumbing in Alaska. That's absolutely true.

The elation didn't last too long. I've always been someone who likes to work. I was soon thinking about my next move.

Part of me thought I should stay in the music industry. I was always going to stay slightly connected. I owned different publishing rights relating to certain people that I had handled, so I was going to make good money from royalties.

I wondered whether I should take on a more

creative role, perhaps as a songwriter. I had been writing love songs for a long time but I had never fully concentrated on them, and I should have.

Two or three years earlier, I had been lined up to write some songs with the rock singer Felix Cavalieri, who was the former lead singer of The Young Rascals and then The Rascals. He was writing an album called *Destiny* and he wanted me to help him with the title song. I hadn't liked the look of the contract his recording company, Bearsville, wanted me to sign so I had backed out.

Tito Jackson and I had started writing songs together at one point too. Aretha Franklin lived around the corner from my parents in Encino and I knew her son. She invited us round and we played a selection of our songs for her. She was really keen to record them but by the time Tito and I had found the time to finish them, she had moved to Detroit and the moment had passed.

The more I thought about it though, the more convinced I became that it was time to make a break from the music business. I wanted to do something different, pursue a new avenue. As I sat in my house in Santa Monica, an idea began to take shape.

It had been Michael Jackson who had revived

my interest in classic movies. Going to the cinema with my grandmother Bess had fired my imagination early on. Watching The Three Stooges, The Marx Brothers and Fred Astaire and Gene Kelly musicals with Michael had rekindled the love affair. My passion, however, was murder movies, classic film noir.

Such was his fame by now that Michael was on friendly terms with some of the Hollywood greats. He had introduced me to Gene Kelly. I was blown away to meet a star of that magnitude. He was such a gentleman, a throwback to another, nobler age, I thought.

It set me thinking. I had seen how big an audience the old musical acts could pull in during my early days in the music business, working for Art Laboe. I would still see ads for shows featuring the old rock 'n' roll stars and they were still packing them in at big venues around LA and New York. I also knew, again from spending time with Michael, how big the old Hollywood memorabilia market was. People spent fortunes on items connected to that golden age of movie-making.

So I figured there had to be an audience for a show, or a series of shows, where people could turn out to meet some of these great film names from the past. Equally, having worked with stars in the music business, I had a hunch that Hollywood was filled with older and retired actors and performers whose egos would love to bask in the limelight once more. There were probably a few who could do with a little extra money too.

I started to cook up a plan for something new, an event that I could produce and that would open the door to a new phase in my career.

As the idea took shape in my head, I bounced it off some friends. I began to see it as a series of events – film screenings, signings, talks and awards dinners – where people could meet the stars of yesteryear. It would be entertaining, with people performing in front of a big orchestra. Above all, it would be very glamorous.

I had a couple of connections with actors. In particular, I was friendly with a guy called Peter McCrea, son of the actor Joel McCrea, who had starred in one of my all-time favourite movies, *Sullivan's Travels*, directed by Preston Sturges. Peter not only thought it was a good idea, he offered to help.

What I needed first was a venue. I wasn't sure

whether Los Angeles was the right place to begin something like this. Wow, how stupid I was. I knew a dealer in film memorabilia in Houston, Texas. When I mentioned the idea to him he got real excited. 'They would love it here,' he said. 'Houston's a money town, an oil town. All the millionaires will come. Do it in Houston.'

I didn't know Texas at all but I trusted this guy's judgement and started sounding out venues there. The key thing now was to line up some stars.

I didn't know that many film people at this point. Peter McCrea was a great help and other friends, like Michael and Tito, helped me to get hold of the numbers I needed. I started making calls.

One of the first numbers I rang was that of Vincent Price, the king of the Hammer Horror movies, in particular those classic movies based on Edgar Allen Poe's stories: *The Raven*, *The Fall of the House of Usher* and *The Pit and the Pendulum*. My powers of persuasion seemed to work as well in the film business as they had in the music industry. I told him that we would devote an evening to celebrating his movies and that all of Houston would be there. I also promised to meet all his expenses, of course. In that fabulous, quiet, gravelly voice of his, he agreed to come along.

Encouraged by this, I called the actress Butterfly McQueen, who had played Prissy in *Gone With the Wind*. Everyone remembers the weeping maid, Prissy. She was the one who twittered, 'I don't know nothin' about birthin' babies' when Melanie Hamilton was about to go into labour. Butterfly said yes too. I was on a roll.

Over the weeks that followed, I talked to more than a dozen Hollywood greats, most of whom agreed to come to the event. My list of confirmed stars soon included Dana Andrews, who starred in *Laura*, Kathryn Grayson, the MGM singing star whose career had ranged from appearing in *Ziegfeld Follies* to classics like *Show Boat* and *Kiss Me Kate*; Mervyn Le Roy, who produced *The Wizard of Oz* and directed films like *Random Harvest* and *Quo Vadis*; Joan Bennett, the leading lady of the thirties and forties, who appeared in *Little Women*; and Debra Paget, who starred in *Love Me Tender* with Elvis Presley and *Broken Arrow* with Robert Wagner.

I spent a lot of time down in Palm Springs, working on the plans. A lot of old Hollywood stars spent their winters in Palm Springs and, thanks to a lady I knew down there, I was introduced to one of my favourite actresses, Gene Tierney, who starred in the classic film *Laura*. I was ecstatic when Gene agreed to have dinner with me on my next trip to Houston, where she resided. We became friends but unfortunately Gene was unstable. She spent time in and out of institutions and it was therefore hard to know which Gene you were going to get when you met her. Once, we were having lunch and she just began crying and left. It was weird but that was Gene Tierney. I was happy to reunite her with her *Laura* co-star Dana Andrews.

I had always been someone who poured myself into my work, and I did so again now. My office at home was soon swimming in film reels, old photographs and posters. I was doing everything myself, putting film clips together and writing material about the various stars for the programmes we were going to produce. I decided to call it The Yellow Rose of Texas Awards.

As things took shape, I was constantly doing the sums, asking myself, 'How much is this going to make?'

In principle, it looked like a pretty profitable enterprise. For instance, I was going to charge a $15 entrance fee for my Evening with Vincent

Price. If 1,000 people turned up that would generate $15,000, more than enough to cover the costs. At the end of the week, I was going to stage a big gala dinner, at which people would have a chance to enjoy a show and then sit down and talk to all these great old stars. I was sure 500 people would be willing to pay $150 dollars to come. That was another $75,000, at least. Some people might pay more to sit at the top tables. On top of this, there were seven days of different events. There were 40 showings of movies. If each of those made a few thousand dollars, things would look even better.

I also figured sponsorship would boost the coffers hugely. A friend with experience in that area reckoned we could easily pull in maybe $250,000 worth of sponsorship from companies that would want to associate themselves with such a prestigious event. I had already put out a few feelers.

There were costs, of course. A lot of them. I had committed to flying all these stars to Houston without getting an airline sponsor and also to putting them up in five star hotels. I also had the expense of hiring the venue and the marketing and advertising to pay for. The bottom line was that I would be happy to break even. If it worked and established me as a producer, I could even live with a small loss. That didn't look likely though. When I added all these sums up, I could see myself making $50,000, maybe even $100,000, clear profit. It was looking good.

All in all, I spent six months planning. The week of the festival was soon upon me and I headed down to Houston full of hope. All of the events were at the Shamrock Hotel.

It was in the days leading up to the first event, when the stars started arriving, that I got the first inkling that I may have miscalculated the costs. In all, I had lined up around 20 movie stars but they had all added on their entourages of make-up artists and agents, some two or three strong. Some had also refused to fly anything other than first class.

I was already forking out a lot of money and I knew some big bills were being run up. I had spent a lot on advertising and promotion, in particular. I was still confident that the shows would be a success at that point, however. It didn't take long for that confidence to be crushed.

The first event was An Evening With *Gone With the Wind*'s Butterfly McQueen. We had hired a

2,500-seat auditorium in the hotel where all the events were taking place. There was going to be a screening of *Gone With the Wind* and a question and answer session with Butterfly, as well as a chance for people to get autographs. Since I owned the concession, all pictures sold would profit me, as well as the programmes for the event. Everyone loved *Gone With the Wind*, and everyone loved her performance in it. I figured this was one of the sure-fire hits of the festival.

When I walked into the auditorium with Butterfly, I nearly died. There were five people there. When I looked at them closely, I saw that they were five people I had invited. I was stunned. I just kept mumbling to myself, 'No people, no people. Why are there no people?'

My mind was in overdrive for a while. I just couldn't understand it. I had spent so much cash making sure the event was advertised. I had advertised it in the papers and had radio stations across Houston plugging the event. The only thing I could surmise was that nobody believed these stars would show up. Or, even scarier, no one cared.

Butterfly bravely went through with the evening.

A few more people turned up during the screening. I got back to the hotel that night and sat awake virtually all night. I thought 'What the hell have I got myself involved in?'

The following day, we set up the event for Vincent Price. Overnight, I had convinced myself there had been some big foul-up with the *Gone With the Wind* event. Perhaps there had been something wrong with the local promotion. Maybe there had been something else happening that night in Houston, although I couldn't for the life of me work out what it might have been. This would be different, I told myself. Wrong.

When Vincent walked into the room there were 15 people there. It was embarrassing. I saw his face sink. Again, professional that he was, he went through the motions, signing the autographs and answering the questions, but when he left he barely acknowledged me. I knew what he was thinking. And he was right.

By the end of the first week, 100 or so people had showed up for the seven days of festival events. When it came to the grand gala dinner, what was meant to be the climax of this week of festivities, 150 showed up. The room was set out to accommodate 500 people. It looked empty. The show went ahead as planned and went down really well. I had drilled the band and performers hard beforehand and they all delivered crowd-pleasing performances but I knew no show was a success unless it had an audience. This one did not!

As I sat there at dinner I kept asking myself the same question. Where did I go wrong?

It was a complete and utter fiasco. I had already forked out close to $1 million. As the bills came in, I realised it was even more of a disaster than I had thought.

I discovered that Joan Bennett had charged something like $20,000 dollars worth of liquor to her room. I couldn't believe it, so I asked the hotel management to explain the bill. They told me that she had been ordering booze from the moment she arrived until the moment she left. She was drinking all the time, and she even took the bottles she didn't drink home with her. It was just nuts.

Some of the other bookings had charged expensive meals, beauty treatments, all sorts of things. When I looked at everything – the hotels, the venues, the staff, the musicians – the bills were gigantic. When I added it all up, I saw that I owed a grand total of $1.5 million, and I was liable for every single cent of it.

The one – very small – piece of solace I could take was that the critics thought the event was a huge success. I had discovered that I had a talent for putting on a show of this kind. People had really loved it. Well, at least those few who had attended. All the newspapers in Houston praised the festival. In fact, one or two of them said Houston didn't deserve such an event if it wasn't going to support it. One said, 'What a night, shame more people in Houston didn't turn out.'

It had been a critical success but there was no escaping the fact that it was a financial disaster. The more I looked at it, the more I realised that there was only one person to blame. That person was me.

It was as if I hadn't learned anything since the day cousin Bob and I had sold 400 editions of *The Dennis the Menace News.* I had never kept track of what was going on. I never added up all the sums. I never saw it coming.

Whatever spin I wanted to put on it, one thing was clear. Less than a year after I had made the fortune I thought would secure me for the rest of my life, I was flat broke. No, it was worse than that. I was ruined.

I had gone from being on top of the world to being at the bottom of the barrel. The Houston fiasco had wrecked my life. The more I looked at the bills, the more terrible the situation became. I quickly realised that I had no option. I put the house in Santa Monica up for sale. It was soon snapped up. I even had to sell my beloved 1981 Mercedes Benz to raise $30,000. Even then I knew I was going to have to work my ass off to make that money back.

A year earlier, I didn't have a financial care in the world. Now I didn't know how I was going to keep my head above water. My music royalties weren't going to be enough to keep me afloat.

As I tried to recover from the shock of it all, I moved all my stuff into my townhouse in Palm Springs. It was much smaller than my Santa Monica place, only two bedrooms, but that wasn't the only difference.

The move was a real culture shock. A two-and-a-half-hour drive south-east of Los Angeles, Palm Springs is set in the middle of a desert. In winter, the winds cool it down so that the temperature is pleasant and comfortable. In summer, it is a completely different place. It can reach 124 degrees there.

I quickly discovered that whenever I set foot outside I was covered in sweat within seconds. Not only that, there were crickets, black widow spiders and snakes in the yard. There were beehives everywhere. It was horrific, and I realised I had gone to hell without even knowing it. Perhaps it prepared me for the Australian outback later on though!

With what little money I had left, I bought myself a second-hand Mercedes. Unlike the last one, it cost $1,000. It was so old and basic that it didn't have air conditioning. In Palm Springs, at the height of summer, when the mercury started rising, this car became a joke. Every time I went out in the car, I was sweating to death. It was like driving around in a sauna.

Palm Springs was a very different community to Los Angeles. Working in the music industry, I had become used to living and working around young people. Everyone was on the lookout for the next step up. Out in the desert, I was surrounded by the older generation. Most of them had achieved all the things they wanted to in life. Now they were enjoying the fruits of all their labours. This made the place much more relaxed. I didn't mind that at all. I needed to recharge my batteries too.

I had always been good at making friends and getting to know people, and I did so again. One of the first people I met was the great actor Joseph Cotten, who had starred in *Citizen Kane* and the classic *The Third Man*, both with Orson Welles. I used to go out with Joseph and his beautiful wife, Pat, about three times a week. He would always introduce me to other people. Thanks to him, I became friendly with the great Ginger Rogers, one half of Hollywood's all-time greatest dance partnership with Fred Astaire. I also got to know Ruby Keeler, the singer and dancer who had starred in films like *42nd Street* and *Gold Diggers of 1933* and had been married to Al Jolson.

I always loved being around Ginger because she always had such great stories to tell. I found Ruby fascinating, particularly when she talked about her life with Al Jolson. I used to pick Ginger and Ruby up and take them out. It was funny. I would turn up in my old Mercedes, which looked fine from the outside. The minute they climbed in they realised there was no air conditioning. They didn't take too kindly to that.

I remember once I picked Ginger Rogers up. She got in the car, sat there for a few seconds, then turned to me and said, 'We'll go in my car. You can drive.'

Jo and Pat introduced me to more people. I met Jennifer Jones, who was the former wife of the late David O. Selznick and the late Norton Simon. She had won an Oscar for *The Song of Bernadette* back in the forties and had kept going into the seventies, when she starred in *The Towering Inferno* with Steve McQueen.

Palm Springs had its share of retired or semi-retired movie executives too. I got close to Anita and Leo Jaffe; Leo was chairman emeritus of Columbia Pictures. I was fascinated by them all. I never got bored of hearing their Hollywood reminiscences. Apart from anything else, it lifted my spirits.

The failure of The Yellow Rose of Texas Awards had taken the wind out of my sails a little. For a while, I found myself drifting, in terms of work.

Once more, I had a mixture of ideas about what I wanted to do. Part of me thought I should try to get back into the music industry. Another part of me thought I should try something completely different again. One idea was to write a book about Ruby Keeler and her life with Al Jolson but I never got motivated enough to finish it.

Then I put together a set of lithographs signed by these various stars from the golden era: Butterfly McQueen, Dorothy Lamour, Janet Gaynor (the first Best Actress Oscar-winner), Ruby Keeler and Kathryn Grayson. I soon realised, however, that there wasn't a big market for them. It was another financial blunder. I still have plenty of the posters left, if anybody's looking for some! The frustrating thing was that I knew what I really wanted to do, and I knew, deep down, that I could do it well. I wanted to be a producer!

Throughout this time, I kept going back to Houston in my mind. The thing that really bugged me was that I knew the shows had been a critical success. I knew I had the skills to pull together something that would really grab people's imaginations.

So within a few months of The Yellow Rose, I decided I was going to try again. This time it would be Los Angeles, not Houston or anywhere else. I was going to put together a single show, an awards dinner, honouring a select few Hollywood figures. I knew it could work.

I called my friend Peter McCrea, who had been one of the most supportive voices, even when things were bad.

'Peter, I am not going to let this bring me down, I am going to do another show in Los Angeles in nine months' time,' I said. I asked him whether he thought his father and his mother, the actress Frances Dee, would be willing to be honoured at the dinner. Peter asked them and they agreed. I asked Ruby Keeler and Joseph Cotten if they would be willing also. They said they would be delighted. Janet Gaynor also agreed.

I've always been someone who bounces back. I was determined to do so again. Instead of getting depressed, I told myself I was going to take the knock and set to work all over again. It wasn't long before I was up and running.

I had a lot of things going for me. I was in the right place, for a start. Palm Springs was home to the older, richer generation of actors, the money circle, which was what had been lacking in Houston. It meant giving up my young life for a while but that didn't bother me because it was fascinating to learn from these people. I loved these people.

My main problem was that I was broke but my friends rallied round. Tito lent me $10,000, as did my mother, although she did insist I pay it back with interest. It was the first time I felt my mother ever showed any sign of caring about me.

Soon I had formed a new organisation. I called it the American Cinema Awards. Michael, Tito and Dee Dee and the McCreas became fellow board members.

It was great being back at work, although it was very different to when I had last had my own business.

When I had had my PR firm, I had been on a salary of $150,000 to $200,000 a year. I had had two homes, a nice car, a great lifestyle. Now I had to cut back on everything. I put myself on a salary of $30,000, a pittance really. It was just about enough to cover the costs of living and travelling back and forth between meetings in Los Angeles and Palm Springs. I worked from home and kept all my costs to an absolute minimum.

I never got down about things, however. I really

believed that I could become a good producer that other people would want to hire. So, once more, I started putting together a show, concentrating on the things that had gone right in Houston and learning from what had gone wrong.

The first American Cinema Awards show took place on 10 September 1983 at the Beverly Theatre in Beverly Hills. As well as Joseph Cotten, Joel McCrea and Ruby Keeler, we honoured two other actresses: Joel's wife of fifty years, Frances Dee, whom he had met on the set of *The Silver Cord* in 1933, and Janet Gaynor, one of the greats of early Hollywood. Janet was one of the few stars to be big in both silent movies and 'talkies'. She was best known for the 1937 original version of *A Star Is Born* and for winning the Academy Award for Best Actress for no less than three films: *Sunrise, Seventh Heaven* and *Street Angel.*

In the run-up to the show, I enlisted two other friends to help out. Angie Dickinson had agreed to host it. She was such a loyal friend, she even helped generate some publicity for me by giving interviews around town. I really appreciated what she did. I remember she told the trade magazine *The Hollywood Reporter*: 'I don't know if this show will go anywhere but I wish David well.' That meant a lot to me, and it also helped sales a lot. I was charging a modest price for tickets to the event: $25 for seats away from the stage, $100 for the ones nearest the entertainment and the stars. I had sold them all in advance. The $100 tickets included a party with the stars at the Friars Club in Beverly Hills afterwards. These tickets sold out.

The other great piece of casting I had done was to ask Robert Wagner, then riding high with his TV show *Hart to Hart*, to be one of the main presenters. As part of the show, I had asked Robert to go around the room introducing all the star guests. He would say a few words about each of them and then ask them to stand up and take a bow while everyone applauded.

When the show got underway that day, I immediately knew that this was an inspired idea. No one had ever put together a show where they introduced everyone who was there. Many of these were old stars who had not been seen for years, so they really relished this moment and the public loved it as well. It took Robert 15 minutes to introduce all these people and the applause they all got was incredible. I knew this was going to be a feature of any shows I did in the future. From the moment I saw Robert host this show, I knew he was my lucky charm.

Everybody was hugely complimentary about the show afterwards. I got dozens of letters saying what a lovely evening they had had, how well organised the show had been and wishing me well for the future. Robert Osborne, who wrote for *The Hollywood Reporter*, really helped me get the ball rolling with this show, and many others. He is one of the most respected men in Hollywood and I owe a lot of the success of that and future American Cinema Awards Foundation (ACAF) evenings to his support. He is still a very dear friend. He deserves a medal for putting up with me for all these years!

As I added up the final bills, I saw that, in contrast to my last venture, I had managed to turn a small – very small – profit. The programme I had produced was filled with well wishes from friends. I had even got the Mayor of Los Angeles, Tom Bradley, to write a note wishing us well. It had had a lot of advertising from restaurants to cosmetics companies, airlines to antiques companies.

The show had made enough money to get me

back on my feet. I was back in business.

I was ecstatic. I knew I was on to something here, something that wasn't being done in Hollywood at that time. It was the era of *ET* and the *Star Wars* movies – big-budget action films made by Spielberg and Lucas. Modern audiences were worshipping heroes that weren't even real. The big stars were robots and moving puppets. I sensed that there was still an appetite for old Hollywood, for real actors with real personalities.

I wasted no time in starting work on a second awards ceremony for the following year. Quite quickly, because of my friendship with Joseph Cotten who became chairman of the organisation, I lined up Dorothy McGuire, the veteran star of hit films like *Three Coins in the Fountain* and Robert Preston, who had starred alongside Dorothy in *The Dark at the Top of the Stairs* and had just had a hit starring alongside Julie Andrews in *Victor/Victoria*.

Shortly afterwards, I persuaded Jane Wyman, the former wife of Ronald Reagan and star of classics like *The Lost Weekend* and *Magnificent Obsession*, to be honoured. That was a real coup, as she also had a huge hit television series at the time, *Falcon Crest*.

I knew that if the awards were going to grow, I would need to draw in even bigger stars. I knew a lot of people but not a lot of the A list. I realised that I needed someone who could get me connected to the real old Hollywood royalty. I found that person in Ruth Berle, the then wife of the great comedian Milton Berle.

Ruth was a glamorous, no-nonsense blonde and one of the greatest women I've ever met. She had been a sergeant in the Army and was tough. She probably needed to be to cope with Milton, who had been married twice before, was renowned for having the largest penis in Hollywood and was still a legendary ladies' man at the venerable age of seventy-five.

I asked Ruth whether she would be able to get some people involved. I gave her some names and she said she would see what she could do. She lived up to her promise – and in spades.

Ruth rang me a few days later to tell me she had spoken to people like Gregory Peck, Kirk Douglas, James Stewart and Henry Fonda. They had all been interested and might be willing to come along to the next awards show. A lot more actors had given her a definite yes.

Ruth was a charming woman and she was a real doer. She rang these people up and told them they had to come because these evenings were for a really good cause. They listened. Ruth was my friend and was really behind me. She helped bring me into the Hollywood game.

As a thank-you, I promised to do an evening as a tribute to Milton. By this time, I had also enlisted the help of an actor called Tristan Rogers. Tristan was Australian-born and was a huge star, thanks to his portrayal of the dashing Robert Scorpio in *General Hospital*. He was keen to get into production as well and wanted to do all he could to help. Tristan and I went to meet Milton at the Beverly Wilshire Hotel one lunchtime. It was a memorable lunch, for all the wrong reasons.

Tristan sat across from Milton. We had ordered sandwiches – me and Milton tuna, and Tristan roast beef. My sandwich was delayed for some reason and Tristan and Milton made a start without me.

Milton loved to talk. He was eating away as he was holding court and was spitting tuna from his mouth, right into Tristan's face. All of a sudden there were pieces of tuna on Tristan's forehead and on his cheeks. I was cracking up but by the time the waitress arrived with my tuna sandwich I had gone off it.

Afterwards, Tristan was wiping himself down in the bathroom. 'I didn't know I would need a shower!' he said. Tristan is still one of my closest and dearest friends.

A few weeks before the second awards show, Ruth rang to say she had had a big breakthrough. She had persuaded Robert Mitchum to be one of the honoured stars. I was over the moon. Bob Mitchum was a genuine Hollywood giant, one of the cinema's greatest actors and hell-raisers. When I met him, I found him a larger-than-life character. He would crack me up with some of the stories he told about life in the golden age of Hollywood.

My favourite story he told me was about the time he was making *Out of the Past*, one of the great film noirs. His co-star in that movie was Jane Greer, one of the most beautiful actresses around. Bob liked the ladies and he developed a crush on her.

Bob thought that Jane was really gorgeous and immediately tried to charm her but he found her a bit cool and distant. She also seemed a bit tired. He noticed that she had bags under her eyes.

Filming went ahead and Bob and Jane worked together all day. Each night she would disappear before Bob had a chance to weave his spell. When she arrived for work in the mornings she would have even bigger bags under her eyes.

Bob was getting really frustrated. So on the fifth day of filming, he finally said to Jane, 'I think you're the most beautiful woman in the world but how come you've got bags under your eyes every morning?'

Bob nearly died when he heard this beautiful, classy lady reply, 'You'd have them too if you spent all night with your legs behind your head.'

Jane Greer was married to the crooner-turned-comic-actor Rudy Vallee and they had a very lively sex life. Apparently, he would make her dress up in all this S&M stuff. She was relieved to get to work for a rest. She divorced Rudy soon afterwards.

By a funny coincidence, Jane Greer became a supporter of the American Cinema Awards and one of my closest friends. Wow, she was still so beautiful, and had a very dry sense of humour. I learned a lot about the delivery of jokes from her. Jane and Bob were reunited at the second of our awards shows, which was even more of a success than the first one.

By the time I was at work on the third show, our list of supporters read like an A–Z of Hollywood. When we honoured Deborah Kerr and Roddy McDowall at the third awards in November 1985, the hosts included Bob Mitchum and Elizabeth Taylor. As a sign of how well established we were, I even had advertising from TV networks like ABC.

I had always intended the show to raise money for charity and we were now fully registered so people could deduct the money they spent from their taxes as a charitable donation. We had also started to give money to Hollywood's leading actors' retirement home, the Motion Picture and Television Country House and Hospital in Woodland Hills, near Los Angeles. That attracted even more big names. We even established scholarships in the fields of theatre arts and dance at colleges and universities throughout the United States.

By now, it took Robert Wagner more than 20 minutes to get round all the celebrities that turned out for the awards. People would applaud until their hands started hurting. It was so exciting.

The awards had turned into one of the high-lights of the year in California. Everyone got dressed up and recreated the golden age of Holly-wood. I got people like Cornel Wilde, James Stewart, Spanky from *The Little Rascals*, Gene Kelly, Guy Madison, Alice Faye, Maureen O'Hara, Maureen O'Sullivan and so many more.

My strategy was to find people that hadn't been seen in years. I found, for instance, Alida Valli, the great Italian star who had starred with Joseph Cotten in *The Third Man*. She had left Hollywood in the fifties to make movies in Europe and hadn't really been seen since. I reunited the cast of *Oliver!* – Jack Wild, Ron Moody and Shani Wallis – to recreate musical moments from the film with a 48-member orchestra. I got Olivia de Havilland and Butterfly McQueen, who both appeared in *Gone With the Wind*. People would travel from around the world to be there. Topol came from Israel, Maximilian Schell came from Germany, Sophia Loren came from Italy.

Everyone was delighted to see these names from the past again. It was always fascinating to see these people come alive as they got their chance to be back in the limelight. The press loved it too. The event provided some much-needed glamour in a Tinseltown that didn't have much tinsel at the time. The *Los Angeles Herald Examiner* said the show was 'well on its way to attaining legendary status'.

It made great copy for the newspapers. There were lots of stories about people who were facing really hard times. In the golden days of Hollywood, the studio system looked after these people. That did not happen any longer.

I found some of them in weird places. Some of them were at the Motion Picture and Television retirement home or were destitute. I found people like Robert Cummings, who between 1955 and 1959 had starred in a big American television show called *Love That Bob* and was also a huge film star. He had left his wife of 40 years and married an Oriental woman. He had lost everything. He had gone from living in a Beverly Hills mansion to a tiny apartment in Sherman Oaks.

The American Cinema Awards were getting bigger and bigger, partly out of necessity. I had learned a lot about staging the event. For a start, it had to be on a grand scale, particularly if people were going to pay the small fortune we were now charging. As our reputation grew, we were able to ask more and more for seats. Tables for ten people were going for $3,600, for what I called the Bronze Circle on the outer edge of the room. We charged $10,000 for the Silver Circle, $15,000 for the Gold Circle and $25,000 for a table in the Platinum Circle, in the best rows. I was planning to introduce a new, even more expensive ticket price at future events. Guests could pay $5,000 for a seat in the first two rows or $50,000 for a table in what I was going to call the Benefactors Circle. For this, they would get an ad in the programme and be able to choose any star – within reason – to sit at their table for dinner.

I knew that to justify this I would have to deliver a really good, entertaining, fast-moving show that had a lot of star names involved. I even got Tom Gleason and Chuck Imhof at American Airlines to sponsor the event. They remained sponsors until the last American Cinema Awards and are two of the nicest guys I have ever met.

I started to go out and put myself around in Hollywood more and more, attending as many functions and meetings as possible. I got to know all these legendary stars and I built a whole web of connections. I was hiring the best musicians and choreographers I could find. The shows were becoming more and more spectacular. The flipside of this, however, was that they were also becoming more and more expensive. We were doing well financially and the charities were really benefiting but I knew I needed some help.

Tragically, Ruth Berle had fallen ill with cancer. She was only in her early sixties and she was dying. She was still working as hard as she could but we knew she probably wouldn't live much beyond the next awards show. She died in April 1989. She was a dear friend who was taken far, far too soon.

When I heard that a lady from Palm Beach, Florida had bought one of the Platinum Circle tables for $25,000 and had been talking about buying even more space at the next awards, I thought I should get to know her.

Celia Lipton Farris was the daughter of a famous English band leader, and had been a jazz singer and actress in England during her teens. She then moved to America but put her career on ice when she married an inventor called Victor Farris. Victor had invented some pretty valuable things, including something called the Farris valve, the cardboard milk carton and a device to hold back sliding hillsides. It had made him a fortune that ran into the hundreds of millions. He had passed away and Celia had thrown herself into doing more and more philanthropic and charity work.

The first time we met, I didn't really pay Celia much attention. I had been involved in rehearsing something in the run-up to the awards and had given her short shrift. When I got to know her better, I discovered she was really keen to get involved.

Ruth had become an executive producer on the show. I quickly saw that Celia could take her place. Celia was very excited by the whole thing and she was a very, very generous woman. With her help, the shows became ever more spectacular. We had a love/hate relationship, and in hindsight I think that's why we worked so well together. She always felt I was using her. To be honest, I suppose I did in many ways, but never really intentionally. I liked to do things on a big scale and that always cost money. But she does have a heart of gold and I like to think she got a lot out of it too.

As the Cinema Awards became more and more established, we raised ever-increasing amounts of money for charity. I moved back to Los Angeles and bought a condo in Century City at Century Towers. The Foundation had already put several hundred thousand dollars towards the building of some cottages at the Motion Picture and Television Country House and Hospital. We had also started to give out university scholarships for young people to study theatre arts and dance. With ACAF money, we had given promising students a chance to go to Boston University, UCLA and many more.

As word of what we were doing spread, more and more big stars joined our board. One of those who joined was Jane Russell, who quickly became like my second mum. Like me, Jane had grown up in Van Nuys. She had that rare ability to use a cuss word and ask God to forgive her two minutes later.

Jane was one of the most decent people I ever met. She had started her own children's charity, WAIF, 50 years earlier and had helped more than 60,000 homeless children get adopted. She looked so great still, something which hit home when I went to host a Rock 'n' Roll Hall of Fame concert in Cleveland, Ohio, in 2004 and was leaving the venue with Jane and her cousin Pat.

The place was in the middle of an area known for its prostitution. Jane looked like a million dollars. A guy rolled up in his car, wound down his window and ushered me over.

'How much for those two?' he said.

Jane nearly died laughing when I told her. Pat was rather curious about how much money he had offered!

As well as the annual Awards show, we also started doing other events. We staged a couple of song-and-dance specials called *Gotta Sing, Gotta Dance*, persuading all sorts of acts to reprise some of their most famous musical roles.

Among those who volunteered were the cast of *Oliver!*, who went through some of the best-known hits from Lionel Bart's show; Rita Moreno, who sang songs from *West Side Story*; and Ann-Margret, who teamed up with Bobby Rydell, Janet Leigh and Dick Van Dyke to perform songs from their hit movie *Bye Bye Birdie*. Janet also joined our board and became my other surrogate mother. I miss her so much; she was a truly great lady.

As more and more people turned up, the events took on a life of their own. On one occasion, I got The Nicholas Brothers, a great dance team from the forties, to reunite. These amazing tap dancers started doing improvised dancing on stage. They were Michael Jackson's inspiration for many of the moves he made so famous. Joining them that night were such hoofers as Buddy Ebsen, George Murphy, Donald O'Connor and Peggy Ryan. All in all, it was quite sensational.

Pretty soon, I learned that you could never know what to expect at our shows. That was never more true than on the night I thought Bette Davis had dropped dead at my dinner table.

Bette Davis was a really regal lady, a genuine member of the Hollywood royalty. I used to go to lunch with her at Jean Leon's La Scala, the premier Italian restaurant in Beverly Hills in the sixties, seventies and eighties. At that time, I used to smoke a lot of cigarettes, as did Bette. Joseph Cotten once remarked that he saw me, Bette and Bette's assistant Catherine Sermack smoking at a table one day and it looked like there was a chimney there, the smoke was so high.

Bette used to love telling stories about the golden age of Hollywood. She told me once how Joan Crawford had come on strong towards her during the making of *Whatever Happened to Baby Jane?* Joan kept sending Bette expensive gifts, which at first she accepted. After a while, Bette started feeling really uneasy about this and told Joan to stop it. She even began returning all the gifts. She was convinced Joan Crawford was trying to have a lesbian affair with her.

Beneath the tough veneer there was a vulnerable lady, I discovered. She had had a stroke and her speech was a little bit slurred. She told me she was always worried about waking up in the morning to find she had had another stroke because of what the first one had done to her.

She had also had a hip replacement and, in private, was mostly getting around in a wheelchair, although she could walk. Even though it was painful for her to walk, she never wanted people to see that she had a problem. She was insistent that she was never seen in public in a wheelchair or with a walking stick, so whenever we went out we had to wheel her through the kitchens so that she could then walk unaided into the dining room.

It wasn't quite so easy when we held the sixth annual American Cinema Awards on 6 January 1989.

This was, by far, the most glittering event we had ever had. It seemed like all of Hollywood had turned out to honour Bette, who was being feted along with Clint Eastwood and Julio Iglesias. It was an incredibly lavish affair. There was Dom Perignon flowing on all the tables. The evening was totally sold out, with a waiting list of 400 people.

We had just sat down for dinner and Bette was taking a bite of her salad when she just slumped forward and fell, face down, into her salad plate. She was motionless and we all thought, 'Oh my God, she's died!' Well actually, I also thought, 'Oh my God, all people are going to remember is that Bette Davis died at the American Cinema Awards and they won't want to come to these dinners any more because they'll think they're going to die here too!'

With the help of the hotel staff, Robert Wagner, Robert Osborne and I rushed her into a private room and called for an ambulance. The funny thing was the group of people who immediately joined me there. On one side of me there was Paul Henreid, who so famously lit the two cigarettes for himself and Bette at the end of *Now, Voyager*. On the other side there was Glenn Ford, the actor whom Bette had mentored at the beginning of his career.

There was always this tension between Bette and Glenn Ford. Back in 1946, Bette had given Glenn one of his big breaks in *A Stolen Life*. They had had an affair but he had dropped her and she had never forgotten it. They had worked together again in 1961, by which time Glenn was a leading man and Bette had needed his approval to get a role alongside him as Apple Annie, the old bag-lady in *Pocketful of Miracles.*

While we waited for the ambulance to arrive, someone gave Bette some mouth-to-mouth resuscitation. All of a sudden she came back to life. She did so, of course, in her own inimitable way.

Glenn Ford was leaning over Bette and tried to talk to her. She took one look at him and said, 'Get him out of here.'

Within a few moments Bette had revived herself. 'Come on, I'm not dying. I'm going to get my award,' she said.

Soon afterwards, Bette was on stage making a speech that seemed to go on and on. She was quite an amazing lady. We all thought she would go on forever but of course she didn't. She died ten months or so later.

In every family there is an emotionally unstable relative. In mine there are hundreds of them. Of all my nutty relatives, perhaps the most unbalanced of all was one of my Spanish-blooded cousins Herp Herpeeze (which rhymes with trapeze). As is so often the case, he was driven mad by his wife.

Herp Herpeeze was a helicopter pilot who flew from his home outside San Diego back and forth across the Mexican border. Herp Herpeeze was single until late in his life when he met the woman he thought was the answer to his dreams.

She was called Herpina and she was an older woman in her forties. Herpina had a real track record with men. She had been married half a dozen times and had produced at least ten children. She had had two sons and two daughters with her last husband, a Chinaman called Lawng Schlong.

When Herp met Herpina, he didn't really care much about her, as she was so overweight. She was an attractive woman, though, and they had a lot in common. Herpina was a trapeze artist in the circus and Herp loved watching her fly. The fact that their names were so similar was a big attraction too. They felt that they were meant to be together after their first date. She ultimately got very thin to please her new husband.

Last but not least, their sex life was also sensational. They did everything together. They spent a lot of their time having oral sex. Herpina loved oral sex. In fact, there were times when that was all she craved. All her ex-husbands apparently loved her for this. She was truly a great fellatio expert. Herp loved to fulfil Herpina's needs as well, so they were pretty happy.

Herp and Herpina went out together for four years before marrying. One year into the marriage, they were about to have sex one night when Herpina said she couldn't because of certain complications. Herp was a bit confused by this but he was respectful and said, 'Don't worry. I can wait.' Herp Herpeeze loved his new wife Herpina Herpeeze. She was his world.

Then, around ten days later, Herp again suggested they have sex. He was really surprised when Herpina again said she had women's problems. This was the first time he had been denied sex twice in one month. He couldn't help mentioning that it seemed a bit soon for her to have this problem again. The moment he did so, Herpina Herpeeze started to cry uncontrollably.

In between sobs, she told him she had herpes. She had kept it a secret from him because she felt that if he knew he would not have married her.

The fact that Herpina Herpeeze had herpes was devastating to Herp Herpeeze. He was shattered that she could lie to him like that. He had himself checked out and found that he didn't have herpes, just athlete's foot and a bad fungus on his big toenail. He was so relieved that he had not caught Herpina's herpes. He was relieved that Herpina had at least had the common sense not to have sex with him while her herpes was active. He still could not forgive her for not having been honest with him, however. What made it even worse was that Herp found out Herpina had given herpes to another female trapeze artist. Herpina had settled out of court with her twenty years earlier. Rumour had it that the other trapeze artist had caught it when Herpina was hanging from her legs while they were rehearsing.

So one day, soon after he had found out, Herp asked Herpina if she wanted to join him on a flight he was making to Guadalajara in Mexico. No one knows what happened exactly. As they were flying over the border to Tijuana, Herpina Herpeeze fell out of the helicopter from 5,000 feet up. She landed in a taco factory, right in a vat of hot chilli sauce. When the coroner came to get her body, they couldn't tell the chilli from the herpes. Mind you, some of the staff thought the sauce actually tasted better.

Herp refused to go to Herpina's funeral because in his mind he couldn't forgive her for not having told him about her herpes before they got married. He was never charged over Herpina's death. The coroner put it down to a moving violation and closed the case.

Herp did want Herpina to have a proper burial, though. He was hoping that the two women he respected most on television, Barbara Walters and Star Jones (both of whom he said had great brains and great looks), would say something at Herpina's funeral. Unfortunately, he never could get in touch with their agents. Instead, he asked the gossip columnist Urah Pill to deliver the eulogy. Urah was so close to Herpina that sometimes it was hard to tell who loved who more.

It was a tragic story but in the years that followed, something rather wonderful happened. Herp met and got close to Herpina's two Chinese daughters, Dong and Wong. After the funeral, he discovered that they had contracted herpes from their mother at birth. He was really moved by this.

So Herp gave up his job as a helicopter pilot and

went to work at a factory making cream for herpes sufferers. More importantly, he dedicated his entire life to a charity, Chinese Girls With Herpes.

In the years since then, Herp has raised close to a million dollars for the charity. The money helps girls with the disease, not just in the US and Mexico but in China itself. As a result of all his hard work, hundreds of Chinese girls with herpes have a much better quality of life.

CGWH has become a charity close to my heart too.

It goes to show that good can come out of even the worst situations.

Oh, by the way, I forgot to tell you that my cousin Herp never did get along with any of Herpina's ten sisters. The one he hated most was called Notalota Towelent. She was, like Herpina Herpeeze, a trapeze artist but with not one lick of talent. Every time Notalota tried to perform, people booed. She didn't try to emulate Herpina but she did copy their mother, Gotalota Towelent, who was a legendary trapeze artist. Notalota hated Americans, I will never understand why.

Notalota was so evil that she always put Herpina down and took whatever money she could get from her. Word around the circus was that Notalota had balls bigger than any man alive. The world knew Notalota was just a plain old nothing, and boy was she ugly. The way she looked reminded me of Joy Behar from The View, who I have always thought had hardly any talent. She also had that unreal smirk of Meredith Vieira. Herpina had more talent in one pinky than Notalota had in her whole lotta and her other sisters hated her.

Notalota met her untimely death when she tried to poison Herp's brother, Twerp, by slipping something into his spaghetti. Unfortunately, she was so stupid she ate Twerp's plate of spaghetti by mistake and died face-down next to a meatball. This was fitting, since her life had been meatless. Her sisters were so excited at the news of her death that they had a spaghetti dinner with lots of meatballs! So goes it!

Control

Sometimes in life you do things that you regret, things that are plain wrong. When you're wrong, you're wrong and you've got to admit it. One of the things I regret most in my life was going back on my word to Janet Jackson.

I have known Janet since she was a kid, when I used to call her 'the heifer'. She has grown up into a brilliant performer; after Michael, the most successful of the whole Jackson clan.

Janet had broken through in 1986 with an album called *Control*, produced by the Minneapolis team of

Jimmy Jam and Terry Lewis. She had had world-wide hits with songs like 'When I Think Of You' and 'What Have You Done for Me Lately'. In 1990, she was about to release another CD, *Rhythm Nation*.

Janet was like my kid sister and I had stayed on friendly terms with her over the years. In January 1988, she had been recognised at the American Cinema Awards, along with Gene Kelly and Shirley Temple. Janet had really enjoyed the night at the Beverly Hilton Hotel and had thanked me profusely for it afterwards.

When Janet invited me to her house, I was intrigued. I knew that she had parted company with her father as manager and was no longer working with John McClain. Might she be after some advice on a new direction? When I arrived at her townhouse on the Bel Air section of Mulholland Drive, she came straight out with it.

'David, you are my brother. I love you,' she said. 'I want you to be my manager. We can do great things together. We will be a team for life.'

I was taken aback. I knew how hard losing her must have been for Joe.

I had seen him mellow over the years. The old toughness had worn off. He had been through so much and he had been given a bad rap.

The thing that really disappointed me was that a few years later La Toya claimed that Joe sexually abused her. I felt really bad for Joe about that. I never thought it was true.

Over the years I got to know Joe pretty well. He was a very strict father who wanted to see his kids succeed and have everything that he had never had. Yes, he overdid it in many ways. Was he tough? Sure. Was he hard? Yes. Would he strap them and spank them? Yes. Would he do it unmercifully? No. Would he try to have sex with his children, as he was accused of doing by La Toya? I don't think so. That was just not his style. He could have sex with any woman he wanted because he was Joe Jackson. I will never believe that Joe tried to have sex with La Toya. I know her allegations really hurt Joe and the family. I felt for him.

This was business, however. I knew Janet was serious about kicking on to a new level, perhaps even challenging Michael at the top of the music mountain.

We talked for a couple of hours. It was a great meeting. In fact, at the end we hugged each other. I was flattered beyond words to have been asked to manage Janet, whose potential was huge. She was still only in her early twenties. I was excited. I could see endless possibilities.

I said yes pretty much immediately. Before I left, we agreed to set the wheels in motion with her lawyer calling mine.

Unfortunately, someone would pretty quickly put a spoke in those wheels.

Later that day, I spoke to Michael to tell him the news. His reaction was immediate. 'No,' he said. 'You can't go with her. You have to come with me. You have to manage me.'

I knew Michael's management situation was in a state of flux. He had parted company with Freddie deMann and Ron Weisner, with whom he had worked for many years. He was being advised now by David Geffen, LA's most powerful music figure and head of his own label, Geffen Records.

'I've given my word to Janet, and my word is my bond, Michael,' I said.

It had been Elizabeth Taylor who had taught me the importance of always keeping my word. I remember discussing it with her one day in the mid-eighties, back in the early days of the American Cinema Awards. I was sitting on her bed at her house in Los Angeles, along with Robert Wagner and Tristan Rogers. Keeping her word was something Elizabeth believed in almost religiously. In fact, she once received a phone call from the President of the United States requesting a meeting. Her response to his secretary was, 'I'm sorry, I have a previous engagement with a friend.'

Elizabeth told me to never, ever change my plans for something better. It has become my motto too. This was to be the first time I would divert from it. I would always regret it and have never done it since.

Michael and I were still best friends. We still had lots of fun together. I spent a lot of time at Neverland, the sprawling new estate he had built in the Santa Ynez Valley, in Santa Barbara County. I had watched him develop it over the past couple of years, turning it into his own personal version of Disneyland.

Michael had his own movie theatre and in those days all the studios used to send their new movies to him. You could go in there and pretty much watch anything you wanted, which we often did. It is funny how with power you can have everything and it only takes one thing to change all of that.

There was also a train network that ran through Neverland, a Ferris wheel and a fairground. I loved Michael's zoo, in which he had giraffes, a hippo and loads of snakes. I even used to play with his chimpanzee, Bubbles.

Michael remained a very generous guy too. He had been really helpful with the American Cinema Awards. In 1990, he agreed to be honoured himself, along with Gregory Peck and Elizabeth Taylor. One day, we were driving to Disneyland for the weekend, talking away about the awards and my plans for their future.

'So who else would you really like to honour?' he asked me.

Then – as indeed I still do – I regarded Whitney Houston as the finest vocalist in the world.

'Whitney,' I said.

He got on the cell phone and called Whitney. Just like that. She agreed to be honoured at our dinner the following year.

In other ways, however, Michael had changed in the past few years.

The turning point had been when his hair caught fire during the making of a video in Los Angeles in January 1984. He was singing 'Billie

Jean' in front of a live audience for a Pepsi commercial when some fireworks went off behind him, setting his hair alight. It was always played down but he was constantly in pain after that. He was on a lot of prescription drugs to take care of the pain.

Since the accident, Michael no longer had his eye on the ball. His vision had deserted him. He wasn't the Michael of old any more.

In the early days of his career, Michael was responsible for every bit of success that he had. I know because I saw it at first hand. He used to stay with me about three times a week around the time he was releasing *Off the Wall* and *Thriller*. Michael was the brains behind it all.

He would say, 'Here's the campaign I'm going to have Epic Records do.' He would explain to me how he wanted to have a billboard on Sunset Boulevard, a billboard in Madison Square Garden, one in Leicester Square and one on Les Champs-Elysées in Paris. He would work out what he needed to do and where he needed to go. He would plan the magazine advertising, the radio stations he needed to talk to – everything.

During that time, Michael used me as a sounding board. We would sit and talk about everything. I was someone he could bounce things off. Then he would call Walter Yetnikoff, who was running Sony then.

Now, however, Michael no longer had that degree of control over his career, as I was about to discover.

On the afternoon after I had met with Janet, Michael called me again and asked me to pick him up. We went record shopping in Glendale and Pasadena. Michael kept begging me to reconsider my decision.

'You've got to come with me. We're best friends. Let me call Janet,' he kept saying.

He knew exactly how to play me. I'm very superstitious about certain things, for instance. I believe that if you step on a line it might be bad luck, so I always avoid stepping on them. It's one of my weird idiosyncrasies, of which I have many! I also had a thing about doing everything in even numbers. Michael loved that. He would play on it and drive me nuts. He would tell me it was bad luck if I didn't knock on wood sixteen times. I would do these things and he would crack up. He knew how to play every one of my vulnerabilities and he did so now.

Michael knew that, in any other circumstances, I would have given my right or left arm to manage him. He knew I was as ambitious as he was and he knew that, even as I was saying no, I was calculating what I could do for him. He kept on talking about what we could achieve together. After an hour or so of this, I finally gave in.

'All right, all right. Provided Janet's OK about it, I will go with you instead, Michael,' I said.

So Michael called Janet. She didn't say anything to me but I knew she would be upset. She just said OK. Michael was delighted, as indeed I was. We were so close, I thought we would be able to move mountains together and have a lot of fun in the process.

It didn't turn out to be that simple.

At that point, David Geffen was overseeing Michael's career. A week or so after I'd given Michael my decision, he asked me to go to a meeting with David and his lawyer, John Branca.

They didn't waste any time in putting me on the spot. Michael had completed *Dangerous*, which was ready for release. They were already planning the marketing.

'So, David, what should Michael do with this

new record?' they asked me. Michael and I had given this some thought. I pitched them my idea.

Ceausescu had just been overthrown and killed in Romania and the world was waking up to the horrors of what had been done to children there. Ordinary kids had been put in mental institutions. Horrendous footage had been playing on the news around the world.

I said I thought it would be a good idea for Michael to go to visit the kids in Romania. It would show Michael's humanitarian side. He could set up daycare facilities there and sponsor the children. They looked blank. They didn't get it at all. Even if they had, they wouldn't have given me any credit.

I could see I was getting nowhere with them. I could see where all this was heading. Even before I left the building, I sensed they were going to make a guy called Sandy Gallin Michael's new manager. As so often happened, my instincts proved right.

To this day, I don't know what was said in the wake of that meeting. I don't know what was said to Michael or what he said to Sandy Gallin, John Branca and David Geffen. All I do know is that later the same day Michael called me. 'I can't have you as my manager,' he said meekly. 'I'm really sorry.'

I felt sick. How could I have been so stupid? How could I have messed up a chance to manage Janet in the vain pursuit of looking after Michael, something deep down I knew was never going to happen? I called Janet almost immediately. She was pretty short with me. She just said, 'David, it's too late.' Who could blame her.

Janet was about to go on tour with *Rhythm Nation* and she had already signed a new manager, Roger Davis. I believe she made the right choice. He would go on to do a remarkable job with her.

This episode put a dampener on my relationship with Janet and it has never been the same since. To this day, she remains more reserved with me than she used to be. It was always a complicated situation and I was a fool not to realise what was going on but I believed in Michael so.

They say things usually work out for the best. Some time after that, Sandy Gallin had to deal with allegations that Michael had had an inappropriate relationship with a young boy. There was a lot of speculation that, in order to make the case go away, Michael was going to pay off the kid and his family. Sandy was the man in the middle and was probably working 24 hours a day to deal with this mess.

I knew Michael inside out and I knew he was innocent. He lived for his work. All he wanted to do was be the biggest star in the world. He didn't care about sex. He was not gay. He called me when all this broke and we spoke on the phone for six hours straight. We spoke from 10 p.m. until 4 a.m.

'Michael, whatever you do, don't settle,' I told him. 'The public will stand by you.' He agreed. He told me that he would stand and fight. Three and a half hours after he put down the phone, at 7.30 a.m., the news broke that he had settled the case. I was mortified. I had just spoken to him.

This to me was a sure sign that he wasn't in complete touch with reality. He told me that his head was in constant pain and he had to take all these pills. He also told me that the pills were having an effect on him. There was no doubt in my mind that the medication he was taking was unbalancing him.

We went through a period after that when we weren't that close. I watched his career going through some pretty rocky waters. We would still talk but we didn't get together that often. I still knew that our partnership was too strong to be broken that easily. I knew we would get back together again one day. Sure enough we did and it was to be two of the best and biggest days of our lives, and together we would make history.

Everyone is prone to vices and when a vice takes hold it can destroy your life.

It was my cousin Elmo Gluk, the igloo plumbing genius, who alerted me to the plight of Eskimos addicted to crack and ice. That's not ice as in frozen water, of course, but ice the drug.

Crack and ice became a big thing up in Alaska back in the eighties. The situation has become worse and worse over the years. There are now thousands of Eskimos hooked on it. They lose their minds on that stuff. A lot of them just jump on their sleds, get their dogs running and head north, never to be seen again.

I don't think the American Government realises what a problem there is with Eskimos on crack and ice. It is making a real mess of their lives and, of course, the lives of their families. So when Elmo told me about the charity Eskimos on Crack and Ice, I immediately said I would do all I could. Now I go up to Alaska every year to hold a benefit on their behalf. It's the least I can do to help.

I always dress very warmly when I go to Alaska. I also make sure I bring Elmo and his family some Eskimo Pie ice-cream bars, as oddly enough they do not sell them up there and Elmo is addicted to them!

It's rare that I've not finished something I've started. In fact, there's only one major project in my life that I've never seen through to the end. There were some pretty good reasons why it worked out that way though, not least the fact that in September 1992 I lost my close friend Anthony Perkins to AIDS.

By that year, I knew I wanted to move into something else, to get away from simply being the producer of the American Cinema Awards. I really wanted to do something different with my life, and an opportunity to do that had arisen with the chance to do a play, in London and the United States.

The play was based on the life of the great Scots poet Robert Burns. It was tentatively titled *Red, Red Rose*, taken from that great opening line of his famous poem: 'My love is like a red, red rose, that's newly sprung in June.'

Burns had always been my favourite poet. It

wasn't just the magnificent, romantic poetry that he wrote. I also loved the fact that he was such a ladies' man, had all these children but would never get divorced. To die poor and forgotten, yet to be remembered in the afterlife seemed to me a brilliant starting point for a play.

I had two amazing partners involved. Gene Kelly had agreed to direct it and my good friend Anthony Perkins had come on board as an executive producer.

Anthony Perkins was one of the most talented and sensitive actors of his generation. He had, of course, been defined by one of his earliest roles, Norman Bates in *Psycho*, but there was so much more to him than the general public knew.

I used to spend a lot of time with Anthony and his wife Berry Berenson at their house in the Hollywood Hills. I spent Christmases with the Perkins, their close friends Dan Aykroyd and his wife Donna Dixon and their other best friends Paula Prentiss and her husband actor/director Richard Benjamin, both of whom I was very fond of. Who could ever forget Paula Prentiss with Connie Francis in *Where the Boys Are*? She was, and still is, one of my favourite actresses.

Anthony Perkins was the smartest man I have ever met in my life. He was so articulate and intelligent. It was Anthony who was responsible for my love of making up so many weird words.

Anthony loved to use big words. He would say to me things like, 'The curriculum of awareness has superlatives and hyperboles.' I wouldn't have a clue what he was talking about half the time and so I would say to him, 'Well the circumference of the luvitanious nature is what allows that to be done soliticiously!'

Anthony would look at me and smile.

'Luvitanious and soliticiously. That's interesting,' he would say. 'I read a lot. I read a book almost every day but they're two new words to me. Now, I'm not saying I cannot learn something from you, but I've never heard of these words.'

'Well, look it up then. Go look at the dictionary. Because those are words,' I would reply, straight-faced.

I would do that every time he used a word I didn't know. I would make up one or two myself. Tony would always catch me out. I've loved playing these kind of word games ever since. It gives me a real sense of lupistinow. (Look it up!)

Anthony and I really enjoyed working together on *Red, Red Rose*. By the summer of 1992, we already had a script from a Scottish journalist I had hired named George Rosie. After doing some auditions we had also found someone we thought would be a great Robbie Burns, a young actor named John Barrowman. John had been born in Scotland but raised in the US. He had done a lot of stage work, was a good song-and-dance man and had the acting depth and looks we wanted. He was a really strong talent, with all the qualities we thought we needed to bring Burns to life.

As the summer of 1992 drew to a close, I headed to London where Anthony and I were going to take the play on to the next stage. We both booked into Claridge's and I was really looking forward to having fun. Sadly, it didn't work out that way.

One day, I went into his room and he came to the door with his shirt off. His whole back was covered in red bumps. I had never seen anything like it. He didn't look well and he said he was tired. I had never seen the effect of AIDS before. His back was ravaged by the terrible, deadly disease.

We were due to meet with John Barrowman that evening but Anthony said he couldn't make the meeting because he was too exhausted. When I tried to call up to his room the following day, I was told he had checked out. I made a couple of calls and found out he had gone straight back to the US.

I had to go back too, to oversee the American Cinema Awards, which were looming into view again. When I saw Anthony back there, he confided in me that he had AIDS.

As we sat and talked, Anthony opened up to me. As a young man he had been gay. He had fallen in love with Tab Hunter and had had relationships with other men, including Rudolf Nureyev and Stephen Sondheim. Then, in the early sixties, he had met a girl and fallen in love with her, Victoria Principal, the star of *Dallas*. She had changed his life. He had never thought that he could fall for a woman but he did.

Things didn't work out with Victoria but then Anthony fell in love with Berry Berenson, whom he married and had two children with. Even though he loved her, he still needed a man every now and again. Somehow, somewhere, he had contracted AIDS.

Anthony was aware that I knew doctors at UCLA, in the heart, burns and plastic surgery departments. He asked me if I could help him find a doctor to treat him. The taboo surrounding AIDS back then was still great. It was common knowledge that some actors had succumbed to this disease but it had never been publicly acknowledged.

I made a call to some friends at UCLA Medical Center. Anthony told me he had been ill with AIDS for only one year. The doctors at UCLA discovered he had had it for nine years and was near death. It was very clear that there was little they could do for him.

While Anthony was at home being nursed by his wife and two sons, I used to go round there to work with him on the play. We would sit and talk and he would make some notes. It really cheered him up. I know he looked forward to those sessions.

In the first week of September, I asked Anthony to rewrite a major scene, inserting his ideas. Everyone knew he was dying. Berry knew it, his kids knew it, Tony himself knew it. I refused to act like he was dying. He had become like the character Norman Bates, a skeleton of himself. It was frightening looking at him. It was the first time I had understood what AIDS was, how it completely ravaged a person. He could barely move his fingers but he scratched out the changes in longhand.

A couple of days later, he died. He passed away surrounded by Berry and the children and friends like Richard Benjamin and Paula Prentiss, Dan Aykroyd and Donna Dixon.

I cried when I heard the news that Anthony had slipped away. I still have those last pages he wrote out in longhand. I will always keep them.

In Anthony's memory, I persevered with *Red, Red Rose* for a while afterwards, working with Shani Wallis and Dominick Allen and staging a couple of scenes for prospective investors in Los Angeles.

My heart was just not in it any more, however. The project soon fizzled out, especially when Gene Kelly also became unwell.

As I looked out at the sea of familiar faces standing and applauding me at the Beverly Wilshire Hotel one evening in 1993, I had to pinch myself. I couldn't quite believe it was true. I was used to springing the surprises on other people, not having them sprung on me. When the Board of the ACAF had first mooted a small party to mark my ten years at its helm, I had no idea they were planning

Michael's incredible *30th Anniversary Celebration: The Solo Years* concert, which I produced, was the highest-grossing non-charity concert in history, breaking all records and taking $14 million. It is also the higest-rated musical TV special ever. This poster was just from the first night

Front covers from the programmes of the American Cinema Awards events, which I produced for eleven years. We eventually donated over £2.5 million to Hollywood charities

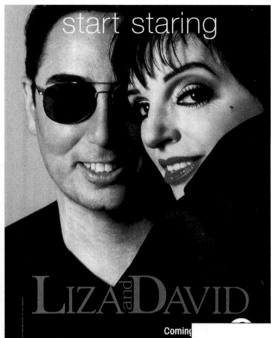

start staring

LIZA and DAVID

Coming

Liza and my aborted
VH1 show

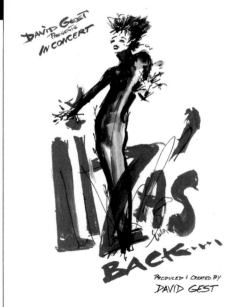

DAVID GEST PRESENTS IN CONCERT

LIZA's BACK...

PRODUCED & CREATED BY
DAVID GEST

Liza's comeback concert
poster, a show I produced
which broke audience
records at the Royal
Albert Hall. I also co-
produced the soundtrack
CD with Phil Ramone

Above left: Michael singing to me and Liza at our wedding

Above right: With Sir Anthony Hopkins

With Tristan Rogers (in the background), Robert Wagner and Michael

I've known Jane Russell for many, many years and she's still as beautiful as ever; she is my second mother. Michael is on the right

In the jungle. My rapping, my snoring, my bush-tucker trials –
an incredible few weeks that changed my life forever. I sure
needed to lose weight and I certainly did. By the way, did I ever
tell you . . . I had a cousin . . .

Meeting Prince Charles at the Royal Variety Performance in December 2006

Performing with my new friend Jason Donovan at G-A-Y in January 2007 an occasion on such a grand scale, with 1,400 people attending.

Standing alongside me was Angie Dickinson, who, ten years earlier, had hosted the first American Cinema Awards show. At the time, Angie had stated she didn't 'know if this show would go anywhere'. Judging by the people standing and applauding, we had achieved a lot in our first decade. Standing in front of me were legends like Kirk Douglas, Robert Wagner, Jimmy Stewart, Janet Leigh, Glenn Ford, Joseph Cotten and Milton Berle. It was hard to express what I was feeling . . . a lot of love.

When I sat down for the show and dinner, however, I realised someone had put in a great deal of work to make all this happen. It was my close buddies Tristan Rogers, Janet Leigh and Anthony Quinn (one of my other best friends, who I loved like a father). The Four Tops, Frankie Valli and The Four Seasons and Petula Clark had all flown out to Los Angeles to surprise me with their perform-ances. Janet Leigh, June Allyson and Margaret O'Brien, three of the Little Women from the 1949 MGM movie classic, had come to present me with an award recognising my work on behalf of the Foundation. I was very, very honoured. I was also very, very proud of what we had all achieved.

We had now raised in excess of $4 million for the Motion Picture and Television Fund. This dinner alone was raising $250,000 for Harry's Haven, the Alzheimer's unit at the Motion Picture and Television Country Home and Hospital, which had been named in honour of Kirk Douglas's father. Both Lew and Edie Wasserman were standing there applauding me.

Over the years, I had become really close to Kirk and Anne Douglas. When Kirk had his stroke, I was one of the people who would go over to see him each week. They were like a family to me and one of my most prized possessions was a letter from Kirk and Anne thanking me for the work I had done for the Motion Picture and Television Fund.

In 1990, we had honoured Elizabeth Taylor, Gregory Peck and my best friend Michael Jackson. There had been a phenomenal turnout. More than 300 stars had come, from current favourites like *Crocodile Dundee* star Paul Hogan, Patrick Swayze, Whoopi Goldberg, James Woods and Rutger Hauer, to genuine Hollywood royalty like Jane Fonda, Clint Eastwood, Esther Williams, Glenn Ford, Kirk Douglas, Sidney Poitier, Clayton Moore, the original Lone Ranger, and Sophia Loren. The music industry had turned out in full force to honour Michael too. Whitney Houston, Lionel Richie, Petula Clark and Michael's little sister Janet were among the throng.

We had sold out the 1,400 tickets way in advance and could have sold them three times over. So many people had wanted to come to the dinner that there was a waiting list of 1,000 names. It had taken Robert Wagner close to 45 minutes to introduce every star attending. By the end, everyone's hands were almost raw from applauding so hard.

Two things stick in my memory about that night above all else. The first was meeting Petula Clark, as *Downtown* was the first album I had ever owned.

Petula had been an idol to many of my friends, including Michael McDonald and Michael Jackson. It was the latter who asked me whether I could get her to perform at the dinner. I was beside myself with excitement when she said yes. I had always dreamed of meeting her.

My first glimpse of Petula was upon arrival at the Beverly Wilshire Hotel, going through the revolving door. I saw her and started behaving like some crazed, star-struck kid. I told her how

Downtown was the first LP my parents had bought me and how I had cycled miles on my bike to buy every 45 she ever made on Warner Bros.

I then demanded she sing all her American hits, there and then, and she did. She sang 'Downtown', 'I Know a Place', 'Round Every Corner', 'You'd Better Come Home', 'Don't Sleep in the Subway', 'The Other Man's Grass Is Always Greener' and 'This Is My Song'. She sang bits of all of them right on the spot for me. You could have shot me dead there and then and I would have gone to heaven a happy man.

Hardly surprisingly, Petula looked at me with an expression that said, 'What a strange chap.' It was the beginning of a long friendship, one I'm proud still exists.

The other hilarious thing that happened that night was when Celia Lipton Farris came on stage. Celia had put a lot of money into supporting the show and had worked hard as the executive producer. On the night itself, she was so excited to be there. She went on stage and sang and made a speech. I was a little worried as a lot of the people there hadn't heard of her.

When Michael Jackson came on stage to take his

final bow at the end of the evening with Celia, she got even more excited. At one point, she wrapped herself around Michael shouting, 'He's the greatest, he's the greatest!' Finally, the musical conductor danced with Celia and Michael could free himself. It was very funny. Even Michael enjoyed it.

The press had never seen anything like that show. CNN called it, 'the largest gathering of stars in the history of showbiz'. 'In terms of star power it is now the number one event in Hollywood,' one of its correspondents said. The *New York Daily News* reckoned 'there were more stars than there are at the Oscars'.

It was Esther Williams who described the evening best. She called it 'a living museum'.

Since then it had become a juggernaut.

In 1992, for instance, we honoured the biggest name of them all, Frank Sinatra. To set the ball in motion, I had talked to the award committee's chairman, Leo Jaffe, and had said, only half seriously, 'We should honour Frank Sinatra.'

'Do you want him?' Leo said.

'Well, yes, of course,' I said. 'Can you get him?'

Three minutes later I got a call. The voice at the other end of the line said, 'Hi, this is Frank Sinatra.'

I was about to say, 'Yeah right,' when he said, 'Leo just told me you want to honour me at the American Cinema Awards.'

I could not believe my luck. I was talking to Frank Sinatra and soon I was producing an evening for him. The show was a glittering success. Frank loved it. I still have a letter from him saying it was one of the great nights of his life.

The success of the show had made me more in demand by other organisations than I had ever dreamed I would be. The ACAF itself never paid me that much money. The most I got out of it was a $100,000 salary and that was in a year when we produced something like five shows in addition to the main event. A lot of other shows started springing up, many of them based on the model I had created of a big, fast-moving variety show that entertained as well as celebrated and honoured the award-winners at its heart. I found myself being asked to produce shows everywhere in the world for huge sums of money.

In 1989, for instance, I had organised and produced an awards show in Italy, the Campione d'Italia Merit of Achievement Awards, held on Lake Lugano. Shortly before her death, I took Bette

Davis there, where she was joined by a glittering line-up of stars I had put together, including Robert Mitchum, Gene Kelly, Ali McGraw, Joseph Cotten and June Allyson.

I was paid a lot for all these new jobs. My fee as an independent producer was four or five times what I made from the American Cinema Awards show. I would earn between $200,000 and $450,000 for each of these events. If I did ten shows a year, which I had done once or twice now, I could make $2.5 million a year. I was suddenly a multi-millionaire, again buying properties and investing wisely. Only this time I realised that I wasn't going to gamble with my own money ever again.

As well as being lucrative, the shows were enjoyable. Back in 1986, the American Cinema Awards had honoured Sophia Loren. Not long afterwards, she asked me over to her house in Hidden Hills, in the San Fernando Valley. I remember she made me pasta. She was a very good cook.

Sophia had been asked to host a major AIDS benefit in Florida. She asked me if I wanted to produce it. I was thrilled because I was offered a quarter of a million dollars. It was going to be a great show honouring Sophia and Julio Iglesias.

Julio was at the height of his career and I had already worked with him on an ACAF salute, so we were old friends. I got all these co-stars of Sophia to come and drew on some old friends like Donna Summer and Michael McDonald to provide the on-stage entertainment. I also got Melanie Griffith and her mother, Tippi Hedren, to host the evening. It was a very successful show. Tippi is one of my favourite people and the work she does for her Roar Foundation is amazing. Tippi always looks at life with a smile.

Working with all these big names taught me important lessons, some big, some small. I learned one small but valuable lesson the night of Sophia's event.

Elizabeth Taylor had hosted the first event of this kind and had raised over $1 million for AIDS. There was always a tension between Sophia and Elizabeth, I felt. They were both Hollywood sex symbols, two of the great beauties of all time. There was respect there, of course. Each respected the other for what they had accomplished. When I honoured Elizabeth at the American Cinema Awards, for instance, Sophia arrived arm in arm with Michael Jackson, which had made me smile a little. Michael was closer to Elizabeth than he was to Sophia. Sophia also wanted to make sure her AIDS event also raised $1 million or more.

Anyhow, on the night of Sophia's AIDS benefit there was an auction to which someone had donated the original painting of Elizabeth Taylor from the film *Raintree County*. The painting, of Elizabeth's character, had featured in the classic movie and the artwork for the posters. I really wanted to have it because I really love Elizabeth so I started bidding on it.

All of a sudden, I felt someone jerking my hand down. It was Sophia. She just shot me a look.

I thought she was joking. But there was this fiery Italian look in her eyes. I realised then that if I wanted to work for her again I wasn't going to bid on that portrait. So I dropped my hand to my side. As Anthony Perkins looked on he just cracked up!

'Oh, Just an Old Friend'

I've always been bothered by people who are holier than thou.

I once knew a priest who thought he was the greatest thing God ever put on earth. His name was Father Merigo. His family came from Spain but he lived in a little town in New Mexico. No one in his parish liked him because he didn't understand how to relate to the people, yet he thought he was greater than Jesus. Until he got run over by a train when his leg got caught in the tracks next to his church one Sunday morning.

There wasn't much left of his body but what there was they scraped up and put in a casket.

They buried him without any fanfare. They took his white robes and placed them over his coffin. Hardly anyone was at the funeral, which proved that he wasn't anywhere near as big as Jesus.

I often think about him. He made me realise that if you can't relate to other people then you are never going to win their respect. I also realised to be careful when crossing railroad racks. He was survived only by his brother, who is a train conductor. He was always trying to get Father Merigo on the right track!

I have said some pretty stupid things in my life but as I stood barefooted, swaying from side to side, at RADA in central London in the summer of 1994, the lines coming out of my mouth seemed completely ridiculous, even by my standards.

'I am a tree,' I was chanting over and over, hoping to God no one I knew could hear me. 'I am a beautiful tree.'

I had headed to London for the summer to get away from Los Angeles, the Awards show and all the things that went with it. Deep down, I knew it was about time I brought that chapter of my life to a close. In one of the programme notes I had written, I had penned an open letter announcing that it was the last show I intended to produce and thanking all those people who had supported me over the years. I knew it was time for a New Day.

The ill-fated *Red, Red Rose* project had really whet my appetite to get involved in the theatre. I had become more and more fascinated by the stage, and Shakespeare in particular. I had loved Shakespeare for a long time and often thought that if I went to heaven he would be the first person I would like to meet. (If I go to hell, I will be meeting a lot of people I know already.)

I booked myself into Claridge's and enrolled in a course on Shakespeare at RADA, the Royal Academy of Dramatic Arts. When I had telephoned RADA, the receptionist said that their summer course was going to be dedicated to Shakespeare. Unfortunately, things didn't quite go according to their proposed plan.

When I arrived, the administrator I had spoken to was no longer there. Instead, the course was being run by another teacher. He turned out to be a nut about all things Russian. He kept talking about how he hated the fact that the Soviet Union no longer existed. He didn't want to discuss Shakespeare. The first thing I did was to learn the Stanislavski technique. I knew all about it, having known many a Method actor. I knew it was meant to connect you with your inner self, to strip you bare so that you could literally become the characters you played. What I did not know is that it would involve me having to pretend I was a tree.

It was nuts. This guy wanted us all to stand around saying 'I'm a beautiful tree. Feel my branches.' Every day. Every day I was cracking up. I was going back to Claridge's and calling Michael Jackson back in the States and saying, 'You think your life's odd. You'll never believe what I did today.'

I was living at Claridge's but I wanted to fit in with the rest of the students. So each morning I would put on a pair of jeans and a T-shirt, jump in a cab and get the driver to drop me off round the corner from the RADA building. I would then walk in with the rest of my classmates. I made a lot of friends immediately.

One bonus was the discovery that I could have been Errol Flynn in a former life. Fencing was part of the acting course and I really loved it. What's more, I found I was really good at it.

After a while, I realised that I wasn't going to be learning anything about Shakespeare. I did not want to be an actor. The world really didn't need another one. I did want to understand the world of English theatre better, so I called my friend Leslie Caron. She had been married to the director Sir Peter Hall. He was working on a new production of *Hamlet* with Stephen Dillane, Sir Donald Sinden and a really good cast in London. Leslie suggested I could sit in and observe them at work.

Leslie was a good friend who had supported the ACAF over the years. She had starred in such classic MGM musicals as *Gigi* and *An American in Paris* with Gene Kelly. Leslie said she would get right back to me. True to her word, she called back within 20 minutes and said I was in.

'This is a serious production, David,' she said. 'You have to treat it seriously.'

She told me that I would have to be there every morning at 8 a.m. and stay there quietly watching through to 5 p.m. I said that was fine. I would be there. So I quit the summer course at RADA and got ready to watch Sir Peter Hall in action.

The first morning of rehearsals arrived and I was there, on the dot, at 8 a.m. I saw Sir Peter standing in the middle of the room sipping a cup of tea and went to introduce myself.

Sir Peter was as cold to me as anyone I have ever met in my life. He was not at all interested to know who I was or why I was there. He had no idea of my background or who my friends were. He really couldn't have cared less. All he knew was that I was a friend of Leslie who was going to be sitting in.

When I thought about it, of course, I knew there was no reason for Sir Peter to take an interest in me. He had a play to produce and was doing me a favour by letting me sit in. As I sat on the sidelines that morning, I could see why he was so wrapped up in things. He had decided to do an ambitious, full, four-hour version of *Hamlet*, which no one had done for a long time. He had a lot on his plate.

At the end of that first morning, I thought I would try to break the ice again. I went up to him and asked if he would like to go to lunch.

'No, I'm busy,' he said.

Fortunately, I had hit it off with three of the actors: Sir Donald Sinden, Gwen Taylor, who played the queen, and Michael Pennington, who played the king. I asked them if I could join them and Stephen Dillane for lunch and we went to a little pub around the corner from the rehearsal room in Chelsea which was actually a church.

I still hadn't quite got the hang of the English theatre philosophy. I offered to pick up the tab for everybody and they looked at me like I was nuts. I could read between the lines. They were saying, 'No, no, that doesn't work here, so don't try to impress us. Your money's no good, we're all the same here.' If I wanted to be one of them I would have to get off any ego trip I might be on. They were not interested in what I had done or impressed by who I knew. They were only interested in me as a person. Which was fine and actually refreshing.

Things carried on like this for the next two weeks. Every day I would turn up on time, and every day Sir Peter was as cold as ice towards me. He didn't pay me any attention. He never even said hello to me. So I just sat there and watched as they went over and over things.

Fortunately, I was fascinated by the whole thing. Apparently, it was the first time that somebody had done a *Hamlet* with nude scenes. That seemed really weird to me but Sir Peter thought it was innovative.

I don't know what he thinks about his version of *Hamlet* in retrospect. I don't think the cast were too sure about it. A lot of them thought it was way too long.

The cast couldn't quite fathom why I was sitting there day in and day out.

'Aren't you bored watching us going over the same thing again and again?' they kept asking me.

The simple answer was 'no'. I was a kid from the Valley who was intrigued by Shakespeare. If I have a choice between a musical, a contemporary drama or a Shakespearean play I will always rather see the latter.

I wanted to get to know Sir Peter a little. Two weeks into the production, I called Leslie again.

'The guy barely says hello and goodbye to me,' I told her. 'Does he know that I have produced Michael Jackson and worked with Elizabeth Taylor and Sophia Loren?'

'Let me talk to him,' she said.

She called me back a few minutes later.

'He'll go to lunch with you tomorrow,' she said.

The next day at lunchtime, I approached Sir Peter. He always went to lunch with his daughter Lucy, who was the designer of the play. She was going to come along as well. Things got a bit more complicated. I had had a call the previous night from the actress Tyne Daly, a star of Broadway and one half of television's *Cagney & Lacey*.

So I said to Sir Peter, 'Would you mind if I bring someone too?' He looked at me as if I had asked to sleep with his daughter.

'No, no. You can't bring anyone.'

So I shrugged my shoulders and said that I was sorry but, in that case, I would have to see my friend.

'She just won the Tony Award for Best Actress on Broadway and I want to spend some time with her,' I said.

He perked up immediately.

'Tony? Who's the actress?' he said.

'Tyne Daly.'

'Oh, of course, you can bring her along any time.'

We had a great lunch, although he spent a great deal of time talking to Tyne rather than to me.

From then on, I went to lunch with him almost every other day for the next four or five weeks. One day, I told him I had an idea about an international version of the American Cinema Awards.

I was going to call it the International Achievement in Arts Awards and was going to honour people in all the arts. I wanted to give him an award for his contribution to theatre.

'What do you think?' I asked him.

'Sure,' he said.

I wanted to work with him on other things too. I wanted to do something in the theatre. My friends all had deep pockets and I was good at raising money. I don't think he ever thought of me in those terms, though. Well, perhaps once he did.

One morning, we were working on a key scene in *Hamlet*, when Ophelia dies. We had been at it for three hours, from 8 a.m. until 11 a.m. Sir Peter didn't feel right about the scene. The problem was the set-up. Sir Peter had the priest leading the king and queen in Ophelia's funeral procession. The problem was that, since she had committed suicide, the priest couldn't really bless Ophelia because it was against church policy. So how come he was leading the procession?

They went over and over this. Everyone was asking, 'How are we going to do it?'

Whatever anyone suggested, Sir Peter would say, 'No, that's not right.'

I said to Donald Sinden, 'This is so simple, an

idiot could figure out how to do this scene.' He advised me to tell Sir Peter my idea.

So I raised my hand. 'Maybe I could help with this scene,' I said.

The expression on Sir Peter's face was priceless.

'Ah, Mr Gest, you've become an expert on Shakespeare have you? So go on then, let's hear what you have to say.'

Everybody in the room laughed. I'm sure they all thought the same thing. Who is this flash guy from Hollywood, with no theatre experience? What on earth can he have to say that the most famous theatrical director in England hasn't thought of already?

They didn't laugh for long.

'Well,' I said, 'since Ophelia can't be blessed by the church, why don't you start with the king and queen leading the procession rather than the priest and put the priest at the end of the procession as if he has been forced to be there. Then you can have the king nod at the reluctant priest to tell him he has to go over and bless her. It's an order.'

I'll never forget the silence. It seemed to last for a minute. I saw that everyone was smiling, as if to say, 'David's got it.'

Sir Peter did exactly what I said. He changed the scene and they rehearsed it and in half an hour they had broken for lunch – on time.

I didn't get any thank yous, of course.

That night, back at Claridge's, I called Whitney Houston and Michael Jackson. Neither of them had a clue what I was talking about.

'You'll never believe it, he used my idea,' I kept saying.

I was so proud. When the production premiered somewhere outside of London, I went along and there was the scene I had contributed to, exactly as I had seen it. I was so pleased with myself.

My plan to stage an International Achievement in Arts Awards had really come together since I had first mentioned it to Sir Peter. I had persuaded Sir Anthony Hopkins, Sir John Mills, Anthony Quinn, Diana Rigg and Ginger Rogers to be recipients of the main film and stage acting prizes. In the music category, Petula Clark and The Four Tops were the main recipients. Sir Peter Hall was the main director to be honoured for his work on the stage.

I had persuaded more than 100 Hollywood stars to come over. Robert Wagner was once more my good luck charm and would be introducing them.

The whole thing was in aid of Great Ormond Street Children's Hospital.

The night itself went amazingly well, despite the fact that no one thought I had a chance in hell of pulling it off. I had hired the Dominion Theatre on Tottenham Court Road but only for one day as it was booked the rest of the week.

I had 24 acts performing, from Michael Bolton to The Four Tops, Elaine Page to Petula Clark and Michael McDonald to David Cassidy. Everyone at the Dominion said nobody could put a show like this together in one day. They said the Prince's Trust always took a week. I did it and it went down a storm!

Alan Bates presented the award to Anthony Quinn and together they did the dance from *Zorba the Greek* for the first time since the movie. The place went nuts. Then Ginger Rogers got out of her wheelchair and walked for the first time in years to accept her award on stage. Everybody stood up and applauded that. There was hardly a dry eye in the house. The next morning, the newspapers were gushing about it. London had not seen a show like this in years. It even made the front pages of two major newspapers.

The only person who wasn't there was Sir Peter Hall. I had persuaded Sir John Gielgud to present the award to him but then Sir Peter got a movie deal and had to be on location rather than in London. I realised then that there were people other than Sir Peter that I could learn from and who might also want to utilise me as an investor.

The evening was memorable in lots of ways but once more Celia Lipton Farris provided one of the most memorable moments, for me at least. She had been very, very generous again in underwriting the show and had spent a fortune to make this happen. When we ran into some trouble with the unions, Celia had once again came to our rescue.

After what had happened with Michael Jackson a few years earlier, I was keen to limit the amount of time Celia spent on stage for her speech. I wasn't going to deny her the limelight. She deserved that and I knew it meant a lot for her to be back on the London stage, where she had apparently once played Peter Pan to glowing reviews. I just wanted to make sure the show ran at a good pace. So I came up with a plan. We were going to give Celia an award for her fantastic contribution to the show.

We knew that, inevitably, she would make a speech. She would probably also want to sing.

Tristan Rogers was still working on the shows with me. Tristan and I decided we would buy a trophy that was so heavy that when we presented it to her she wouldn't be able to do anything other than make a short speech and then get the hell off the stage as fast as she could.

Back in Los Angeles, Tristan went to a place in Beverly Hills and bought a trophy that weighed something like 150lbs. He then brought it all the way to England. When I saw it I couldn't believe the weight of this thing. It was a monster. On the night itself, I had to haul it up there on to the stage.

When the moment came to present the award to Celia, she held it in her arms as if it were a bouquet of flowers and proceeded to make a ten-minute speech. Tristan and I were dying. It didn't matter what this thing weighed. She stood there and made that speech. No one was going to deny Celia her moment back on the London stage, and when you think about it, who could blame her? She sang as well and did a pretty damn good job. I was very proud of her and so was the audience.

That was the last time Celia did a show with me.

I will always be grateful to her for the support. She did a hell of a lot to make these shows a success. I was never entirely sure why.

I loved being an American in London. I loved living in Mayfair, not far from Hyde Park and the West End. I also loved living at Claridge's.

I was friendly with Ronald Jones, who was the general manager of Claridge's and had given me a generous rate to live there. At the time, there were only a handful of us living at the hotel but what we lacked in numbers, we more than made up for in colourful behaviour.

There was a very rich couple from South America living at the hotel. One night, we were in the dining room and the husband had drunk too much. He wanted more but the staff wouldn't serve him. He clearly wasn't happy about this. So he took out his penis and had a pee in the dining room because he was too lazy to go to the toilet. He just stood there, in the middle of this elegant room, and made a puddle on the floor. No one knew where to look.

That was the end of his stay at Claridge's. He was very wealthy. He had been living there for ages. They asked him to leave the next morning. It was hysterical. I always think of him whenever I walk by where he relieved himself. I can't help imagining whether the carpet is still just a little stained.

One of the things I really loved about London was the social life. There was always so much going on. I already had a lot of friends living in England. I was soon rubbing shoulders with all sorts – even the Queen and future king of England.

What happened was that I developed a liking for the mezzo-soprano Cecilia Bartoli. I had seen her in California, at a Christian College in Pasadena, singing Verdi and had been blown away by her voice. I had never really been into opera but she really was impressive.

While I was living in London, I saw a little ad in the paper saying that Cecilia Bartoli was singing in Windsor in the presence of Prince Charles. Tickets were £60, which at that time was quite a lot of money. I called up to buy 20 tickets. I thought that I would introduce this great singer to a load of friends.

Perhaps tickets weren't selling that fast because, to my surprise, the guy at the other end of the line asked me whether, given that I was buying so many,

I would like to consider jointly hosting the party that was going to be held to accompany the concert.

'Jointly hosting it with whom?' I asked.

'Prince Charles.'

'Prince Charles!' I thought.

I put my hand over the receiver for a second, in case this guy heard my scream of joy. I composed myself and in a very calm voice said that would be OK.

'Thank you so much,' the guy said. 'We will be in touch with more details soon.'

I immediately called up some of the people I knew in London: Sir John Mills, Shirley Bassey and Petula Clark. I also rang my old friend in LA, Freda Payne, inviting her over for this party.

Thus it was that a few weeks later we all headed off to Windsor to see Cecilia Bartoli. During the interval, we all headed into this room and I was introduced to Prince Charles.

It was really informal; everyone seemed much more relaxed than I had expected.

'Hi, so great to meet you. How are you doing?' Charles said.

'Great,' I replied. 'Let me introduce you to

everyone here. This is Sir John Mills,' I said.

'I know Johnny. How are you Johnny?' Charles said.

Then I introduced him to Freda Payne, who he thought was very attractive, which she is, of course. I knew he liked The Three Degrees and black music. He asked when she was next playing in London.

Charles and I talked throughout the hour-long intermission. He told me how Barbra Streisand, who was now performing again, had shown footage of him in her show. He also talked about how he loved opera. I was honest and told him that I was just getting into it. He then proceeded to tell me about Montserrat Caballé, who was about to come to town.

'You really must see her,' he said.

So a couple of weeks later, I went to see Montserrat Caballé as Charles had suggested. I didn't know he was going to be there too but he was. When he walked in everyone stood up. When he saw me he came straight over and shook my hand.

'Hi, how are you?' he said. 'Good to see you again.'

I was with another large group of people. Everyone was in shock. When Charles left, I turned around and said, 'Oh, just an old friend.'

They didn't realise that I had just hosted a party with him. They were dumbfounded.

(When I met Prince Charles again, at a Royal Variety Performance the day after *I'm a Celebrity . . . Get Me Out of Here!* completed, I mentioned to him that we had hosted that evening and he was kind enough to pretend to remember.)

I was really impressed with Charles. We talked about soul music and The Three Degrees. He loved the Philadelphia Sound. He was very charming. I could identify with him. He is someone who has also been given the wrong rap. It's so easy for people to say things about you, and then when they meet you they discover you are totally different. It's something that has happened to me.

A few weeks later, I bumped into Prince Charles's mother.

One of my favourite events is the annual Chelsea Flower Show. I always try to go to the opening, and this year I went once more, with Sir John and Lady Mills. I had met them years before. I often used to come to London and spend time at their house.

Anyhow, the Queen was there to cut the ribbon on the first day of the Chelsea Flower Show. I said I would really like to meet her. They all kind of laughed nervously and said, 'Oh no, you can't. She's here in an official capacity. It doesn't work like that.'

As we were walking around looking at all the flowers and garden displays, who should be standing there with her security but the Queen.

I yelled out, 'Oh, Queen Elizabeth! How are you?'

People looked at me like I was insane.

She gave a thin little smile.

'Fine,' she said.

'I'm here with Sir John Mills,' I said.

'Oh, Johnny, how are you? Mary, hello.'

So she talked to us while all her security people looked around, scared to death that something was going to happen.

I took the same tack as I had with Charles.

'You look great, absolutely great,' I said, meaning it. 'I want you to know something – Americans love you.'

She kind of smiled and chuckled. I don't think most people talk to her that way. Everyone was probably thinking, 'Oh, my God, what is he going to say next?' I was polite though. I'm not that much of an idiot.

Afterwards, Sir John said to me, 'It's unbelievable. Whenever you want to meet somebody it always just happens.'

I hadn't thought about that before. I guess it's true.

I loved Sir John's etiquette. He was the most polite person I have ever met. I took the edge off that a little for him though.

One day, we went to a restaurant in Buckinghamshire, near where he lived. He had told me that the food was supposed to be great but it was actually terrible and I couldn't eat it. The roast wasn't cooked properly and the vegetables were swimming in water which looked like it had parasites in it. Sir John was laughing.

When the owner came out to see us and asked how the food was I said, 'Inedible, absolutely inedible.'

I could see Sir John shrinking in his chair but I didn't care.

'You should be ashamed of yourself,' I said. 'I'm going to allow you to take it off the bill.'

They did.

The really funny thing was that Sir John called me a month later and told me that he and Mary had been to a restaurant and had done exactly the same thing. He told them that the food was inedible and refused to pay for it.

He learned that from me. He was too English to have had the nerve to do that before. God bless him. I miss him. Fortunately he has two wonderful daughters, Hayley and Juliet, to carry on his acting dynasty.

East Side Stories

London had given me a new lease of life but I knew my future lay in America. At least for now. So, after a year and a half living at Claridge's, I headed back across the Atlantic, my batteries recharged, ready to throw myself back into more awards shows.

The International Achievement in Arts Awards show I pulled off at the Dominion Theatre in London had been such a hit that I repeated the formula three more times, first in New York in 1995, then in Beverly Hills in September 1997 and then in Los Angeles in 1998. The three shows honoured, among others, Gregory Peck, Jennifer Jones, Celine Dion and the great Smokey Robinson. Proceeds went to two charities run by friends of mine: the Michael Bolton Foundation and the Whitney Houston Foundation for Children.

Despite my promise to quit, in November 1996 I also staged the 11th American Cinema Awards in honour of Bob Hope, Richard Dreyfuss, Morgan Freeman, Shirley MacLaine and the daytime television actress Susan Lucci. The show was a great success, with former President Gerald Ford and Elizabeth Taylor attending.

The latter wasn't as satisfying as it used to be. The kick I had once got out of drawing in the Hollywood crowd back in the eighties had faded. This time, when I brought the curtain down on the show, I knew it really was going to be the last.

I was growing restless, with Los Angeles in particular. It suddenly seemed an unpleasant place to be.

The final straw came one night when a very rich friend of mine organised a double date for me and him. We took these two girls out for dinner and afterwards went back to his place.

I had known this guy for a while. What I did not

know was that he possessed a violent temper. I was with one of the girls when I heard a noise and ran to investigate, only to discover he was hitting the other girl. I saw him whack her really hard and this made me furious. I stepped in straight away and broke it up, then got the girls out of there.

That was the end of our friendship. I never spoke to this guy again. That incident made me realise that I had fallen out of love with the whole Beverly Hills scene.

The very next day, I said to myself, 'You know what? I've had enough of this.' I put my place in Century City up for sale, booked myself on a plane and flew to New York a few days later. I knew I was ready for a change and this proved to be the perfect move.

My feelings for New York as a city had changed completely since my unhappy times at London Records 25 years earlier. Back then, I had been a square peg in a round hole. Now I felt like I fitted in there.

I had had some great experiences in New York during the past few years. I had held the second International Achievement in Arts Awards at the New York Hilton and Towers. We had had a great night honouring the old western movie hero Gene Autry, my old friend Leo Jaffe and – most enjoyable of all – Whitney Houston. She was one of the main reasons I was so happy about going to New York.

Since Michael Jackson had first introduced us, Whitney and I had become really good friends. She had a charity of her own, the Whitney Houston Foundation for Children, which I did all I could to help.

Whitney had also been really generous to me and my awards. When the ACAF honoured the charity work done by the music mogul Clive Davis, at the tenth Annual American Cinema Awards show, I surprised him by getting Whitney to sing to him.

Clive and I hadn't always seen eye to eye but I think there had always been a mutual respect between us. In the run-up to the event, Clive told me that Whitney would show up but she wouldn't perform. So when she was about to go on stage, I asked her if she would sing a song.

Boy did Whitney sing. She performed 'The Greatest Love of All' and tore the house down in front of more than 1,200 people, including 300 stars who turned out for the event. Clive was stunned and really happy.

As a thank-you, I thought that Whitney would like a nice gift. Knowing she was a huge fan of Ginger Rogers, I got Ginger to sign a pair of her dancing shoes from the Fred Astaire days. She signed them 'to the greatest female vocalist in the world' and I had them framed with a picture of Ginger and gave them to Whitney. She has never forgotten it.

One of the things I liked about Whitney was that we shared the same pranksterish sense of humour. I'll never forget going to see her in concert in Atlantic City soon after she had released the album *My Love Is Your Love* in 1998. She wasn't performing much at the time, so it was a rare opportunity to see her sing to a large audience. Her husband Bobby Brown had just gone to jail and Whitney was really feeling the pain of being alone. I brought along my friend Deborah Cox, who had just recorded a duet with Whitney, and Gloria Gaynor and her then husband.

Halfway through the show, Whitney filled in the break between songs with a few words to the audience. The minute she started speaking I had a feeling I was about to be the butt of some kind of joke.

'Ladies and gentlemen,' she began, 'in the audience tonight is the National Association for the Advancement of Colored People's white man of the year, a man who has been recognised for having so much soul. Please welcome David Gest.'

I stood up and took a bow. Sheepishly, it has to be said.

'In honour of this great man, I'm now going to sing David's favourite song,' Whitney announced, straight-faced. She then proceeded to sing the old southern song, 'Mommy's Little Baby Loves Shortening Bread'.

Now, the audience that night was 80 per cent African-American and I was prepared to bet they were all thinking, 'How on earth can he love that song?'

I was dying in my seat. I had to cover up my face because it had turned so red. Whitney totally got me. She knew I would cringe, and I did.

After she had sung just a few bars, she stopped and made me stand up again. I just saluted her and admitted defeat. She had totally embarrassed me. Not many people are able to get one back on me, but Whitney did.

I had a cousin Ada, who lived on her own all her life and died a virgin at the age of ninety-nine. She never felt the warmth of her womb.

Ada never married or had children. She wasn't religious at all either. She was lonely. There was never anyone to buy her a gift or bring her a birthday cake. She didn't have any friends. She lived alone in a one-bedroom apartment and all she did was watch TV.

No one wants to leave this world an old, lonely virgin like her. Oddly enough, she died with her finger between her legs.

Cousin Ada made me realise that all you need to make you happy is good company. That is the most precious thing in the world.

I began my new life in New York, living in a hotel: the Plaza Athenee. Soon I discovered this great building on the Upper East Side, at West 67th Street. It was a condominium tower and was full of high-rollers, from Wall Street bankers and investment brokers to famous showbusiness people. The actor Liam Neeson, American television star Regis Philbin, rock star Jon Bon Jovi and radio talk show host Howard Stern lived there, amongst many others.

The first time I visited the place and asked to see an apartment, I was shown around by a guy named David Weild, a Wall Street genius who was vice president of the NASDAQ exchange. I really liked his apartment and did a deal to move into a similar one, a few floors below on the 29th floor. It was a great apartment. It was big, with three bedrooms and a magnificent 2,000-square-foot living room that looked out over Central Park and the whole city. From the moment I set foot in the place I loved it.

I was ready for New York now. I was older, wiser and, in the words of that great Billy Joel song, in a 'New York State of Mind'. I don't think I had ever been as happy living in a place as I was at the tower on West 67th Street. I have always been someone who enjoys people – and this was a place filled with interesting and unusual ones.

When I moved in, I immediately made contact with David Weild. We came from very different worlds but opposites attract and we were soon close friends.

One of the first things I did when I moved in was to redesign my kitchen. When I threw one of my first parties, I decided it wasn't big enough to cope with dinners for 200 people! Somehow, I don't know how, I persuaded David and his then fiancée Christie to let me use their kitchen, which was twice the size. Their apartment was five storeys above mine, on the 34th floor, so I commandeered one of the service lifts and had all the food brought down that way.

My apartment was really well suited to parties. So I was soon having lots of them.

Whitney and Bobby Brown spent a lot of time at my place. Whitney and I would host these charity parties, often for her foundation. One time I had Whitney, The Four Tops, Michael Jackson, Michael McDonald and Ashford & Simpson all performing in my living room. I remember Whitney singing 'I Believe in You and Me' with The Four Tops and Trisha Yearwood, who is now married to Garth Brooks. It was incredible.

Whitney and I were always teasing each other and making each other laugh. We were like brother and sister. As with Michael Jackson and me, people weren't always sure how to take our playful relationship.

Whitney and I would go through these elaborate charades where she would suddenly say she was leaving in the middle of the party. I would pretend to be upset and stop her. We would play out this dramatic scene and she would eventually agree to stay. It was all an act. People didn't quite know whether we were fooling around or being serious.

I had such fun in New York, not least because there were so many fun people in my life there.

David Weild helped me to pull off an outrageous joke on his wife Christie and this girl who worked for my friend Marc Anthony.

She needed a gynaecologist. I happened to be with Marc when I heard her talking about this. I told her I knew a great gynaecologist who lived in my building.

'Her name is Christie.'

This girl asked me whether she was an OBGYN or Obi-Wan Kenobi or whatever the qualification is.

I said, 'Yes, of course.'

So the girl called Christie at her apartment and before Christie could say anything she was talking away.

'I have some things wrong with my vagina and this is what I would like you to do.'

She then went on to describe in very intimate detail exactly what was wrong with her vagina.

After a while, Christie managed to get in a word or two.

'Are you sure you've got the right person?' she asked.

'You are Christie, aren't you?' the girl said.

'Yes,' Christie replied.

'Well, I've been told that you're the best gynaecologist in New York.'

'Are you out of your mind? What are you talking about? Who told you this?'

'David Gest,' she said.

'Oh,' Christie said. 'That explains everything.'

Both women were so embarrassed. When I saw Christie next, she called me every name under the sun. When the girl who worked for Marc told him what had happened he was hysterical with laughter.

Another couple I had become close to were the brilliant Canadian R&B singer Deborah Cox and her husband, the music producer Lascelles Stephens.

Like Whitney, Deborah 'got' my sense of humour.

I will never forget the first time Deborah sang at one of my awards shows. We were introduced and started talking about the numbers she was going to sing that night.

'Now, about you performing it topless,' I said. 'I think it's great that you're willing to sing topless. It will make this a much more interesting evening for everyone.'

She looked at me, dumbfounded, for a moment.

'What are you talking about?' she said.

It didn't take long for her to get the joke.

After that, Deborah and Lascelles knew to expect anything when I was involved and they would be happy to join in the fun. While I was living in New York, they helped me pull off a great joke on the legendary Dionne Warwick, one of my favourite singers and truly a great artist.

Dionne wanted to get in touch with Deborah and rang me asking for her number. I told her that she needed to go through her manager, who was also her husband.

'OK. What's his name?' she asked.

I guessed she would assume he was a 'Cox' too, so I told her his name was Big.

'Big,' she said.

'That's right,' I said, 'just ask for Big.'

So Dionne called up Deborah and Lascelles.

'Hi, I'm looking for Big Cox,' she said, completely oblivious to what was coming out of her mouth.

Lascelles didn't know what was going on then either and thought the call was from a disturbed person.

'I'm sorry, you have the wrong number,' he said.

Dionne assumed she had made a mistake and redialled.

'Hi, this is Dionne Warwick and I'm looking for Big Cox,' she said this time.

Once more, Lascelles was as polite as could be, knowing now that this was Dionne Warwick calling.

'Oh, I'm sorry, Dionne, but you have the wrong number.'

She immediately called me back and said the number was wrong.

'Dionne, it's the right number, I promise you that. Just say you are looking for Deborah Cox's husband,' I told her. 'Maybe they misunderstood who you were asking for.'

So she called for a third time.

'I'm looking for Deborah Cox's husband. I'm looking for Big Cox. Is there a Big Cox at this number?' Dionne asked.

Lascelles had, by now, guessed that something was going on and was having to suppress a laugh. Deborah was there with him and was listening in.

'Well, this is Deborah's husband but my name is not Big,' he laughed.

'You're not Big? Not Big Cox?' Dionne said, her voice slowing down as she spoke. Suddenly the penny dropped.

'Did I just say what I think I said?' she said. Then, after a pause, she started shouting. Lascelles and Deborah began laughing hysterically!

'I am going to kill him! I am going to kill that David Gest! I'm so sorry, sir, this is the most embarrassing thing. I am so sorry.'

Dionne rang me straight away.

'That was not funny,' she said, laughing down the line at the same time. I didn't hear much of what she said after that. I was on the floor, wetting myself!

I'm not someone who can sit back and do nothing. I needed to get to work on a project. I rang up a guy named Frankie Blue, who worked at one of the big New York radio stations, WKTU 103.5. I had known Frankie for a couple of years. You could say the way we met was unusual: we had once shared a jacuzzi with Michael Jackson.

Michael and I had attended a big event at the Epcot Center in Disneyworld in Florida. It was the weekend before his American Cinema Awards salute with Elizabeth Taylor and Gregory Peck. Disney Studios had sent a jet to take Michael and some other people from California to Florida. We flew over with a small group of people, including George Lucas and his daughter and Carrie Fisher and her boyfriend.

When we got to Florida, they didn't know who I was. They put Michael in this huge two-bedroom suite with a jacuzzi and they put me in this tiny little room next to his.

I took one look at the room and said, 'That's it. I'm leaving. Get me out of here.'

'No, don't do that. We'll share my suite,' Michael said.

One of the bedrooms was very large and the other was medium-sized. Naturally, I moved Michael into the smaller one.

I said to Michael, 'There's only one star here and that's me.' That's the way our relationship was. And he moved!

In the outside world, of course, the roles were very much reversed. The following day I said we should go shopping. Michael looked at me as if to say, 'Are you crazy? Don't you know what will happen?'

I told him it would be OK.

The moment Michael walked into this shop, crowds started appearing. All the aisles were pushed down and people were trampling on every type of Disney item. It turned into a riot and they had to call in 20 police.

Michael turned to me and gave me a little smile and a shrug of the shoulders.

'I told you so. All that damage was because of you,' he said. 'That's why I get them to close a shop when I go there.' He was right; the damage came to $25,000, all because I thought I knew everything!

Anyhow, one evening while we were at Disneyworld, we got into a jacuzzi at the hotel. Among those relaxing in the jacuzzi was this guy named Frankie Blue. He was a programme director at WKTU and we stayed in contact.

Once I had settled into life in New York, I rang Frankie and set up a meeting. I told him what I had been doing in LA and elsewhere and that I was now going to be based in New York. He suggested that I produce some shows for the station. I wasted no time in getting down to it.

New York had much more energy than LA. It gave me energy too and I began to be more creative and take more risks with the shows I put on.

In March 2000, Whitney and I were putting on an event to honour a very popular American radio personality called Scott Shannon. We had hired the Marriott Marquis Hotel in New York and had lined up a lot of strong acts. I felt the show needed to be raunchier, however. It needed something new and controversial.

I had heard a new singer called Pink on KTU and had loved her. I called her manager and asked if she would like to perform at this event. Whitney's name being connected to it obviously helped. They said yes.

My shows always had a full orchestra and included one or two hit songs by each artist. This time I wanted to do something shocking.

Pink was going to sing her new hit 'There You Go', backed by a dance troupe of eight girls and eight guys. I directed the dancers to act as if they were making love to each other in a really hardcore way. To really get people's attention, I had them all drop their clothes at the end of the routine.

Around 1,400 people came to the event, including some close friends of mine. When it came to the climax of Pink's act, while she remained fully clothed, everyone was stunned to see all these dancers stark-naked on the stage for a few seconds, penises and vaginas everywhere.

People were a little nervous and scared that I was doing something new like this. Michael McDonald and Tommy Johnston from The Doobie Brothers had brought their families along. Dionne Warwick turned to me and said, 'Has it come to this?'

Everyone was amazed. They had never seen anything like it.

I thought it was great, and it certainly got Pink noticed around New York. It made a great impact. I'm not saying it got the party started for her but it certainly helped!

The success of that show gave me the impetus to go on with the event I was planning for Frankie Blue of WKTU. I had come up with the idea of staging a big Christmas show at Madison Square Garden on 34th Street. Frankie had come up with the name, Miracle on 34th Street, after the much-loved Christmas film of the same name.

I pulled out all the stops and Frankie and I got together some of the hottest young acts around, from Christina Aguilera, Toni Braxton and Destiny's Child, to Ricky Martin, Marc Anthony and 98°, featuring Nick Lachey. I met a lot of rising new stars through the show. Michael Jackson made an appearance and was particularly impressed with Destiny's Child, the new three-piece, all-girl band led by Beyoncé Knowles. Afterwards, I told Beyoncé that Michael had a crush on her. She blushed. That night, Beyoncé and Kelly presented me with a humanitarian award from KTU.

I have formed some unlikely partnerships in my time, but none as odd as that which I forged with Liam Neeson. We joined forces at the tower on West 67th Street and together we staged a revolution, of sorts.

I loved living in this building. The only problem was the way it was being run. When I looked at the accounts in detail, I realised that all the hefty maintenance fees we were paying were not going towards fixing up the building but to what seemed to be more trivial things.

One day, I got talking to Liam and learned that he felt the same way. He said he had also been looking at the building's accounts and shared my feeling that a lot of money was being wasted. He had gone over the figures with a fine-tooth comb and discovered that funds for maintaining the building were being spent on flowers and things like that. The priorities seemed to be all wrong.

I really liked Liam. He's a giant of a man and has real fire in his belly. We instantly became friends. We made a deal to raise these issues at the next homeowners' committee meeting. We also agreed to try to change the leadership, replacing the current committee with a new one, led by us, if necessary.

In the run-up to the meeting, we went around the building canvassing people. There was no shortage of other tenants who felt the same way. A lot of them had complaints against the current committee but were too reticent to do anything about it. We pledged to raise their grievances for them. Soon we had a real political movement on the go. There was a whiff of revolution in the air.

The climax came at the annual meeting, where the guy running the place would talk through the accounts and other building business. He had been in charge for something like nine years and had been used to having his own way. I thought I would make a show of strength.

So I got two huge black bodyguards to accompany me. Their nicknames were Freddie Bigballs and Johnny Longcocker and they were big, big guys. No one in their right mind would have argued with them.

The crowd at the meeting was pretty straight. There were a lot of Wall Street people who were used to conventional board meetings. When Freddie and Johnny walked in on either side of me, everybody's jaws hit the floors.

There was a pretty heated debate. We proposed a vote of no confidence in the present committee. When it came to a show of hands, we won.

Things weren't quite that straightforward, of course. I demanded that we elect the new officers that night but they wouldn't do it. They hid behind the rules and said we had to wait three months for a re-election. We weren't going to be put off now, however, so David Weild and myself ran for office. Along with Liam's support, we won.

Even then, the existing committee did not want

to accept defeat. They tried to argue against our taking over but we said no way. 'You lost, we won. We are in charge now.' I remember Liam and I having a victory dinner when we took over the committee.

After this little coup d'état, I really got involved in the running of the building. This didn't make me very popular with everyone. The doormen, for instance, didn't like the fact that I wanted to stop them taking breaks all the time and being on the phone from dawn till dusk. Another big issue was that we felt anyone with a dog should use the back elevator, unless the dog was on a leash. The reason behind this was that someone had been hospitalised after a dog had bitten a chunk of his arm off.

Even though I ran the place like a tight ship and with the best interests of the residents in mind, there were some who didn't like me being in charge. I didn't care too much. If people resented the fact that I stood by what I believed in, that was their problem. Besides, I was having too much fun living there.

I have never been able to look after myself. I don't even know how to make toast. So I've always relied on having maids to cook and clean for me.

My apartment in New York really needed looking after, so I employed two full-time maids. Their names were Big Yvetta and Cocka Lavaca, who was from Czechoslovakia.

Big Yvetta was a big African-American girl with a huge laugh. She is one of my best friends to this day and the best housekeeper in the world.

I thought Big Yvetta could take a joke, so the day she started working for me I asked her to go across the road to Starbucks and get me a skinny latte and some 'poontang'. (It's a slang word that caught on in America after the Vietnam war. It means pussy.)

So she went into Starbucks and asked for a skinny latte and poontang. The person in there looked at her strangely and told her she could have the coffee but the poontang she would have to find elsewhere.

Yvetta went around to all the coffee houses and restaurants in the area asking for poontang. She got the same reaction everywhere. People either looked at her like she was nuts or laughed in her face.

Yvetta had been out for maybe half an hour when she finally went into a hardware store and a guy there took pity on her.

When he explained it to her, she said, 'Oh my

God!' She immediately came back and read me the riot act. I was on the floor laughing! I used to play all sorts of jokes on her.

Another maid who worked for me while I lived in that building was from Nigeria and her name was Betty. She had been with me for six months when I told her she had to go downstairs to the concierge to take a urine test. If she passed, she could carry on working in the building. It was a rule of the building, I told her. Anyone who had been working for more than six months had to take this test. She would urinate in a bottle and leave it at the front desk for a doctor to run tests and approve her continued employment.

Well, that day Betty headed downstairs to ask the guys at the front desk for a bottle. They didn't have the first clue what she was talking about. It just so happened that I had gone to a concert the night before and had left a bottle of wine downstairs. When they produced it she just shook her head.

'No, not that,' she said. 'I need to urinate in one and give it to you for testing so I can continue working here.'

'Who told you that?' one guy said.

'Mr Gest.'

When the guys realised what was happening, they were more than happy to play along. There was an African-American maintenance guy working there. He went to the water cooler and unhooked one of the giant drums of water.

He dragged it over to Betty and said, 'Here, fill this.'

They all started laughing. Betty came back up and she was laughing too. No one ever walked out on me. They loved it. I kept Betty on part-time until she moved with her boyfriend to North Carolina. Anyone who gets my sense of humour like that is OK by me.

Miracle on 34th Street

It's odd how inspiration can sometimes appear as if by magic. The idea that set off a sequence of events which would change my life forever began one morning in New York in January 2001 when I woke up and turned on the radio.

It was a cold, grey morning in Manhattan. A thick shroud of mist hovered over the trees in Central Park. The mood was very different in my apartment though. The minute I heard the familiar music blaring out of the radio, on WCBS FM, it was as if a ray of sunshine had burst through the clouds.

The record was 'The Love You Save', my favourite Jackson Five song. I first heard it back in 1969, when The Jackson Five had taken the world by storm with a string of four number one hits: 'I Want You Back', 'ABC', 'I'll Be There' and 'The Love You Save'. The group generated incredible excitement and the world was crazy about them. Since that time, the band had broken up and Michael had gone on to become the biggest pop star in history. The group had come together again once for the Triumph Tour in 1984. It was now 17 years since the Jackson Five had last performed together live.

As I listened to the song, one single thought kept going round in my head. 'It's time for The Jackson Five to get back together,' I told myself.

In the ten years or so since he had tried unsuccessfully to make me his manager, Michael and I had remained friends. The closeness we had shared in the late seventies and eighties had faded a little because we were both so busy but we still spoke frequently.

One of my most recent long conversations with Michael had taken place towards the end of the previous year, 2000, when he had called me for a chat. We talked for ages, just like the good old days. I made him laugh, he made me laugh. I think Michael felt the same way I did, that he missed his old buddy.

'David, we really should start doing some things together,' Michael said as the conversation came to a close.

As I thought about our conversation on that January morning, I realised this was the opportunity of a lifetime. Michael had released his first solo single, 'Got to Be There', in 1971. This year would mark his 30th anniversary as a solo artist.

This was not only the perfect occasion for a celebration of Michael's life and for The Jackson Five to reunite, it was a great opportunity to produce a show that would be truly historic. Moreover, this show would lend itself naturally to television, potentially making it an even more lucrative venture.

I was wise enough to realise that I was not the only person who might be thinking along these lines. In 1992, Jermaine Jackson had teamed up with producer and writer Suzanne de Passe, who had worked with the Jacksons at Motown in the early years. Together they had made a hit miniseries for television called *The Jacksons: An American Dream*. Prior to that time, de Passe had made a very successful music special for television, *Motown 25: Yesterday, Today and Tomorrow*. It was one of the best specials I have ever seen. A show to mark Michael's 30 years as a solo star was just her kind of project. Michael had been talking to her but nothing had come of it. I knew I had to move fast.

I picked up the phone immediately and called Michael at Neverland, where he was living in those days. His reaction was swift and predictable.

'David, no,' he said.

Ever since I had had my first job on the *Valley News & Green Sheet*, 'no' was a word I had a lot of trouble accepting.

I knew I had amazing powers of persuasion with Michael. I decided to get the first plane out to California, went down to Neverland and put those skills to work.

'Michael, this is going to be done,' I said, 'and this is why . . .'

I ran through the potential of the show, both in terms of profile and finances. Handled properly, this could be a huge payday for him: millions upon millions upon millions. His career was nowhere near the level it had attained during the golden days of *Thriller*. I knew this would appeal to him. He began to show that big smile of his and slowly started to relent.

'Michael, people want to hear all those old songs. They want to hear them,' I said. 'They want you and The Jackson Five.'

Michael understood. We drew up the papers and formed a company called World Events LLC. It was our company, we were co-presidents. He trusted me and I trusted him. We went on a vacation to San Francisco and Carmel to celebrate. We felt like the kids we used to be 30 years ago.

From the outset, I was determined to run the show. I now had years of experience of producing similar events. I also knew Michael, particularly when it came to money.

Once, at Disneyland, he bought so many bronze and porcelain figures of characters from the film *Fantasia* that we had to call four extra limousines because there was no room in the car. Michael was very giving. This stuff was worth a total of $200,000 and he gave $100,000 worth of it to me! He was always incredibly generous but he never kept track of his money.

It was the same when it came to his concert tours. He had always been one to overspend. Although he might make $100 million, he would spend $102 million because there was nobody to check him. I was determined this was not going to happen here.

So from the very beginning, I ran the whole show. Michael had to have my approval to do anything. When he would call me with some request, if it was not financially sound, I would say, 'No.' Point blank.

A couple of times early on, Michael called me with ideas for stage layouts that were going to be very expensive.

'No, we're not going to do it,' I said. 'End of conversation. Do you want a pay-cheque at the end of this or not, Michael?'

I had been here before and I wasn't going to have another Houston on my hands. I would not let the budget get out of control. If this show was a success, I knew I would never have to work another day in my life. If the budget was not managed properly, I could just as easily find myself working at a Kentucky Fried Chicken.

I booked Madison Square Garden for the

concerts, which were to be held over two nights on 7 September 2001 and 10 September 2001. Thanks to the Miracle on 34th Street concerts I had produced the previous three Christmases, I already had a good relationship with the place.

I had also come up with the concept for the *Michael Jackson: 30th Anniversary Celebration, the Solo Years* show. It would be spread over the two nights and both shows would be split into two halves. The first half would be in honour of Michael, who would sit in the audience while many performers paid him tribute. In the second half of the show, Michael would perform with his brothers and other famous acts.

Already I had begun to shape the running order. I knew the opening needed to be spectacular, so I put Whitney, Mya and Usher, three of the hottest singers around, together for a version of 'Wanna Be Startin' Somethin''. The choreography was being staged by a brilliant guy called Brian Thomas and his partner. I had hired Brian for other shows and he was great to work with. To really make this opening number stand out, we decided to have a real African tribe dancing in the background as Whitney, Usher and Mya performed the finish.

This opening song would set the standard for the whole evening. It had to be perfect.

Strategic planning was well underway. I asked Marc Anthony to sing 'She's Out of My Life' and teamed a real powerhouse trio, Luther Vandross, Usher and 98°, for a version of 'Man in the Mirror', backed by a 100-member gospel choir. Additionally, I persuaded Missy Elliott and Nelly Furtado to duet on a version of 'Get Your Freak On' (one of Michael's favourite songs) and a really talented kid called Billy Gillman to sing one of Michael's first and best-loved songs, 'Ben'. I also asked my old friend Gloria Gaynor to sing her signature song that really summed up Michael's life in recent years: 'I Will Survive'.

The more I worked at it, the more I realised that this could be the highlight of my career so far, without a shadow of a doubt. Almost every day I felt hairs standing on the back of my neck at the thought of it all coming off. Every now and again, however, I also felt sick at the prospect of the whole thing being a disaster.

As we prepared to release tickets for the shows, we decided to charge between $75 and $5,000 per seat. This was the most anyone had ever charged for a non-charity event in New York. In my estimate, no one would ever see another show with 100 major acts, so what the hell! It was expensive but no one was forcing anyone to buy tickets!

The news of the ticket prices caused a real storm in the city. A gossip writer, Richard Johnson of the *New York Post*'s Page Six column, wrote a critical piece (the beginning of a trend with him!) predicting that it was going to be a fiasco because we were charging so much money for an event that wasn't even for charity. He also cast doubt on whether I would be able to get the Jacksons together again. There had been rumours of rifts within the family, particularly between Michael and Jermaine.

I knew that I had the family safely signed up but at that time Page Six was an influential column and I was worried what impact its coverage of the ticket prices might have. (Oddly enough, recently Page Six went through a number of scandals and is no longer in many people's minds as important as it was back then. The allegations of paying people for stories undermined its importance. I had heard talk that there were all manner of bets in Las Vegas that I would never pull the show off. No one believed I could get the Jacksons together because of the tensions. But I knew that any publicity is better than no publicity, and we were getting a ton of it.

Thankfully, the following day, Yoko Ono, who was a close friend of Michael, spoke out on our side. She said that the fuss was ridiculous. She said, 'This is America. David and Michael have the right to charge what they want. If you don't want to go, don't go. If you do want to go, then you'll pay the money.'

Yoko probably saved our backsides. I will always be indebted to her.

I'll never forget the day the tickets went on sale, at the end of July 2001. We sold out 90 per cent of both shows in nine hours and sales were over $10 million dollars on the first day! The rest of the tickets soon went too. We knew then that we had a huge smash on our hands – it was the hottest ticket there was. Michael and I had only laid out $20,000 so far. It was absolutely extraordinary.

By August, with a few weeks left until the show, things were looking good. There were still plenty of problems to overcome, however. The biggest worry was Michael himself. What I had noticed back at the beginning of the nineties was even more prevalent now.

The difference between the old Michael Jackson and the new one was that he just wasn't as focused as before. What was even sadder to witness was the way Michael seemed to be playing people off against each other. For example, he would hire one lawyer and then hire another one. These people would hate each other, so he would never get the best out of them. He had tried the same thing with me, of course, successfully spoiling my chance to work with Janet. I had learned a lot from that experience. This time I didn't let him get away with it.

By now Michael was being managed by John McLain, who I had known since our childhood, when he was at a private school called Walden with Michael. John and I had been friends. He had been executive producer of Janet's early recordings and had helped sign her to A&M. Two of my old pals, Ed Eckstine and Mike Merkow, were also pals of John.

Two weeks before the show, Michael rang up to say that he had been talking to John and that he was going to bring in Suzanne de Passe to co-produce the show with me. My response was instantaneous.

'Are you out of your mind?' I said.

I knew immediately this was John trying to make a power-play, and it was typical of Michael and his tendency to pit one person against another.

I had always tried to do the opposite and get the best people working together. I would hire the top lighting and sound directors, the best choreographer and I would work with all of them. I would use their expertise to make the shows great. While I always had ideas, I never told them what to do because they were experts in their fields and I wasn't. I couldn't tell a sound man how to mike something up. I have always hired the best.

Michael loved creating fire. As far as I was concerned, it was his worst habit and I think it contributed to his downfall. This time I simply wasn't going to stand for it.

'Michael, let me tell you one thing,' I said. 'We have a contract. I will take you to court and I will fight you. It's two weeks before the show and there is no reason to bring anyone else in. You can tell John McLain it ain't going to happen.'

Before Michael could say anything else I carried on. 'If you want to see another side of me, then get ready.'

Michael got the picture.

'OK, forget it,' he said. He backed down. He called John and he didn't mention his name again after that.

Moments like that aside though, Michael was not as interested as he used to be. Back in the eighties he was the ultimate detail man. He looked at every aspect of his career, forgetting nothing. He would always deliver the greatest performances, especially when he needed to.

Not any more.

Two days before the first show, 'N Sync, then one of the biggest bands in the world, led by Justin Timberlake, informed us they were about to pull out. The only way they would stay on the bill was if Michael would perform with them on the MTV Video Music Awards, which were taking place just a couple of days before our show. We were due to have our main rehearsal that very day. The old Michael would never have bowed to a threat like that but he had changed. Without my knowledge, he meekly agreed to 'N Sync's demand, not even telling me.

I could not believe it. Michael went to the MTV awards show, then arrived late for the run-through of the most important two shows of his life. He allowed only two hours to rehearse a complex sequence of songs and dances that included not just his brothers but other acts as well.

I was absolutely furious with Michael but I had to let it go. Fortunately, I had a girlfriend to turn to, who was also performing on the show, but that's another story altogether.

Even though I had to rehearse all the acts without Michael, I could see that the show was absolutely brilliant. That made the situation all the more frustrating. I knew I was doing a good job, even though Michael seemed disengaged and distant. This attitude made me very angry and I did not understand it. Everything else aside, I knew that – barring any major disasters – we were on course for a huge financial success. As well as selling out at the box office, there was a bidding war for the television rights, which I had personally been negotiating.

I had made a tentative deal with ABC for around $4 million, which was one of the highest figures ever paid for a two-hour television special. There were problems with the fine print, however. During negotiations, ABC agreed to pay half the money up front. Now we were close to drawing up contracts and they suddenly said they didn't want to handle it that way. While ABC argued over the contract, their rivals at CBS offered to pay much more. I couldn't turn this offer down and thus went with CBS instead. In addition, I got CBS to agree to let me and Michael have all rights to the television show, something that was pretty much unheard of in television. Michael and I owned it, CBS did not.

A long list of overseas broadcasters, from Europe to Australia and the Far East, were offering big money for deals in their regions too. The money for worldwide television rights could be more than twice what CBS had paid.

So, as the date of the first show drew close, I felt like everything was set fair. Nothing could go wrong. Yeah, right!

On 7 September 2001, Madison Square Garden was packed. More than 200 celebrities had shown up. Friends of mine like Liam Neeson, Angie Dickinson, Robert Wagner, Jane Russell, Janet Leigh and Sir John Mills had been joined by entertainment and sports stars, from Quincy Jones to Muhammad Ali. By 7.30 p.m., virtually every seat was filled, ready for the start of the show – and the television recording – at 8 p.m.

There was one rather conspicuous space in the front box of the auditorium, however. When the show started, Michael was supposed to be sitting in the audience while people performed to him. He was nowhere to be found.

I had stressed the importance of Michael being on time to everyone, including the star himself. It was important because we were filming and the contract with the Garden stipulated that the concert must finish at 11 p.m. to avoid overtime: costly, costly overtime. At first, I just put it down to Michael wanting to make a grand entrance but when 8 p.m. came and went, I knew it was more serious than that.

I went backstage and started making frantic calls. I was assured he was on his way and would be there any minute. The clock kept ticking.

It was exactly 9 p.m. when Michael turned up with Elizabeth Taylor at his side. I took one look at him and my heart sank. He was subdued and almost disinterested. It was as if he wasn't there.

Everyone had been pretty concerned. When word spread of Michael's arrival, all sorts of people tried to get backstage to see him. I remember one of the senior guys at his record company, Tommy

Mottola, coming backstage, saying that he needed to talk to Michael.

I just said, 'No, go to your seat.' I was fit to be tied.

As well as the potential damage to the show, I knew this was going to hit us hard financially. Keeping the Garden open for an extra hour would cost us an additional $100,000 or more.

I was scared. I wasn't quite sure what I was going to do but I knew I had to be cool. So I got everyone ready, told them to get the show started in a couple of minutes and led Michael to his chair. He sat there looking half asleep.

When we finally got the show started, it was after 9 p.m. and we were already a full hour behind the running schedule. Then, when we started filming, I discovered the problems were far from over. I had never really done a show of this magnitude for television before.

We started the show with Samuel L. Jackson, who came on stage and talked about Michael. Next we kicked off with Whitney, Mya and Usher's spectacular version of 'Wanna Be Startin' Somethin''. This all went well but then we needed a break of ten minutes for the lighting to be reset and the cameras refocused. This had to happen after each song thereafter. Being a novice at television, I thought it would go like my usual live shows: straightforward. As the technicians tinkered between songs, the audience was growing restless. There was nothing for them to do but talk amongst themselves. I was going nuts.

As part of the deal with CBS, I had complete control of the show. They had put so much money into it, however, that Jack Sussman, one of their senior executives, was on hand. He was looking at me in a way that said, 'Do you really know what you're doing here?'

As the show progressed, things went from bad to worse.

Marlon Brando lumbered up on to the stage and made a 25-minute speech. He was talking about stuff that had nothing to do with the show: child poverty and the plight of immigrants, all sorts of things that were happening elsewhere in the world. A lot of people didn't seem to know who this Godfather was and were screaming 'Get off!' and booing. I had given Brando a scale payment, like everybody else, for being in the televised part of the show. Michael had also paid him privately, as I found out afterwards. Eventually, Brando was booed off. We had to turn the lights off and say thanks to get him off the stage. It was a nightmare.

Throughout all this, I had a terrible knot in my stomach. It felt like the whole thing was sinking towards disaster. Every time I looked at Michael I just felt worse. He seemed totally out of it. He just sat there, stony-faced, and watched the show, moving his hand to say thank you to people as they sang to him.

The show eventually finished just before midnight. People had been sitting in their chairs for four and a half hours. They looked relieved to get out of there.

Afterwards, there was a big party at Tavern on the Green, which a lot of people had paid big money to attend. As we were all leaving Madison Square Garden for the limousines, Michael came up and told me he wasn't going.

Inside I exploded. I knew I had to stay calm and be firm.

'Let me tell you one thing, young man. If you don't go to this party, you will not see one pay cheque from me,' I said, keeping my emotions in check as best I could.

'Also, if you are not here at four o'clock on Monday for the second show you will lose $5,000 per minute from your pay cheque. I am serious. I sign the cheques. One minute over, you lose $5,000. If you are an hour late again you will owe me $300,000.'

We had gone $150,000 to $200,000 over budget that night alone and I was furious. Michael's late arrival, coupled with the flabbiness of the show, the stopping and the starting, had made the concert endless. Michael had pulled himself through the performance, which wasn't bad by any standards, but it wasn't his greatest. It just didn't have his usual electrifying quality. Something was wrong with him and he knew I knew.

I made sure Michael went to that party but he was as disinterested as he had been at the concert. At one point, we met the actress Patty Duke. We both loved her TV show and the film *The Miracle Worker*, for which she had won an Academy Award for Best Supporting Actress. Michael just looked at her without expression, as if he didn't know her. Throughout most of the party, he sat at a table with Yoko and Sean Lennon. He was out of it and didn't know where he was. Everyone thought he was acting strangely. I believed it was the painkillers.

The next day, I called everybody who worked on the show to my apartment for an early morning meeting. I told them that the first show had been abominable, a debacle. If we didn't buck up our ideas in the three days between now and the next concert on 10 September, then the whole thing would go down as a disaster.

If the second show was to be up to scratch, I knew a long list of things had to be addressed. First, we had to do something about filling time while the television people got their cameras ready between acts. So, to give the concert continuity, I arranged to play some great video footage of Michael performing on giant screens whenever there were dead moments.

I also went through the running order again, making sure those people who were talking were short and sweet. The biggest change, however, needed to be in the star of the show.

I gave Michael a day to recover before I went to see him and deliver the lecture of all time. 'How could you do this? We could have lost a fortune,' I said. 'What the hell was wrong with you? How could you have been so stupid?'

He tried to justify his behaviour but I did not want to hear it. 'Don't even speak to me again until Monday,' I said. 'Just be there at four o'clock.' I have always been direct with Michael and he respects me for that.

I spent the remaining time before the second concert cutting things from the running order so that this show would run on time and to plan. As we rehearsed some of the sections again, I checked and re-checked the timings with a stopwatch.

On Monday 10 September, I arrived at Madison Square Garden just before four o'clock. I had hardly taken my coat off when Michael showed up, bang on time. Clearly the idea of losing $5,000 a minute had woken him up a little.

From the moment Michael arrived, I could see he was back to normal and ready to kick ass. He looked like a new person, focused and ready to perform. Whatever had happened a few nights earlier had been put behind us. He was 'on'.

I was never more proud of Michael than I was that night. He showed his real artistry and reminded everyone why he had become far and away the most successful star on the planet.

The show started on time at 8 p.m. and moved

along as smoothly as a baby's bottom. Throughout the first half, Michael sat in the audience, beaming and waving to everyone, unrecognisable from the zombie-like guy who had turned up the first night.

When the second half of the concert began, Michael was electric. He walked out on stage carrying a small case. He placed it down, pulled out his black sequined jacket, hat and white gloves and burst into 'Billie Jean', complete with the legendary Moonwalk dance. The audience went crazy! Everyone jumped out of their seats and from that point forward the place was on fire. Britney Spears joined Michael on stage for a version of 'The Way You Make Me Feel', Slash from Guns 'n' Roses backed him on guitar for 'Black and White'. The show came to an end with just Michael on stage, singing and dancing up a storm.

This time the show ran like clockwork. It finished at 10.30 p.m. precisely.

I was so relieved. Michael had come alive and given the greatest performance ever. The reviewers came backstage afterwards and said it was the best show they had ever seen. They were all going to write reviews the next morning saying so. I'm sure they headed to work with that in mind.

After packing up, we all left Madison Square Garden just before midnight on 10 September 2001. The next morning, the world changed.

If the terrorist attacks of 11 September had happened a day earlier, I would have been bankrupt. As it was, we successfully completed the shows the night before and were able to retreat to the editing studio. First, though, we mourned for five days those we had lost and the losses of others. My friend Berry Berenson, who had been married to Anthony Perkins, died on the Boston plane that crashed into the World Trade Center. When I found out, I cried. I had loved her. Now her two children had lost both parents within a few years.

New York was in a state of shock for weeks afterwards and life would never be the same again. The age of innocence had died. The world had changed overnight.

On 17 September, I sat down with one of the best editors from Sony and started to put the footage together. I knew we had some great stuff but I also knew that most of it was in the second night's show. I needed to put together two hours of footage for

CBS. I set about picking the best segments to construct the special.

The television broadcast wasn't due to go out until later in the year so I took my time, two months to be exact. I also spent an extra $100,000 editing and polishing everything so that it looked as slick and stylish as it possibly could.

I found myself being creative. I learned how to edit and spent endless hours in that suite, cutting and pasting, editing and mixing. By the time I had finished, I was exhausted but I also knew that the finished show was something special. This proved to be very true.

The two-hour broadcast went out on CBS on 13 November 2001. It was the highest-rated non-charity musical special in television history, breaking every record. The audience was in excess of 44 million people. One out of every four households in the United States tuned in to watch it. The reviews were great too. The critics loved it as much as the audiences did. It was an amazing moment in my life. I knew that for the first time I had really found what I thought would be my niche.

If it was a critical success, it was a financial

sensation. When we added up the final receipts, including television rights, receipts for the concerts and everything else, we had cleared $20 million. I wrote Michael the biggest cheque he had received in the last few years. I wrote myself the biggest cheque I had ever seen in my entire life. I was on cloud nine!

In the weeks running up to the *30th Anniversary Celebration*, Michael had kept going on about this friend of his who he wanted on the show. Her name was Liza Minnelli.

I really wasn't sure. This woman, even though she had won Tonys, Emmys, Grammys and an Oscar, didn't fit in with the show I was producing. *Michael Jackson: 30th Anniversary Celebration, the Solo Years* was for contemporary and hip artists.

I had worked with Liza on a couple of American Cinema Awards shows. I think we had dinner at Frank Sinatra's house once. She had never made any impact on me. I certainly wasn't a fan. I did think she was very talented. I thought she was great in a movie called *The Sterile Cuckoo* and I must add that I did really like her in *Cabaret*, for which she had won the Best Actress Oscar. She had a kind of nutty quality on screen, and I've always liked nutty people. She was very Broadwayish and middle of the road, however, and I didn't feel she would fit on this show. Michael was insistent.

'You've got to have her on. You've got to have her,' he kept saying.

I really wasn't convinced so I said, 'Look, before we have an out and out argument about her, let me send my conductor Joey Melotti over to hear her sing.'

Joey was in charge of conducting all the acts who were singing to Michael in the first part of the show. He went over to Liza's house in July or August of 2001. He called me afterwards and said, 'Her voice is really strong, although she's not in perfect shape.'

I said, 'Do you think she can cut it? I just don't want her to make a fool of herself.'

I went over to Liza's house the next day. She knew I was coming to check her out. When she opened the door the first thing I saw was the most incredible pudge nose, the kind La Toya had before she had her plastic surgery. This nose went in all these different directions and it wasn't perfect. I have always liked imperfect beauty. I think the most beautiful people in the world are those who have imperfect faces. Lord knows, I do.

I looked into Liza's eyes and I knew I was in love with her. Just like that. It was odd because she had none of the qualities that I normally fall in love with, except she was a brunette, which I have always been fond of.

I listened to Liza sing. Immediately I saw this little girl inside of her who was dying to come out. I asked her if she would like to have dinner.

Frankie Blue and his wife Jamie came out with us. In the cab going back to her house after dinner, we looked at each other and knew we were thinking the same thing. Within a week we were living together, commuting between my house on the West Side on 67th Street and hers on the East Side on 69th Street.

We didn't go to a lot of places. We travelled back and forth to London, went to shows and had loads of fun, even if we were just reading books in bed. Liza has a great personality and made me laugh. She also took such an interest in me and made me feel like the most important person in the world. As I was completing the Michael Jackson television show, she kept reassuring me that what I was doing was great. When we were apart, we would talk on the phone for hours. I knew I loved her more than life itself at this point.

When we staged the Michael Jackson concerts in September, no one knew we were dating, even though we had been together for two months by then. After the show was over, Whitney Houston was coming out of her dressing room and saw Liza and me kissing madly at the side of the stage. Whitney later told me she knew the two of us would marry from what she saw that night.

I had had many girlfriends over the years, some of them long-term. I had even come close to getting married once before but somehow it had never felt right. I don't think anyone had been able to cope with me and all my odd idiosyncrasies before. I certainly hadn't been ready to commit myself to another person.

When the dust of the *30th Anniversary Celebration* settled, I saw that things had changed. I saw the rest of my life with complete clarity. Liza had changed my life for the better, or so I thought.

I knew that I was in love with Liza and she was in love with me. I knew we were going to get married and that we would stay married for the rest of our lives. Every night I would go to sleep with her in my arms. For the first time I had found someone who really, really loved me. Who knew what was about to happen? Maybe I was the most naïve person in the world as I did not really even know what an alcoholic was. Why is it people find it hard to tell the truth? Everyone should always find out about a person's medical condition before they get married.

Liza

Bad Dreams

We got married in New York on 16 March 2002. By July 2003 we were separated. Before my marriage, I had been someone who was happy to stay in the background, producing, orchestrating and controlling things without revealing my real face. Yes, I had an ego but it was an ego that was satisfied by the world in which I moved, the people I knew and the successes I enjoyed. I was friends with some of the most famous and talented people in the world. I didn't need the public's acknowledgement. I didn't set out to be famous in that way.

The minute I married a world-famous woman, I stepped out from behind the curtain and all that changed. I became one half of a marriage that was analysed and talked about all around the world. In the 15 months we were together, our faces featured on dozens upon dozens of covers of countless magazines. Strangers who assumed they knew me made judgements and cast opinions, even though they had never met me. I became a tabloid king!

Anyone who has been through a marriage break-up knows how hard it is. No one goes into a marriage without love. I certainly didn't. When it doesn't work out you have to grieve. For me, being in the public spotlight while I got on with this process only made it harder.

I couldn't feel too sorry for myself, however. I didn't have to look far for examples of people who had suffered far worse fates than mine.

I had admired Luther Vandross for many years and we had become friends when I put him on the Michael Jackson special. I had had the idea for Luther to sing 'Man in the Mirror' with Usher and 98°. Luther sang the climax of the song. When he came out he took the song to a whole new dimension; his voice was awesome. He took it beyond what I had expected.

After that concert, we stayed in touch on a regular basis. I knew he was going through problems with his recording company and I tried to help him. I recommended a friend, Peter Asher, brother of Jane Asher, who had been part of the singing team Peter and Gordon. Peter didn't think it was something he wanted to do, so I was looking around for someone else to look after Luther.

In April 2003, Luther and I were due to get together to talk about this. I had just got back from a trip to Europe. Liza was in the hospital with a broken patella. Luther called me to arrange a dinner a couple of nights later, but we got talking – and talking and talking. We spoke for about four hours.

We both had a lot to get off our chests. I was having my problems with my marriage. He had just recorded the album *Dance With My Father*, which was to win numerous Grammy awards.

Luther was very upset because his record company, Arista, didn't seem to be supporting the album as much as he thought they should. He had lots of grievances. The boss of his label had put him through to someone who was third in command, rather than dealing with him directly. They didn't want to release the title song as the single, something Luther was very passionate about. In general, they didn't seem to be confident about the album. They didn't know whether it was going to cross over to a pop audience. Luther seemed mortified.

Luther felt humiliated at having to go through this after such an incredible career. It was one of those conversations you have every now and then in your life when everything comes out. That night, Luther and I spoke about life, his problems with Arista, everything. We spoke until two in the morning.

I put down the phone hopeful that I might be able to ease some of his worries. It wasn't to be. The next morning Luther had a massive stroke from which he never recovered. He died in July 2005. The album came out posthumously and was a number one bestseller, platinum record and Grammy winner. *Dance With My Father* was the hit he believed it to be and in the end he got his way because the public loved it and him.

The last two years had been the worst of my life

due to the head concussion. I couldn't function the way I used to. I was fed up with the way things were going. For the first time in my life I was very, very ill. It was tough being married to an alcoholic.

What happened to Luther gave me some perspective, however. Things had been bad but they weren't worth losing my life over. It marked an important moment in my journey back to recovery.

From June 2003 through June of 2004, I lived on the island of Hawaii. Ironically, I had bought a house there so that Liza and I could avoid the press. I didn't go back to that house. I remained in a hotel for anonymity.

Moving to Hawaii didn't seem to make any difference. The press wrote about me anyway. I suffered from severe head pain and spent a lot of time in hospital in Hawaii. I had to take large amounts of medication to control the pain. In fact, an American television show, *Dateline*, filmed me getting 80 shots in the head, something I had to go through every three weeks. People then realised I was telling the truth about my concussion.

Liza is currently being sued for $100,000,000 by her former bodyguard and best friend M'Hammed Soumayah, the man who nurtured her back to health after she was struck down with encephalitis, for beating him and forcing him to have sex. She is currently defending the suit.

Since becoming a tabloid king, I had had to acquire a security guard. The guy I had hired was from England and was a karate champion. His name was Imad Handi. While I was in Hawaii, he and my American security guard, Willie Green, looked after me. Other friends would visit me too including James Ingram and his wife Debbie, Mya, Deborah Cox, Gloria Gaynor, Candi Staton and so many others. Without them I might have never recovered.

During that period of my life, I hit rock bottom physically. I had been down before but my health had not suffered. Now it was like I was living in a bad dream. It was all due to the concussion. The blood vessels in the back of my head had been broken.

I stopped caring for myself. Imad would bring me seven pieces of Boston cream pie every day. I would eat five or six sandwiches. I went from 140lbs to 235lbs.

I was taking about 29 pills per day to take away the pain. All I would do was take my medication to get rid of the pain and just lie in bed, day after day. I suffered from memory loss. It was the lowest point of my life. I never thought I would recover.

My cousin Ein Stein was a lovely man and he was married to a lovely woman named Pinkney.

Ein and Pinkney Stein were two of the brightest scientists in Russia. They both loved to study the planets. They were fascinated by them. Their favourite planet was Uranus, and when they had a little daughter they named her after it.

Little Uranus was one of my favourite cousins. We always played together whenever she came to America. Funnily enough, when I was living in England in 1993, I introduced her to a friend of mine in the music industry named John Smelz. They fell in love, married and she became Uranus Smelz.

Uranus and John had a beautiful wedding. The maid of honour was Uranus's best friend, a girl whose father was an inventor of soda in Russia. During Communist times, the most sought-after commodity was any type of good, flavoured soda. This man was so proud he actually named his daughter Sodas.

Now, at the wedding, Uranus introduced her

maid of honour to the best man, Tom Yours. Sodas and Tom fell in love on the spot and eventually got married.

Uranus and Sodas remained the very best of friends. Whenever they walked down the street together, people would say, 'There goes Uranus Smelz and Sodas Yours.'

I've never quite understood why all my cousins have such odd names.

Anyway, the tragedy of this whole story is that one day, as Uranus Smelz and Sodas Yours were walking to an art gallery, a sewage truck driving by went out of control and hit a car.

The accident sent the truck's cargo flying through the air and it all fell on top of Uranus and Sodas. I do not know whether it was the smell or the quantity of the sewage that actually killed them but what an untimely death. Who would have guessed that Uranus Smelz and Sodas Yours would be killed by smelly sewage. It seems incongruous but it's true. No bull.

In June 2004, I left Hawaii and headed for Los Angeles for my first public appearance in a year, the funeral of my very good friend Ray Charles.

Additionally, Kirk and Ann Douglas gave a dinner party in my honour at Mr Chow's with Angie Dickinson and other friends present. I was still not very well.

Memphis had always been a city I loved. I had had a lot of great times there, especially working with Al Green and Willie Mitchell back in the seventies. I felt it would be a great change to move back there.

Throughout the dark times of my marriage break-up, the one consolation I had was that I was financially secure. I had watched money slip through my hands in the past. That wasn't going to happen again. I had saved the money I had made from the *30th Anniversary Celebration* and didn't intend to waste it. So I bought a great house, a beautiful, three-storey place on the river, in an area that I knew was becoming popular with celebrities.

The actress Cybill Shepherd lived a few doors down from me in a house on an estate facing the Mississippi and Justin Timberlake owned a property nearby. It was a really tranquil spot, just the place to get my life back on track, I figured.

While the sale went through, I stayed in a small residence, the Talbot Heirs. It turned out that the place was filled with the cast of a new movie being filmed in Memphis, *Walk the Line*, about the troubled life and times of singer Johnny Cash. The guy who was playing Jerry Lee Lewis was next door to me on one side, the guy playing Elvis was on the other. They were young guys but great fun to be around. We started hanging out and going drinking. It made me feel like I was getting out into the world again.

Within a couple of months, the house was ready for me to move in. It too gave me a boost. Pretty soon, I began drawing up plans for a concert at the end of the year.

I called up some old friends: The Doobies, Deborah Cox, Mya, Dionne Warwick, Petula Clark, Jerry Butler, Gene Chandler, Mel Carter and a group of others, including the original Box Tops, featuring Alex Chilton, Three 6 Mafia and Lil' White, and booked them to do a show at the Cannon Center in Memphis that Christmas.

Deborah and Michael McDonald had come over to Hawaii to take part in a concert the previous year, while I was very ill. It had been misjudged from the beginning. I had wanted people to know I was still alive, even though I was mentally dead. I had put on two concerts, one at a big sports stadium and another at the Mandarin Oriental on New Year's Eve 2004. I hadn't been on top of my game at all. The shows hadn't made any money because I wasn't all there physically. The head concussion had made me very, very ill. I didn't even stay to watch them. I had left my long-time colleagues Tristan Rogers and Joey Melotti to get on with it. It would have been smarter not to have done these concerts at all. I just wanted people to know I was still alive, unfortunately it was barely.

In Memphis, however, I sensed I could get back into the rhythm and put on a good show.

As I got out and about in the city, however, I realised that Memphis wasn't the way it had been in the seventies, when it had been a really happening place. It showed how little I was in tune with what was going on around me. One day it suddenly hit me that there were people living rough on the streets. Everywhere it seemed that shops and offices were closing down.

Somebody told me that 65 per cent of the population was destitute. There was a bad atmosphere in the city. There was a lot of racial tension and bigotry. I hate bigotry and will not tolerate it.

So I decided I was going to take whatever profits I made from the Christmas events and feed the city's homeless. I stuck adverts around the city and got ten restaurants to open from noon until 8 p.m. that Christmas Day. All people had to do was prove that they were a senior citizen, from a low-income family, homeless, physically impaired or a student who had no money and they could eat for free on me.

That Christmas, around 100,000 people, most of them African-American, had a great Christmas dinner. It caused a real stir around the city. All the news stations covered it. Once again, people didn't believe that all these people would turn up but they did. I felt better about that than I had about anything since 2001. It gave me a real lift. At least I was doing some good. At least I felt alive again. Just.

Before I moved into the new house in Memphis, I knew I had to get a maid. A friend of mine recommended a lady who had worked for an athlete friend of theirs and arranged for her to come and meet me at the hotel.

She said her name was Vaginica. Immediately I started laughing.

She said, 'I don't find it very funny that you're laughing.'

I had a friend over and he was laughing too.

So I said, 'Can I ask you, sweetheart, how you got that name?'

She said, 'My mommy, she loved her own body part so much. She loved the smell, the feel and she loved the beauty of it. She always said that if she had a little girl that was as lovely as her body part she would name her Vaginica. When she looked at me she said, "Oh, this is the sweetest thing I've ever seen. This is my little Vaginica."'

My friend and I had to run to the bathroom because we couldn't take it.

It was hard for me to understand how any mother could give a child that name. But as I got to know Vaginica, she told me more stories about her mother.

Vaginica's mother expressed her love to all these different men that she met by letting them get to know her vagina. She said it with such honesty. Vaginica married her high-school sweetheart in the 8th grade when she found out she was pregnant. His name is Harry Ceaman. She became Vaginica Ceaman!

I eventually found out that Vaginica had two daughters. One was named after her mother's parents, Clive and Tina, little Clitina.

I said to her, 'Do you understand what Clitina means?'

She said, 'Yes, Clive and Tina put together.'

It is odd when you think of Vaginica having a little Clitina but they're southern. She has another daughter, Beulah Belle. She told me that both her daughters were going to be singers, that they both had beautiful voices, that Clitina looked just like Whitney Houston and that Beulah Bell looked like Angela Bassett.

When I met Clitina and Beulah Belle I was shocked. Vaginica is a pretty woman, apart from the fact that she has a gold tooth in the middle of her mouth in the shape of a star. She has these cute little aprons with 'Vaginica' embroidered on them in different colours. Beautifully done.

Little Clitina, however, was 375lbs and Beulah Bell was about six foot four and about 475lbs. They wore these polka-dot mini-skirts they got from Wal Mart and these spandex leotard tops with go-go boots. They also had big pink and white bows in their hair. They looked like they belonged in the *fifties. They were two of the ugliest creatures I had ever seen in my life but still very sweet. The only resemblance to Whitney Houston I could see was that Clitina swept her hair over her face.*

When Vaginica said, 'Do you see it?' I was speechless and she said she understood. The other one didn't look anything like Angela Bassett either.

The girls sang like two dogs in heat. They were probably the worst singers I've ever heard in my life. They kind of howled together. They both wanted to be in show-business, though, and they had this wonderful love for life.

I was stunned. I had never realised that Vaginica had been using my bidet as a water fountain. She thought you got water from there to clean the floors.

I saw her turn it on one day and it went right in her face because she had it on too high. She had no idea what it was. She thought it was a waterfall in the middle of the bathroom. Her two daughters got such a kick out of playing with the bidet that they wanted to get one in pink and put it next to their refrigerator for their father. They also wanted to get one for their pastor. They both live in a very bizarre world.

Vaginica drives a huge truck.to work. When I talk to her about her mother she tells me that her mother wants to donate her vagina to science. She says she wants to do the same.

I said that I had never heard of anyone donating their vagina to science. Vaginica told me that people donate beautiful things to science so other people can get enjoyment out of them.

I said I had heard of people donating their hearts and their livers but never their vaginas. She's insistent that she and her mother are donating them. She wants her daughters to do it too but having seen the girls I think a donation from them might scare people!

Holy
Focaccia

Your childhood has a big influence on who you become. You don't need to be Sigmund Freud to know that. I know, for sure, that a lot of things about me are explained by my early days growing up amidst the paddy fields of Taiwan. For a start, that place put me off rice for life . . .

In October 2006, while passing through Los Angeles, I organised a dinner party for some friends: Tito Jackson, Freda Payne, James Ingram and the two original lead singers of The Fifth

Dimension, Marilyn McCoo and Billy Davis Jr. I booked a table at the Roosevelt Hotel, the original home of the Oscars, where I usually stay when I go to Los Angeles.

It was great to see everyone and to catch up on old times but the evening felt a bit weird. I wasn't going to be able to stay throughout because I was supposed to leave early for the airport. At 11 p.m. that night I was due to catch a plane to Brisbane, where I was supposed to be taking part in a British television show. I was really torn about whether or not to go.

I had been approached to do a show called *I'm a Celebrity . . . Get Me Out of Here!* I really wasn't that interested when I first got the letter from ITV. I had been approached by British companies about similar things before, including the Channel Four show *Celebrity Big Brother* and a show called *The Farm* but I had turned them all down. A few months earlier, when the people from ITV had arranged to have tea with me at the Grosvenor House Hotel in London while I was in London for a party honouring me and Smokey Robinson, I hadn't expected to be persuaded. Then they told me what they were willing to pay. It was unbelievable.

I really hadn't seen *I'm a Celebrity* before. I understood pretty quickly that it was some kind of survival show, where you were dumped in the middle of the jungle with a bunch of other celebrities and then had to do a load of tasks. The public voted on who they liked – and didn't like – until someone emerged as the winner at the end of the three weeks.

I found some clips on the internet. I'm not real good with computers but I watched a clip on the show's website. I saw Margaret Thatcher's daughter, Carol, eating some bugs and the show's presenters, a pair named Ant and Dec, doing a dance. I thought it was funny, especially those two.

The person who wanted me for the show was a girl called Emma Ford and she set up a meeting at Grosvenor House with Richard Cowles, the executive producer of the show. We hit it off immediately.

My first reaction after the meeting was: 'I can't say no to this kind of money.' I also reckoned that if I did this show, it might help sell tickets for the four concerts I was planning for the end of the year at Cadogan Hall in London: David Gest's New Year's Weekend All-Star Soul Spectacular, featuring Peabo

Bryson, Russell Thompkins Jr and the New Stylistics, Candi Staton, Bonnie Tyler, Freda Payne, Martha Reeves & the Vandellas, William Bell, Carl Carlton, Billy Paul and my dear friend Deniece Williams.

I signed a contract committing myself to the show. The doubts set in pretty much immediately but with so much going on I put it out of my mind.

It was only at the Roosevelt that night in Los Angeles that it began to sink in. I am going off to do this show now. Oh my God, why?

My friends were not all for it. On the other hand, my bodyguard Imad, who lived in England and knew about the show, said this would be good for me. He said I should let the public see who I really am.

There were two problems with that. First, I thought that the British public knew who I was. Of course they didn't. My ego got in the way there! More to the point, I wasn't sure if even I knew who I really was at that point. Truthfully, I had really let myself go again. In the two years since the break-up of my marriage I had become fat and lazy because I was so ill. I had lost touch with the real me. The migraines were still there, in fact they have never gone. I just deal with them each day by taking four Excedrin Migraine pills. Even today I am still on them.

That night, my friends finally told me to go for it and have fun. 'What is there to lose?' one of them said as I left the Roosevelt Hotel and headed to the airport.

Their words of encouragement didn't have an effect for long. As I sat on the plane, flying over the Pacific, I thought to myself, 'What am I doing here? What the hell am I doing, period?'

A couple of days later, I was feeling even worse. By then, I was camped at the Palazzo Versace Hotel on the Gold Coast of eastern Australia, near Brisbane, where everyone was being gathered for the start of the series. Since arriving in Australia, I had got to know a lot more about the show and the other people involved in it. The more I learned, the less I liked the look of everything about it, including myself.

I knew I had put on weight since the break-up of my marriage but I hadn't realised quite how bad I really looked. When I saw myself in the mirror, I was actually 85 pounds heavier and had tits and man boobs. I was disgusting. The sight of all that blubber made me sick.

So I thought I had better do some groundwork and prepare the British public for this gruesome sight. They were going to see me as I am in the show, so I thought they had better not expect too much. I had been a good body-surfer when I was hanging out on the beach in Marina del Rey as a kid. I decided to go body-surfing and invited a couple of the press photographers who were there covering the show to join me. I had to do this so that nobody would be startled later at the sight of my obesity. Boy, did they make money on that shot. The photo still haunts me today. It didn't leave me in the best mood.

Then, on the night before we were supposed to go into the jungle, someone rang me from London and read me all these quotes from one of the other contestants, a woman called Lauren Booth, a journalist who was Cherie Blair's sister. She had really been shooting her mouth off, saying I had had bad plastic surgery, my eyebrows were patched on, etc. etc. I thought to myself, 'I've never met this woman!' What she said was so mean and malicious that I called the producers.

The producers and I had been talking about how the show was going to begin the following day. As

I was used to hosting things, they asked if I would be the first one out at the 'meet and greet' party. Then I would greet the next person and the next person after that and so on. I would say hello to them one by one. I knew who I wanted to greet first. I had a real welcome planned for her.

'Either you bring Lauren out second or I'm out of this show,' I said.

They got freaked and came running over to my suite. I really laid into them.

'This bitch said all these things,' I said. 'How does she know about my eyebrows? Look at my eyebrows. Do they look like they are tattooed on? How does she know what plastic surgery I've had done? How can she make all these assumptions? She hasn't even met me.' I was furious.

They agreed.

So the next day it all began and Lauren came out to meet me on the rooftop where it was being filmed. 'So you've been talking about me. Isn't it great that you think I'm an asshole? You've never met me before,' I said.

At that point I was in such a mood I really didn't relate to anyone. When the rest of the contestants came out, I didn't pay much attention. I didn't really know who any of these people were. I was an American and none of them were huge names to me, apart from Jason Donovan, the actor and singer.

I had lived at Claridge's when Jason was a big star on record and in the West End version of *Joseph and the Amazing Technicolour Dreamcoat*. I had met only two of the others. A couple of weeks earlier, when I had been a judge on a TV show, *The All Star Talent Show*, the pop star and presenter Myleene Klass had been one of the hosts and another of the people there, the DJ Toby Anstis, had been a contestant. I had been cheered for saying I thought Toby was a good dancer.

As the cast of the show got together, I didn't feel like talking much during that first hour or so. When we were sent off to get changed into our 'jungle gear', I spent an extra hour in my room. I really wasn't looking forward to whatever lay ahead. I made them all wait!

To get to the jungle where our camp was based, we had to fly in helicopters. I got into a chopper with four others. Once it was up in the air, it started dipping up and down, behaving like it was in *Top Gun* or something.

My experience of almost falling out of a helicopter that time when I had been with Al Green had cured me of any fears. I was laughing but I could see that Toby, who was sitting next to me, was suffering and was not far from throwing up.

Once we were dropped off, we had to canoe the next leg of the trip. I used to canoe as a kid but the vessel they had lined up for me was a kayak. I shared it with actress Phina Oruche. It wasn't a good start.

We did fine for about four minutes, then lost our rhythm completely. All of a sudden the others were passing us and we were just moving aimlessly from side to side, going nowhere basically.

It was then that I felt the strangest thing. I suddenly thought, 'What if you were here on your own? What if this was all you had in your life?'

I realised then that I had to make the best of it. So I just got on with it, refused to give in and kept paddling. It took us an age but we got there in the end. It was kind of an epiphany.

I knew that the production team saw me as a wild card. They were very worried I would leave within 24 to 48 hours. My contract even stipulated that I would get no money if I left before the first person was evicted. After that I would get a pro-rata fee. During those early hours, there were times when I wanted to walk – I'm sure that thought crossed everyone's mind – but from that moment on I knew I would stick it out.

We had to make the final trip to the camp on foot. One thing I worked out pretty quickly was that I needed to make this a team effort. It was a team show. It really was all for one and one for all. Anyone who didn't feel that way was going to be dead. So I tried my best to get along with people.

I put the flare-up with Lauren behind me and got on with it. I actually liked Lauren once I got to know her and I have always felt that if someone apologises, which she did, then you should put any grudges behind you and move on. You get more with honey than with vinegar. She happened to be a very nice person and we have become friends.

I didn't get off to the best start on the first night. I didn't realise that I snored. None of my girlfriends had ever told me. So I was very surprised when they told me the next morning that I had been making an almighty noise. I thought they were kidding but apparently not.

Pretty quickly, I saw that Jason was going to be

the guy I bonded with best, although in the end it was both he and Matt Willis who became my closest buddies in the camp, as well as in London. On our first day in camp, I said something to Jason. It was a joke and he knew it. He just looked at me and said, 'Fuck you!' Right then we became best friends. Jason immediately knew how to deal with me.

Over the following three weeks, our relationship went through a pretty interesting evolution. It started out that I was Jason's father. Then he became my brother. By the end, I was the child and he was the father. It was weird.

Life quickly settled into a routine of sorts. We spent a lot of time doing really menial things, with a lot of it revolving around mealtimes.

The food was terrible. We had to eat a lot of rice and beans, which I hated and simply couldn't eat.

They also expected us to do household chores, which presented a bit of a problem for me. I had been happy to clean out the latrine, usually with Matt. We became the poopy cleaners. One night, however, Phina said that it was my turn to do the washing-up after dinner. I said, 'I don't do dishes.'

It didn't go down too well but I made sure I

didn't get asked again. I washed the pots with shampoo and conditioner and moisturiser, which I thought got them very clean.

I found out later that Myleene and Jason had washed them again because they smelled of soap. I thought they looked good. They had been eating off things that were much filthier. At least it made sure that I wasn't asked to do that again.

When I was picked to do the first task, or Bush-tucker Trial, for which we would earn real food, I was pleased. It gave me a real focus. I couldn't wait to get something decent to eat. They led me to a place where I had to sit in a tank of water that was then filled with all sorts of creatures. As these things poured in, I had to collect as many stars as possible, each one corresponding to a meal for the camp.

Talking to the production team before the show, I had made out that I was terrified of bugs and lizards and all sorts of creatures. Reverse psychology. Never fails.

As all sorts of things dropped into the tank, I thought it was hilarious. Here I was, my feet chained to the bottom of the tank and I still felt totally in control. Ever since I had been a kid I had loved playing around with frogs and lizards. At Neverland with Michael, I had had the time of my life with the alligators and crocodiles. I suddenly found myself performing like I was some kind of stand-up comic.

When a little baby alligator dropped in I looked at it and said, 'Weren't you at my wedding?' When I tossed it aside, I started singing, 'See you later, alligator!' I was on a high.

In fact, looking back, I realise I would have done better if I had not talked so much. I got six stars but could have gotten all ten if I had taken the task more seriously. At that point, no one had gotten that many stars and my fellow camp mates were impressed.

As time wore on, I formed a bond with the guys. Matt had been in a really successful boy-band called Busted. We started playing around with words in the way I had done with Anthony Perkins years before. Two other camp members, Jan Leeming and the former EastEnders actor Dean Gaffney, were our victims. Dean, although ambitious, was a really nice guy and I liked him immediately.

Toby and I also had great fun coming up with a rap song. The chorus went:

I'm A Celebrity! No food
I'm A Celebrity! No booze
I'm A Celebrity! No nookie
I can't even find myself a bloody chocolate cookie!

Myleene was nice too, and what a body she had! She looked like a goddess. She was very sweet and was willing to help pluck my nose hairs. She was also kind to me about the food situation.

My camp mates were giving me rice in the morning and I would take handfuls of it and throw it in the river. One day, Matt found me with my hand full of rice, ready to get rid of it. That didn't go down well because he knew I was starving myself. Myleene would always give me extra vegetables because I wasn't eating the meat.

I also enjoyed getting to know the actress Faith Brown and the designer Scott Henshall. I thought they were both great people.

I got on fine with most people. The only person I didn't hit it off with was ex-BBC newsreader Jan Leeming.

After I had been chosen to do the first task, Jan had to do pretty much every one for a week after that. Every time she was picked, she complained about it. I tried to explain to her that the more she complained, the more the public were going to pick on her. She just would not listen.

After a while I started to feel a bit sorry for Jan.

At one stage I realised that she liked to talk about show tunes and musicals. Having been involved with so many Hollywood stars, I thought I could relate to her on that level. She responded to this and sang a number, I think it was 'Summertime' by Gershwin.

I wanted to vomit it was that bad. It was like a cow meeting a moose and the two of them having an orgasm. I didn't want to say, 'You suck,' so I just said, 'We'll work on this tomorrow.' I wanted to give her confidence because I felt sorry for her.

I know some people had probably gone into this thing with some kind of game plan, but I decided I just had to be myself as much as possible.

I couldn't swear as much as I did normally, so whenever I felt the urge to let loose I taught myself to say 'focaccia'. It is much better for a kid to say this than the 'F' word. Given the amount of beans and rice I was being asked to eat, I found myself saying it quite a lot. 'Holy focaccia' became my catchphrase. Other than that, I was the same, slightly eccentric person I was in the outside world.

I never realised that the stories and characters I was talking about in the camp were having such an impact back in the UK.

As people were being voted off the show, I didn't really analyse where I was going right or wrong. I was too hungry. I could feel myself wasting away, which wasn't such a bad thing, of course.

As time wore on, I started to regress, to get in touch with the person I really am, rather than the one I had been forced to become in recent years. When you have that much time to yourself, you can't help thinking things over, taking stock of where you are in your life. As I did so, I started to realise that all the material things I had acquired meant absolutely jack all. So what that I had a lot of money and material possessions, collections of antiques and gold records? That didn't mean anything out in the jungle. I saw that I could survive without those things. I began to enjoy myself more and more in my new outdoor home.

With a couple of days to go before the end of the show, Matt, Jason and I were given a task to do together. The competitiveness in all of us had come out by now.

We had to throw ourselves down a slide, armed with an arrow which we had to throw at a balloon hanging in the air. It took a lot of precision to be able to arch your arm back so that you could hit the balloon. I really wanted to beat Jason but hadn't been told to bring my glasses. I am near-sighted, so I could barely see the target as I flew by. I missed it by an inch and Jason hit it. So goes it.

That night, back in camp, I realised that I could carry on living outdoors for even longer. I didn't want to get out of there at all, quite the opposite in fact. I wanted to do all the trials. I wanted to be the one at the end to eat all those bugs and things. I would have eaten them.

But it wasn't to be.

Three weeks into the show, with only one more day to go, there were only five of us left: Jason, Myleene, Matt, Dean Gaffney and me.

Whenever it was time for one of us to leave after a public vote, Ant and Dec would come into the camp and read out the name of the one to go. They would always milk it for every bit of drama they could get. They came in twice that day. First they announced that Dean had been voted out by the public. Then, with the usual dramatic pause, they told us that the one who had come fourth in the show was . . . 'David'.

I felt fine about it. The others were kind of shocked because they thought I was going to win the whole thing — certainly Matt and Jason thought that. As I got myself together and made my way out of the camp, I told myself that this was a fair result. Matt, Jason and Myleene deserved to win more than I did. For a start, they had done more of the chores and were better athletes.

I also felt that I didn't need to win the show. As far as I was concerned, I had already won in ways I would never have thought possible three weeks earlier. I had proved to myself that I could stick at it and wasn't afraid of anything. I had done well enough to make it all the way to the top four. For me, that was as good as winning.

When I left the camp, I did a live interview with Ant and Dec in which they showed me some clips from the past three weeks. It was odd as I couldn't see myself without my glasses. Hearing them talk about me left me feeling a little emotional. I'm not a person who really cries, so it takes a lot to get me to shed tears. I felt like I wanted to but held them back. I felt really moved by the two of them talking about me.

As Ant and Dec tied up the interview, one of them said I had become an unlikely national hero.

I thought, 'Yeah right.'

It was when I crossed the footbridge leading from the jungle that I began to suspect things had changed.

As soon as I got to the other side of the bridge, someone from the show handed me a letter. It was from ITV, saying they wanted me to do my own television series. I had barely recovered from this emotional ride when I met with the company's head of programming, Paul Jackson. He was really complimentary and told me ITV had plans to turn me into a big star. At that point I was in shock still. I really thought this couldn't be happening to me, that they must have made a mistake. Let's face it, I'm fifty-three and not exactly a knockout to look at.

I met more and more people from the production and the press and everyone was saying, 'You're a national hero.' I was still saying, 'Yeah right.'

I didn't understand what they meant.

It was only when I called some friends that it began to sink in.

I called Petula Clark back in London. She said the sweetest thing.

'David, I'm so glad the nation now knows what I've always known: what a funny and warm person you are.'

I could feel the tears in my eyes.

Then I called another friend.

'You won't believe what's happened to you. The public loves you,' she said.

'Oh, come on,' I said.

'David, you have no idea,' she said.

I didn't.

When I got to the hotel, my publicist said I had had five other offers to do TV shows. The staff of *I'm a Celebrity* had sent me a list of the newspaper clippings from the past three weeks. There were dozens and dozens of them. As I started reading them, I just sat there shaking my head.

The *Sun*, never an easy paper to please, said, 'Everyone thought he would be a Hollywood fruitcake, but he has turned out to be a fantastic, charming man.'

The *Guardian* said that I had 'all the physical attraction of the elephant man on a bad hair day', which I thought was nice and probably true. 'But who could not warm to the man. He has turned out to be a quirky man with a heart and soul.'

Another paper talked about how 'suffering loony Leeming's singing he was the soul of diplomacy'. Even Simon Cowell had been saying nice things.

'He's really funny and great on camera,' he said, which I was touched by.

My head was spinning. I couldn't quite come to terms with what was happening. I needed some time to take stock. Fortunately, ITV flew Tito Jackson out to greet me and at that point I just choked up and cried. It was a long overdue shedding of tears.

I stayed on for the last day of the show, in which Matt emerged as the eventual winner and King of the Jungle. I was so pleased for Matt, who is one of the most gifted kids I have ever met in my entire life. I believe he will become a huge music and TV star. He has that special quality that turns women on and makes men want to emulate him. I love this kid. He is like my brother.

After that, I immediately headed back to London, where ITV wanted us to do a 'coming home' show. More importantly, however, I was heading for a meeting with Prince Charles and Camilla.

It was when I got back to Heathrow that the

reality of what people had been saying in Australia dawned on me.

As I came out through customs, people were applauding. That had never happened to me in my life before so, naturally, I thought there must be someone famous behind me and turned round to see who it was. There wasn't anyone there.

People were shouting, 'David, good job.'

'Holy focaccia.'

'Where's Vaginica?'

Before I knew it, there was a small crowd around me. I signed like thirty autographs, then there were ten more, then there were photographers. Soon there were a hundred people all around me. I was telling myself this must be a dream.

I got in the car and on the way into central London asked the driver if I could get some throat drops. I had picked up a bad throat on the way back from Australia.

As I walked into the pharmacy people were reacting in the same way they had at the airport.

'Holy focaccia, it's you,' the person at the checkout said.

The same thing happened when I got back to Grosvenor House.

It was odd, because I had become so used to being out in the open air that I found myself needing to go out and be outdoors every now and again.

Whenever I did so, people would come up and say hello or shout greetings.

There was a construction site opposite the hotel. When I walked past, the guys working on the site started shouting.

'Yo Davey, where's Vaginica?' one said.

'I don't do dishes,' another one shouted.

Even walking around the rather grand streets of Mayfair, I was besieged by people coming up asking for their photos to be taken with me and for autographs.

I was almost in tears. I couldn't quite get all this love. I didn't have a chance to properly take stock. It was as if my life had been put on to a permanent fast-forward.

That first night back in England, I was asked to appear at the Royal Variety Performance at the London Coliseum. When I got there, the hundreds of people outside were all asking for my autograph. Inside, I met some of the stars of the show. It appeared that everyone in the country – perhaps even the world – had been watching *I'm a Celebrity*.

Rod Stewart came up to me and said, 'Job well done.'

Barry Manilow, an American, came up to me and said, 'You are a superstar.'

I said, 'Come off it.'

'No, David, you are all the public has been talking about. I've been over here. You're so funny.'

The reaction when I came out on stage to introduce one of the acts was unbelievable.

'Holy focaccia!' I said. They went crazy.

'I'm here for two reasons,' I said. 'Firstly, I support this charity and secondly, my housekeeper, Vaginica Ceaman, loves this act. She's seen them 16 times and would have seen them 17 times but her daughter got encephalitis.'

They went crazy again. I couldn't believe how everyone had latched on to Vaginica.

Backstage, I was introduced to Prince Charles and Camilla.

'My housekeeper Vaginica is your biggest fan,' I told Camilla when I shook her hand.

'Tell her I said hello and that I hope she is very well,' she smiled.

For once, I felt secure. I loved the UK and they seemed to love me!

In the weeks that followed, things continued in the same, strange vein. The series of concerts I had planned for the New Year weekend sold out. We even had to plan an additional concert. People flooded in to see Martha Reeves, Candi Staton, Freda Payne, Deniece Williams, Billy Paul, Russell Thompkins, Jr. and The New Stylistics and the rest. For the first time in all my years producing, they wanted to see me too. Each night I would be front of stage, introducing the acts and telling tales from the jungle. I loved telling the stories and making people laugh. More importantly, it felt great to put a smile on people's faces.

Soon afterwards, I was moved when I got a call from Simon Cowell asking me to tea. We sat there talking for two and a half hours. I admire Simon immensely. He said that we were so much alike, and he was right. He asked me if I would star in *Grease Is The Word*, his next series. I immediately said yes and we shook on it. Like me, his word is his bond. A handshake is as good as a contract. I am excited about being a judge on *Grease Is The Word* and will give it my very best. I am enjoying working with Sinitta, David Ian and Brian Friedman, who are also judges on the show.

Most excitingly of all, Paul Jackson was as good as his word and offered me my own Sunday night series on ITV1, *The David Gest Show*, a fly-on-the-wall-style documentary show. It had been commissioned by Layla Smith, the classiest of executives and a wonderful human being. The even better news was that it was going to reunite me with many of the team that had worked on *I'm a Celebrity*. I was really pleased that I was going to be working again with Marty Benson, whose first interview with me for the show at the Lanesborough Hotel weeks before going into the jungle had reaffirmed for me that I was doing the right thing. I was also delighted that Emma Ford, Craig Blackhurst and Andy Burgess, as well as the producer of *I'm a Celebrity*, Natalka Znak, would be the production team behind *The David Gest Show*. I also got two of the craziest camera crew ever, Matt Smith and Ben Bradley. And I found a fabulous make-up artist, Lisa Armstrong, Ant McPartlin's wife.

Only a week after I returned from the outback, their cameras were following me around, recording seemingly every detail of this exciting new life of mine. I even went back to one of my first loves, songwriting. Matt Willis introduced me to James Bourne, another ex-member of Busted. Along with Chris Leonard and Jake Gosling, James and I co-wrote the theme song to my new television show, *The David Gest Show*, called 'This Guy Is Crazy'. Tito's kids, 3T, recorded the song and this tune will hopefully revive their careers. I know Dee Dee is smiling that her kids and I are finally working together.

My life has been a series of new beginnings. I've lost count of how many times I've said 'New Day'. Now, here I am at the start of another one. How long it will last and where it will take me is anyone's guess. I certainly don't know. Who would have ever thought I would become a television star!

As I take stock of my life so far, I am certain of a few things though.

What I thought was going to be the worst experience I ever had turned out to be life-changing in every way. My three weeks in the middle of the Australian nowhere put me in touch with the things that matter in life, things like nature, human frailty, feelings and learning how to work with and around other people.

It reminded me too of something I've always valued: friendship.

One of the reasons I can count my friends on the fingers of fourteen hands, which is fourteen hands more than most people, is because I am caring. I have friends who have been friends for 40 years. Most of my friendships have lasted. When I make a friend, it's usually for life, although there have been a few exceptions. In the jungle, I made some friends that, I hope, will remain friends for life too.

Predictably, perhaps the greatest lessons I learned there, however, were about myself.

I learned, for instance, not to care so much about the way I look.

Deep down, I've always been insecure about my appearance. It wasn't so bad when I was at school and I could get the girls by making them laugh or just being odd but ever since then I've always thought that I was the ugliest person alive.

What I realised is that beauty is in the eye of the beholder and just because you've got a bald spot in the middle of your head, use eye shadow to make your hair look fuller, snore and are a middle-aged old fart, it doesn't mean that people can't accept you for what's inside. I never realised that until *I'm a Celebrity.* From now on, people are going to have to deal with me as I am. They can either take it or leave it.

Most of all though, *I'm a Celebrity . . . Get Me Out of Here!* made me realise that I had lost something. Ever since I was a kid at elementary school, growing up in California, I've been a different kind of person, someone who's drummed to a different beat. I think that's what people have always liked about me: the fact that I'm a kid at heart. Throughout my successes in life – making it in the music business, befriending some of the biggest stars in the world, staging shows that have earned millions around the world – I had stayed in touch with that kid. Then, for a while, I lost touch with him, allowed him to slip away.

When that happened, I think a part of me died. I certainly think that in the period before I went to Australia I was dead inside. I needed an awakening. During those three weeks in the jungle, I got one. I thank God Imad made me do the show. I will always be grateful to him for realising it would be good for me. That's when I rediscovered the little boy inside me and that's when I became – once more – a kid at heart. I intend to stay that way now.

When it comes down to it, when you strip the rest away, that's who I am: a kid in love with life and people, a kid looking for a little bit of the love he didn't have when he was young. Wherever life takes me from here, I'm going to take care not to lose him again.

I was a kid when I first heard the story of my cousin Ruth.

She came from Liverpool and was the family's one connection with showbusiness.

Ruth was a fan dancer and did striptease and burlesque in the thirties and forties, mainly in London. Her act was pretty famous. She used to have a parrot on her shoulder that would sing as she sang and stripped. It was a great feature of the act, along with the parrot feathers Ruth used to wear on her nipples and would twirl around like crazy windmills. I think, for a while, Ruth was the queen of the West End.

Anyhow, Ruth's reign came to an end one day in a really unfortunate way. She was in the middle of her act, twirling her nipples away like a lunatic, when the parrot got agitated and suddenly, without any warning, bit off her earlobe. It just leant over one night and chewed it off. There was blood everywhere.

It ended Ruth's career there and then. It wasn't so much that it spoiled her looks. It was more that it gave her lockjaw and she couldn't sing.

My family always used to shake their heads and mutter whenever her name came up. She was a lesson to us all, they would say. Showbusiness is a weird profession. You never know what is around the corner. One minute you might be on top of the world, the next you might be out of work, without an earlobe. Don't get involved.

Ruth was a role model to me, however. She had been her own person and done what she wanted to do. She had had her moment in the limelight, and no one could take that away from her.

We never did find the earlobe. It either fell on the floor or the parrot ate it. While I was in the jungle, many people sent my cousin Ruth jars of peanut butter for her birthday. Unfortunately, her gums got stuck together and she had to go to hospital. She found out what was really bothering her was a bad case of gas, as she is allergic to peanuts. The staff at the hospital could not decide what smelled worse, the peanut butter or the gas.

She's still around somewhere, probably waiting for her comeback, even though she's ninety-seven now. The parrot is dead, of course.

They seem to never end, the problems of my family members.

My cousin Telly, named after the actor Telly Savalas of Kojak fame, was recently rushed to the hospital where they had to do an emergency graph. He didn't die, but it was the worst tellygraph he ever received . . .

By the way, did I ever tell you . . . I had a cousin . . .

Someone Like Me

MILES KINGTON

If you liked *Angela's Ashes* you'll hate this.

For the last twenty years Miles Kington has written a
humorous column in which everything has been made up
and nothing can be trusted. Now he has written an
autobiography by those same exacting standards.
Was his father a German spy? Did his mother insist
on permission from the Vatican before dancing on Sundays?
Was baby Miles the victim of pram napping?
Who cares when a book is as brilliant as this one?

Prepare to be amused (and occasionally bemused)
by the amazing adventures, hilarious happenings and
other alliterations that make up Miles's formative years.
Filled with tales of Dadaist dog training, borrowed
lawnmowers, anti-squirrel devices and visions of the
Virgin Mary this is one of the funniest and most
original books you'll have read in decades. *Someone Like Me*
is quite simply too good to be true . . .

NON-FICTION / HUMOUR 978 0 7553 1357 0

Now you can buy any of these other bestselling
Headline books from your bookshop or
direct from the publisher.

FREE P&P AND UK DELIVERY
(Overseas and Ireland £3.50 per book)

Could It Be Forever? My Story   *David Cassidy*   £7.99
A searingly honest autobiography from the seventies TV and
pop star, revealing the highs and lows of his stardom and
success.

Playing with Fire   *Nigel Havers*   £7.99
With characteristic modesty and a captivating eye for the
absurd, the much-loved TV and film star treats us to the
highlights and lowlights of a life like no other.

By Myself and Then Some   *Lauren Bacall*   £8.99
A remarkable story of the life of the iconic, award-winning
American actress whose career has spanned over six decades.

Treasure Islands   *Pamela Stephenson*   £7.99
The wife of Billy Connolly and author of the bestselling *Billy*
follows in the intrepid footsteps of Fanny Stevenson, wife of
Robert Louis.

TO ORDER SIMPLY CALL THIS NUMBER

01235 400 414

or visit our website: www.headline.co.uk

Prices and availability subject to change without notice.

CIDER
MAKING

TRADITIONAL
BEER
AND
CIDER
MAKING

by
Ian Ball

PAPERFRONTS
ELLIOT RIGHT WAY BOOKS
KINGSWOOD, SURREY, U.K.

Made and Printed in Great Britain by
Cox and Wyman Ltd, Reading

Contents

INTRODUCTION

WHY BREW?

Pub beer is worse than ever. Never in English history has so much money been charged for such weak, gassy brews.

Never has our choice of ale and beer been so limited. Even the "real" ales, boasted by breweries today, would have been tipped down the drain by our great grandfathers.

We are told our quality of life has never been so good. Maybe, but one thing is certain, our ale and beer have never been so bad.

Traditional and modern ales and beers brewed to the recipes and simple instructions given in this book leave pub beer way behind in quality and you have a wide selection of types of ale, beer, lager and stout to choose from. All the brews can be made from pure, natural ingredients, without adding chemicals or sugar (sucrose) and your beer can be bottled or barrelled and ready for enjoyable drinking within a few weeks of making it. In addition you can adjust flavours, textures and strengths to suit every occasion, as did our ancestors.

Many of the ancient brews revived here were once an essential part of English daily life and diet, but time-honoured methods of making beer which they embodied were forced out of existence by the large breweries' mediocre, mass-produced beer. Nowadays such recipes are unlikely to be found elsewhere.

Brew your favourite modern beer; sample the ale King Alfred enjoyed, the sack Shakespeare's characters loved, the herb ale Queen Elizabeth I drank and many other traditional country ales and beers brewed for centuries to bestow good health (and long life!) on the drinker.

Making your own beer is easy, takes little time and the finest pint costs only a fraction of the price you would expect to pay over a bar.

Having home-brewed ales, stouts, ciders or whatever available means you may quench your thirst whenever you like; hold inexpensive home brew parties; take your social life *home*, away from pubs, smokey bars, noisy computer games and rowdy aggressors.

Enjoy beer with your meals and use it for preparing and flavouring exciting new dishes. Some superb recipes are included in Chapter 14, starting on page 48.

Home brewed beers are full of vitamins, nourishment and energy-giving goodness. A pint of country style, traditional brew has a higher energy value than a pint of milk and accompanied by a

hunk of fresh, crusty wholemeal bread and a slice of cheese is a satisfying, nutritionally excellent meal.

To enable you to locate brewing methods instantly an easy-to-use index is given on page 57.

Cider, made from fermented apple juice, has ancient and sacred associations with pre-Christian religious ceremonies. Cider was regarded as a sacred beverage that possessed special health-promoting and healing qualities, and was believed to bring happiness and love into the lives of those people who drank it.

Cider was the traditional drink of the Celts in Britain, and as the Anglo-Saxon settlers from Germany gradually occupied England and forced the Celts into Wales and the west country in the fifth century A.D., the displaced Celts took with them their cider making secrets and techniques and continued to plant and care for their orchards and sacred groves of cider apple trees.

The craft of cider making was also continued in Gloucestershire, Herefordshire, Kent and Norfolk. An old Herefordshire legend states that if a cider apple orchard is destroyed to make way for a field of hops to flavour ale or beer, it will be cursed and the venture doomed to failure.

Cider production in Britain reached a peak in the seventeenth century, when large shipments of cider were taken to London, where good quality cider was preferred to medium grade French wine.

Cider was, however, never as popular as ale or beer and heavy taxes levied on cider steadily reduced public demand to the point where, by the eighteenth century, commercial apple growing and cider production was in rapid decline. Today, however, cider is enjoying a revival in popularity and commercial cider made in Devon and Somerset is renowned world-wide for its high quality.

Few rustic crafts can be more ideally suited for those of us who enjoy making things ourselves, or be blessed with more tangible results!

Cider made at home is an economical and delicious beverage with all the natural goodness of apples.

In this book cider making begins at Chapter 20 and *there is a special quick index to help you locate principles and methods on page 108.*

1

BEFORE BEER

In the beginning was ale. Beer came a hop later.

Ale is the traditional English drink. Anglo-Saxon settlers brought it with them from their German homelands in the fifth century A.D.

Ale was brewed from barley and flavoured with honey, flowers, fruit and herbs. There were many kinds of ale and it was drunk for pleasure, nourishment, health and fitness.

Ale was enjoyed in large quantities at social gatherings. It formed an important part of daily diet and nutritional intake, and addition of medicinal herbs gave ale a highly valued healing quality.

The Romans, who frequently warred with Angles and Saxons, noted how they often drank ale before battle and fought like demons.

Vikings also drank a honeyed ale before going berserk in battle. Berserkers were Vikings who led attacks. Their courage and indifference to wounds and pain is legendary.

Ale played an important part in every aspect of English daily life.

Beer came to England a thousand years later. It was introduced by Dutch protestant refugees, who drank a weak ale, flavoured with bitter tasting hops, which preserved it in storage. They called this drink beer.

Initially, beer was universally disliked by Englishmen, who regarded it as an insipid, sleep inducing, fattening brew. And "beer guts" was a term of abuse applied to the fat Dutchmen.

Beer was not as strong or nourishing as honey, herb, flower and fruit flavoured ales.

Today, the only distinction between *commercial* beer and ale is the lighter colour and hopping of some ales compared with bitter beer. Often, there is no discernible difference.

With this book, as well as brewing modern ales, beers, stout and lager, you have the opportunity to sample some of the lost olde ales of Merrie England.

Of course you are not allowed to *sell* your home-made beers and ciders; for this you would need a special licence by arrangement (in the U.K.) with H.M. Customs and Excise. Home-made brews are therefore only for consumption by yourself and your family and guests to whom you serve them.

2

BRIEF HISTORY

Ale was brewed in ancient Mesopotamia in 800 B.C. Laws were passed governing its sale by tavern keepers.

It was also taxed!

The ancient Egyptians believed Osiris, god of agriculture, taught humans the secret of successful brewing. They recorded several recipes.

Ale was known to the ancient Greeks and Romans. The Romans occasionally drank hopped ale, or beer. However, inhabitants of vine growing countries preferred wine to ale.

When wine sipping Normans invaded England in 1066, they

found ale quaffing Saxons with well established breweries and ale houses.

The Domesday Book, compiled in 1086, records the existence of forty-three sizeable breweries in England. Saxon recipes suggest their ale was at least three times stronger than modern beer.

Most households brewed ale. Brewing was a woman's work and the wife was brewmistress.

Norman aristocrats continued drinking French wines; Saxons preferred ale.

Drinking competitions were held regularly and a Saxon's manliness was judged by the amount of ale he could drink. Pegs fitted into tankards marked the amount of ale to be drunk in one swallow. The longer a contest lasted the higher pegs were raised. This is the origin of the phrase, "to bring him down a peg or two." If an opponent could no longer compete, his pegs were lowered. But this type of contest is certainly not to be recommended today; we know more about the health risks!

Pubs began as ordinary houses alongside much-travelled routes where the good wife, to earn a few pence towards housekeeping, brewed ale and offered it for sale to thirsty, travel-worn passers-by. A broom was stood outside the house as a sign that ale was sold. Brooms were probably the first pub signs.

Ale was first taxed nationally in the twelfth century. Quality and prices were firmly controlled in the thirteenth century, when official ale tasters were appointed to sample and approve a brew before it could be sold. There was considerable competition for their jobs!

Oxford and Cambridge University Colleges were busy brewing their own distinctive ales in the fourteenth century and the Church joined in on a large scale in the fifteenth century. Justices of the peace were given power to grant and revoke licences to ale houses and innkeepers. Hopped beer made an appearance.

In the sixteenth century Dutch settlers planted hop fields in Kent. The Church reduced ale production and breweries increased supplies to ale houses, inns and taverns – many had previously brewed their own ale. Exports of ale were made to France, where it was favourably compared with medium quality wine.

Tax on ale and beer was considerably increased in the seventeenth century and became a major source of Government revenue. Many families still brewed their own supply of ale and beer for mealtimes.

The eighteenth century saw the formation of large breweries. Among names familiar today are: Bass, Charringtons, Courage, Guinness, Watney, Whitbread and Worthington.

Licensing hours were first introduced in the nineteenth century.

After the First World War, bottled beer became popular and widely available. The twentieth century has been a sorry time for beer drinkers. Breweries have combined, stopped producing local brews of character and distinction and brewed bland, nondescript beers designed to appeal to everyone. Many recipes have been discontinued and lots of highly individual, special brews have disappeared.

So that brewers could save on production costs, counter rising taxation, and increase profit margins, the alcohol content of ale and beer, always high in the past, has plummeted.

The strongest draught beers commercially available to us are about 4.5% alcohol by volume (8% proof).

The average commercial beer is about 3.5% alcohol by volume (6% proof).

Compare alcohol levels of some popular mid-nineteenth century brews with our nearest commercial equivalent:

	Nineteenth century	*Today*
Stout	14% alcohol by volume (24.5% proof)	about 4.5% (8% proof)

Old Ale	10.5% by volume	
	(18.5% proof)	about 5% (9% proof)
Porter	8% alcohol by volume	
	(14% proof)	Not available
Pale Ale	6% alcohol by volume	
	(10.5% proof)	about 4.5% (8% proof)

Quality and strength were combined in nineteenth century brews. Today, most commercial beers have neither.

It is up to us now, to make our own superb quality ale, beer and stout at home and continue the tradition of brewing excellence established by our forefathers.

3

YOUR GOOD HEALTH

Ale, beer, lager and stout are brewed from barley. Other grains are sometimes added to give extra flavour and colour. Hops are used for their bitter flavour and preserving quality.

Traditional country ales were flavoured by honey, herbs, flowers, fruits and spices. The health promoting and healing properties of many of these additives were clearly understood by Anglo-Saxon ale brewers.

Nutritional and medicinal qualities of ingredients are extracted by brewing and passed on in the matured ale or beer. The toast, "to your good health" is a statement of fact when you drink traditional brews!

Here is a list of ingredients recommended in recipes included in this book, together with health-giving and healing properties popularly credited to them through centuries of folk medicine.

Caution

Please note that no claims are made for the healing qualities of any of these ingredients. The list is included for your interest and information only and is not intended as a guide to alternative medicine. If you are unwell, consult your doctor and ask him if it is safe for you to drink home brew while taking any medication he might prescribe. Remember also that drinking to excess can lead to hangovers and ultimately alcoholism.

A list of some of the health promoting and healing characteristics traditionally ascribed by folk medicine to ingredients in recipes included in this book

Barley: The main ingredient in all ales and beers. Barley is extremely nourishing and renowned for its body building and strength giving properties. It is easily digested in liquid form and a valuable source of food for the sick and convalescing.

COUNTRY ALES

Apple: Stimulant and health tonic. Contains vitamins A, B, C. Beneficial in cases of anaemia, poor complexion, skin disorder, arthritis and asthma. Helps reduce emotional tension and headaches.

Balm: Soothing. Calms nerves and relieves headaches, toothache and colds. Aids digestion.

Bay leaves: Tonic. Assist digestion and relieve wind and stomach cramps.

Borage: Tonic. Purifies the blood and heals ulcers in the mouth. Eases catarrh and reduces fevers.

Bran: Nutritious, body building. High in vitamin B. Helps relieve arthritis and rheumatism.

Carraway seeds: Effective in treating colds. Help digestion, ease indigestion and release wind.

Cinnamon: Stimulant. Improves digestion. Remedy in cases of diarrhoea and nausea.

Cloves: Stimulant. Improve digestion and raise body temperature. Mild anaesthetic effect in relief of pain.

Comfrey: Nutritious – contains a substantial supply of protein. Wide medicinal properties; purifies the blood and is beneficial in treatment of skin disorders, anaemia, arthritis, asthma, catarrh, colds, coughs, diarrhoea, internal bruising and pain.

Dandelion: Tonic. Purifies the blood, cleanses the liver and acts as a diuretic and mild laxative. Remedy for skin disorders and anaemia.

Fennel: Rejuvenating. Since Roman times believed to improve eyesight. Remedy for stomach acid, cramps and wind.

Ginger: Stimulant. Cure for colds, sore throats and indigestion.

Honey: Rich in essential nutrients. Calming and rejuvenating. Strengthens heart muscles and valuable in treatment of anaemia, arthritis and rheumatism.

Lemon: Natural antiseptic – cleanses the system of impurities and relieves asthma, colds, coughs, gout, rheumatism and sore throats.

Marjoram: Tonic. Restores lost appetite and aids recovery from coughs, headaches and toothache.

Mint: Soothing. Eases pain and relieves colds and headaches.

Nettles: High in vitamins B and C. Remedy for asthma, colds, bronchial coughs, backache and rheumatism.

Nutmeg: Particularly effective in treating nervous disorders and rheumatism.

Parsley: General tonic. Rich in minerals and vitamins A, B, C. Used to treat a variety of ills, including anaemia, arthritis, catarrh, high blood pressure, dropsy, dyspepsia and rheumatism.

Rosemary: Stimulant and tonic. Remedy for colds, sore throats and nervous conditions. Tones body muscles and strengthens the eyes.

Rue: Stimulant and aid to good health. Beneficial in treatment of stomach troubles, headaches, sciatica and gout.

Thyme: Tonic and antiseptic. Helps cure colds, coughs and headaches. Assists digestion and eases asthma.

Woodruff: Stimulant and tonic. Uplifting, restorative effect. Cleanses the liver.

MODERN ALES AND BEERS
Barley: See above.

Hops: Natural antiseptic. Cleanse the liver and purify the blood. Relieve earache and toothache. Sleep inducing.

Maize: Nutritious, body building food. Contains vitamins A, B, C.

Rice: Nourishing and body building. Beneficial for stomach disorders and relief of diarrohea.

If you have not already done so, please refer to the *Caution* at the beginning of this list.

4

COMMERCIAL BREWING

Breweries use a lengthy and complex process to produce beer. Home brewing is simple by comparison. But commercial methods are worth examining.

Technical terms, the jargon loved and habitually used by some home brewers, are bracketed next to the items and procedure they describe.

Ale and beer begin life as barley grains, soaked in water for two to four days. The water is then drained and the barley left for five days at a temperature of 16° C (58° – 60° F) to germinate (malting).

During this period a natural chemical reaction in the barley turns its starch into fermentable sugar (maltose). Nutrients, which nourish and encourage the beer yeast's fermentation of sugar also develop. Tiny shoots show from the dried barley at the end of this stage. These are removed and the barley is cured by further heating (kilning) before being used for brewing.

The final colour of a brew is decided by the temperature at which the barley is heated (kilned). A high temperature results in a darker colour and subtle difference in flavour. Caramel is sometimes used to colour a brew. Any addition of cereals like maize or rice also affects colour and flavour.

Next, the barley is ground (cracked), mixed with hot water (liquour) and kept at a constant temperature of 62°–68°C (145°–155°F). When extraction of flavour and goodness (mashing) is complete the liquid (wort) is filtered from the barley which is rinsed (sparged) with hot water or liquid (wort) to make sure everything of value to the finished beer has been removed. The barley grains (grist) are discarded and sold as animal feed.

The liquid (wort) is boiled with hops for two or three hours to acquire their flavour, bitterness and aroma. Some hops are added towards the end of this process (dry hopping). Hops are then strained off and sold as fertilizer.

The natural sugar (maltose) content of the liquid (wort) is measured and sufficient processed cane and beet sugar (sucrose) may be added to raise the combined sugar content of the liquid (wort) to the amount necessary to produce the desired level of alcohol.

Next, beer yeast is placed (pitched) in the liquid (wort) which is often fermented to non-sweetness (dryness) in a day or two. During fermentation frothing surface beer yeast is skimmed off occasionally.

Natural, "real" ale and beer is casked just before fermentation is complete and beer yeast present in the unfiltered (living) beer finishes fermentation in the cask, giving the brew its natural life and sparkle.

Keg, bottled and canned ales and beers are filtered and all beer yeast destroyed. Their sparkle is due to the artificial injection of carbon dioxide gas (carbonation).

5

WHAT BREWS HOME BEER?

All types of ale and beer are brewed from four basic ingredients:
1 **Barley malt**
2 **Hops, or alternative natural flavouring**
3 **Water**
4 **Beer yeast**

1. Barley malt

Barley grain, properly germinated and dried is called malted barley grain. Crushed and then boiled in water, it provides flavour, nourishment and natural sugar (maltose) for brewing. Beer yeast turns sugar into alcohol during fermentation.

You can buy barley grains ready malted and cut out the tiresome task of germinating and drying the grain. Malted barley grains need only crushing and boiling.

The easiest way to make superb home brew is to *buy pure malt extract* from your local health or homebrew stockist. This saves you crushing large quantities of grain and reduces the need for boiling to a minimum.

Recipes in this book use pure malt extract and small amounts of grain to achieve brews of excellent quality.

Pure malt extract, designed for home brewing, is available as syrup or powder. The powder is easier to handle but must be stored in a dry place if not required immediately. Syrup should be kept somewhere cool.

Buy *unhopped* pure malt extract and look out for special types prepared for particular styles of beer. Any pure malt may be used but superior brews result from using dark malts to make strong bitter, brown ale and stout and light malts for ale, light bitter and lager.

Pure malt extract is sold in containers ranging in size from 2 lbs (907 gms) to 56 lbs (25½ kgs) in weight. You can economise by buying in bulk, but aim to use it within a few months of purchase.

The quantity of pure malt used in a brew affects the fullness, flavour and alcohol level of your beer.

Your brew will be improved by adding some cereal grains. Here is a list of adjuncts recommended in this book. Full instructions for their preparation and use are included in recipes.

ADJUNCT	BENEFICIAL EFFECT
Black malt grains	distinctive colour and flavour
Bran	increased body and texture
Crystal malt grains	improved colour and body
Flaked barley	extra flavour and body
Flaked maize	enhanced flavour and texture
Rice	fuller, rounder texture and body

All these ingredients are stocked by health and homebrew shops.

2. Hops

Add bitterness to beer and help it keep longer.

Several varieties exist.

Fuggles and Goldings are most commonly used for brewing ale, beer and stout.

Hallertau give a more delicate flavour to lager.

Dried hops, ideal for home brewing, are readily available from health and homebrew shops.

3. Water

Hard water is generally preferred for brewing light ale and bitter beer.

Soft water is favoured for mild ale and stout.

If you do not mind putting chemicals in your brew, you can adjust water for special results by adding:

Epsom salts (magnesium sulphate) to harden water.

Salt (sodium chloride) to soften water and round the brew's flavour.

Directions for the optional addition of Epsom salts or salt are given in recipes.

4. Beer yeast

Beer yeast (saccharomyces cerevisiae) is available as dried granules in single packets or tubs and as a liquid, natural culture in a phial.

It ferments rapidly on the surface of your brew and converts natural sugar (maltose) and any added household sugar (sucrose) to alcohol.

Beer yeast works best at a temperature of about 18°C (64°F) and imparts extra flavour to your brew.

Lager yeast (saccharomyces carlsbergensis) ferments from the bottom of your brew; lends a unique taste to lager and is marketed in the same way as beer yeast.

6

SUGAR-FREE BREWING

Traditional English country ales and beers relied on beer yeast fermenting the natural sugar (maltose) found in malted barley grains to provide the alcohol content of a brew. These ales and beers were of exceptionally high quality; full flavoured, strong and nourishing.

Processed cane and beet sugar (sucrose) was not widely employed by British commercial brewers to ferment alcohol until the late nineteenth century. The main attraction of cane sugar for brewers was its cheapness compared with pure malt. By replacing some of the malt with processed cane and beet sugar (sucrose), brewers were able to maintain the level of alcohol in a brew while considerably reducing the malt required to supply natural malt sugar (maltose) and cut production costs. This practice was loudly criticised by drinkers at the time but to no effect. As a result commercial ale and beer has become steadily more bland and insipid.

German law forbids inclusion of processed sugar (sucrose) in a brew and refuses to recognise beer not brewed wholly from malt.

About 75% of pure malt extract syrup is fermentable natural sugar (maltose). Dried pure malt extract powder consists mainly of natural sugar (maltose).

Recipes in this book offer you the opportunity to brew true ale, beer, lager and stout in the finest Anglo-Saxon tradition by making use of the natural sugar (maltose) present in pure malt to ferment alcohol. Malt only brews are high quality, delicious and nutritious.

7

MONEY-SAVING BREWS

You may like to make especially economical, quality brews by replacing some pure malt extract with granulated household sugar (sucrose).

Recipes in this book give clear instructions to enable you to produce first class, money-saving ales, beers, lagers and stout using pure malt and a minimum of granulated household sugar (sucrose).

Your economy brews will have a lighter colour, taste and texture than traditional whole malt brews.

For a little extra money you can change the flavour, body and "feel" of each of your economy brews by replacing any measure of granulated household sugar with an equal amount of brown sugar, demerara sugar, golden syrup or pure honey. You may replace all the granulated sugar, if you wish.

To help with your adventurous economy brewing, here is a table describing the influence these pure malt substitutes are likely to have on your finished brew.

PURE MALT SUBSTITUTE	INFLUENCE ON BREW
Brown sugar	Subtle deepening of colour, texture and flavour.
Demerara sugar	Strong, rich golden colour, flavour and body.
Golden syrup	Smooth texture and taste.
Granulated sugar	Neutral – emphasises the natural malt and hop or alternative flavouring of the brew. Otherwise, no discernible effect, except that it tends to reduce the fullness of the flavour.

Pure honey   Full, round, rich flavour and silky "feel".

Endless permutations of blends are possible and it is rewarding to experiment and develop secret recipes and special brews.

8

EQUIPMENT

You do not need a lot of equipment to start brewing. Visit your local homebrew stockist and browse through the items on display. It is a good idea to get to know what is available. The specialist staff are always willing to advise and help.

Bucket or brewing bin with lid

What you require depends on how much beer you intend making. One gallon (4½ litres) fills eight one pint (½ litre) bottles. This amount is easily brewed in a two gallon plastic *food grade* bucket. A headspace of 2 – 4 inches (51 mm – 102 mm) should be allowed for frothing during fermentation.

Larger quantities of beer are best brewed in a 3¼ gallon (15 litre) or 5½ gallon (25 litre) plastic brewing bin. These are sold with lids. You need a well fitting (but not airtight) lid or covering for your bucket or bin to keep out insects, dust and airborne bacteria. A large square of clean material fastened with string is adequate.

Metal containers are NOT suitable for fermenting beer because the alcohol produced can absorb mildly poisonous chemicals from the metal.

Saucepans with lids

One or two large saucepans capable of holding 7–8 pints (4–4½ litres) of liquid are desirable, together with lids. One large saucepan will suffice if you are brewing one gallon (4½ litres) of beer at a time. You may use several smaller saucepans instead, if you wish.

Syphon tubing

Plastic syphon tubing about 4–5 feet (1.2–1.5 metres) in length is always useful and a small plastic on/off tap can be bought to fit standard size plastic tubing. It is wise to invest in such a tap.

Polythene funnel

A polythene funnel with a mouth 4–6 inches (102 mm–152 mm) in diameter is worth having.

Strainer

A finely meshed nylon sieve, or suitable strainer is an important piece of equipment.

Kitchen scales

You probably already have these. A set of kitchen scales is necessary for accurate measurement of ingredients.

Measuring jug

A calibrated measuring jug helps keep an accurate account of ingredients included in your brew.

To bottle or not to bottle . . .

You can choose to bottle or to barrel your beer. There are advantages in both methods.

Bottling

Brews mature quickly in beer bottles and remain in excellent sparkling condition for many months. Beer bottles can be stored in convenient places and easily moved to new locations. They are easily chilled in a fridge; may be offered as gifts, or taken on picnics or to parties. However, bottling beer takes longer than barrelling it.

Barrelling

Barrelling beer in plastic pressure barrels, specially designed for home brews, is quick and easy. The beer is draught in character and drawing your own pint from a pressure barrel is a satisfying and rewarding experience. A pressure barrel is particularly useful when holding a party and saves collecting and rinsing empty beer bottles. The disadvantages are that barrelled beers take slightly longer to clear and mature; do not keep their condition for more than a few weeks once several pints have been drawn off and are heavy to move, requiring a semi-permanent resting place.

A happy medium

Many home brewers bottle strong and special brews and barrel lighter, less costly ones intended for regular consumption.

Bottles

Buy 1 pint (½ litre) beer bottles *specially designed* for your home brewed beer from your local homebrew stockist.

Some home brewers bottle beer in screw-top lemonade or cider bottles, or ordinary non-returnable commercial beer bottles bought from an off-licence. Such bottles will not withstand the pressure of carbon dioxide gas formed naturally in your beer after it has been bottled. Bottles not manufactured for home brew are likely to explode and can cause *serious* injury – **NEVER USE THEM**.

Bottle caps

Metal caps to fit 1 pint (½ litre) home brew beer bottles are also stocked by homebrew specialists.

Capping tool

You need a capping tool to crimp the edges of the metal caps securely around the mouth of your bottles and guarantee an air-tight seal.

Several designs of capping tool are commercially available, ranging from inexpensive hand held capping tools – which are gently tapped with a hammer to fasten the metal caps in place, to more sophisticated lever action models.

Pressure barrels

When barrelling brews use only specially designed *plastic pressure barrels*. Wooden barrels are difficult to keep clean and sterilise satisfactorily, admit too much air and generally fail to keep the brew in tip top condition.

There are many designs of plastic pressure barrel for you to choose from, in sizes holding from 2½ gallons (11½ litres) to 5 gallons (23 litres).

As you drink your barrelled beer, so its natural sparkle and condition fades. Towards the end of the barrelled brew you can recondition the beer by injecting carbon dioxide gas into it with an *injector unit*. These small units screw into the tops of pressure barrels and are usually sold as optional extras, complete with operating instructions.

Bottle brush

A wire handled bottle brush is invaluable for reaching into awkward corners when cleaning bottles and barrels.

9

HOME BREWING

Cleanliness

Never risk bacterial infection and spoilage of your brew. Before brewing, clean equipment with warm water. Use a bottle brush for reaching into awkward corners. Then sterilise ALL your equipment by rinsing with sulphite solution (see below). This kills bacteria.

Sulphite solution

This solution is made by mixing sodium metabisulphite with water. Sodium metabisulphite is available from your chemist or homebrew shop as powder – ½ lb (227 gms) is a handy quantity, or in the more expensive form of Campden tablets.

Dissolve 1 oz (28 gms) of sodium metabisulphite powder or 9 crushed Campden tablets in 1 pint (½ litre) of warm water.

Do not breathe the fumes given off when the chemical mixes with water as these can cause momentary irritation to your nose, throat and lungs.

Store sulphite solution in a cork-stoppered bottle. After being used to rinse equipment, it can be poured back into the bottle. In this way, it may be used repeatedly and remains potent for months.

Always remove traces of the solution from equipment before brewing by rinsing with warm water.

After use make sure equipment is thoroughly cleaned and dried before being packed away.

Brewing

Pure malt extract is used for brewing all recipes in this book, cutting out the long, tedious business of malting and temperature controlled mashing of barley grain. A small measure of fresh grain is added to increase quality, bite and flavour.

Beer yeast

All types of beer yeast will activate automatically when added directly to your brew, but for best results always follow the manufacturer's instructions.

Starter bottle

By making a starter bottle of activated beer yeast before beginning to prepare your brew, you guarantee a rapid start and faster finish to its fermentation.

METHOD

1. Activate beer yeast

Activate the beer yeast in your starter bottle by pouring the quantity of beer yeast suggested in the manufacturer's instructions through a sterilised, rinsed polythene funnel into a sterilised, rinsed one pint ($\frac{1}{2}$ litre) bottle. Dissolve 1 heaped tablespoon of pure malt extract syrup OR 1 level tablespoon of dried malt extract powder in $\frac{1}{4}$ pint (142 mls) of hot water (malt extract supplies natural sugar – maltose – and essential nutrients to nourish the beer yeast). Cover and allow to cool. When cool, pour into the bottle and add 1 level (5 ml) teaspoon of pure lemon juice (to speed initial fermentation of beer yeast in the starter bottle). Then three-quarters fill the bottle with warm – not boiling – water. Loosely cover the top of the bottle with a 4 inch (102 mm) square of sterilised, rinsed polythene, or silver cooking foil, secured around the bottle neck by an elastic band and put it aside while you prepare equipment and ingredients. Most types of beer yeast will normally be active, frothing and ready for use in approximately an hour. Some types of beer yeast take longer. Check any instructions that come with your beer yeast for precise details.

2. Assemble equipment

Next, assemble your equipment:

a) *Bucket or brewing bin with lid*
b) *Saucepans with lids*
c) *Strainer*
d) *Kitchen scales*
e) *Measuring jug*
f) *Large spoon for stirring*

Clean all equipment and sterilise with sulphite solution (sodium metabisulphite mixed with water, see page 32). Pour the solution back into its storage bottle and fasten cork stopper. Rinse your equipment with warm water to remove traces of sulphite solution.

*TIP

Fast fermentation and clearing

To encourage rapid fermentation and quick clearing of your brew by natural means, a small measure of brewed tea (tannin) and pure lemon juice (citric acid) is included in each recipe.

3. Assemble ingredients

a) *Pure malt extract*
b) *Hops or alternative natural flavouring*
c) *Any grain additives*
d) *Sugar (sucrose) IF BEING USED*
e) *Epsom salts (magnesium sulphate) or salt (sodium chloride) IF BEING USED*
f) *Tea and fresh lemon*

4. Make tea. Extract lemon juice

a) Make tea and allow to cool, or use leftover tea from an earlier pot
b) Extract juice from lemon

*TIP

Lemon juice

Remove small quantities of pure lemon juice by pricking the lemon through its skin with a sterilised, rinsed needle and squeezing out the required amount. The lemon reseals itself and may be kept fresh stored in your fridge.

5. Simmer about 5-6 pints (3-3½ litres) of water in large saucepan

a) Add pure malt extract; ½ total quantity hops or alternative natural flavouring and any other ingredients, as directed in recipes.
b) Stir until malt extract is dissolved.
c) HOME BREWERS USING HOUSEHOLD SUGAR (SUCROSE) OR GOLDEN SYRUP. Stir in the required amount until dissolved.
d) Cover with lid and simmer gently for 15 minutes.

e) Add remaining ½ of hops or alternative natural flavouring and any pure honey being used. Cover and simmer for 10 minutes. Then switch off heat and allow to cool.

*TIP

Pure malt extract syrup

Soak jars or tins of pure malt extract syrup in a bowl of warm water for a few minutes to loosen it for easier pouring before brewing.

6. When liquid is cool

a) When cool, pour the liquid from your saucepan or saucepans through a sterilised, rinsed nylon sieve or suitable strainer into a sterilised, rinsed plastic (food grade) bucket or brewing bin. If you find the saucepan too heavy to lift safely, scoop up the liquid in your measuring jug and strain it into your bucket or bin in easy stages.

b) Discard hops and all other solid additives. If you have a garden, they make excellent compost.

c) Pour in activated beer yeast from starter bottle.

d) Add strained cold tea and pure lemon juice.

e) Add cold water to bring the total liquid in your bucket or brewing bin to the quantity of beer required.

f) Allow at least 2 inches (51 mm) – 4 inches (102 mm) head space at the top of your bucket or bin for frothing and foaming. Cover.

g) Remove somewhere warm to finish fermenting. A temperature of about 18°C (64°F) is ideal.

7. Judging when fermentation has finished

Fermentation has finished when your brew has fermented to dryness (non-sweetness). Dryness is reached when all natural sugar in the malt (maltose) and any additional processed household sugar (sucrose) has been converted to alcohol by the beer yeast.

Signs to look for

Fermentation has ceased when bubbling and frothing has stopped; the surface is still, beginning to clear and the brew tastes dry (non-sweet) and is not fizzy on your tongue.

The warmer the temperature, the sooner a brew ferments to dryness. At a temperature of about 18°C (64°F) fermentation usually takes from 6–14 days to finish. Brews strong in alcohol can take longer to finish fermenting than brews relatively low in alcohol. Recipes in this book give you an idea of when to expect your beer to finish fermenting.

When fermentation is completed, your brew is ready for bottling or barrelling.

10

BOTTLING, BARRELLING
AND STORAGE

When you are satisfied that fermentation has finished (see page 36) the time has come to bottle or barrel your brew. **WARNING** – when bottling your brew, use only the beer bottles specially designed for home brew, available from your local homebrew stockist. Other bottles *may explode* and can cause serious injury.

METHOD
1. Sterilise equipment
Clean, sterilise with sulphite solution (sodium metabisulphite mixed with water, see page 32) and then rinse with warm water:
a) Home brew beer bottles or plastic pressure barrel
b) Home brew beer bottle caps
c) Syphon tubing
d) Polythene funnel

2. Prime your brew
To give your brew sparkle and life in bottles or barrel and keep it in good condition, you must prime it. Priming is achieved by adding natural sugar (maltose) found in pure malt extract, or granulated household sugar (sucrose) to your brew immediately before bottling or barrelling. The pure malt extract or granulated sugar is fermented in the bottles or barrel by beer yeast remaining in the clearing brew and this second minor fermentation produces a protective blanket of carbon dioxide gas naturally, giving the brew sparkling, lively appeal and protecting it against bacterial infection.

To prime your brew:

a) Pour two or three cupfuls of your brew into a sterilised, rinsed saucepan and gently heat until simmering. Then stir in and dissolve 2 level tablespoons of pure malt extract syrup (maltose) OR 1½ level tablespoons of pure malt extract dried powder (maltose) OR 1½ level tablespoons of granulated household sugar (sucrose) for each gallon (4½ litres) of brew you wish to prime. Cover and allow to cool. **WARNING** – Never exceed the recommended measure of pure malt extract or granulated sugar, or your bottles may explode!

b) When cool, pour the sweetened priming beer from the saucepan into the bucket or brewing bin holding your fermented brew. Stir two or three times, taking care not to disturb too much the thick layer of beer yeast at the bottom of your bucket or bin. Cover and leave for about ten minutes to blend and mix thoroughly.

3. Filling bottles and barrels

a) After allowing sufficient time for the dissolved pure malt extract or granulated sugar to permeate your brew, rest the bucket or brewing bin on a strong, solid surface at a higher level than the bottles or barrel to be filled.

b) If your tube is not long enough to reach, then place the polythene funnel in the neck of your barrel or first beer bottle.

c) Put one end of your syphon tubing in the bucket or brewing bin containing your brew so it rests just above the bed of beer yeast at the bottom of the bucket or bin; suck beer into the syphon tube and hold the other end in the mouth of your funnel. Beer will flow through the tube into your bottle or barrel provided that the end of the tube outside the brew is kept at a lower level than the surface of the brew in the bin.

Filling beer bottles

Fill beer bottles to within 1 inch (25 mm) of the top of each bottle. Then stop the flow of beer through the syphon tube by pinching the end and raising it level with the top of your bucket or brewing bin. If you have invested in a small plastic on/off tap, simply switch off the flow of beer. Then fill the next bottle.

Filling plastic pressure barrels

Fill your plastic pressure barrel to its shoulder, allowing 2–3 inches (51–76 mm) air space between its cap and the surface of your brew.

*TIP

Beer yeast

After your first purchase of beer yeast, if you intend to brew regularly, you need never buy any more. Just follow these instructions:

a) Remove two heaped tablespoons of beer yeast from the bottom of your bucket or brewing bin after bottling or barrelling your brew. The beer yeast will ferment another brew and stored in a covered sterilised, rinsed cup or jar keeps fresh in a fridge for a week, or wrapped in a sheet of sterilised, rinsed polythene in a freezer for up to six months. Whichever method you choose, activate the beer yeast before use in a starter bottle by adding warm water, pure malt extract and pure lemon juice as described on page 33. When it is fermenting and frothing it is ready to pour into your brew and will ferment up to 5½ gallons (25 litres) of beer.

OR

b) Pour a fresh brew directly onto the bed of beer yeast in your bucket or brewing bin after bottling or barrelling. Fermentation starts almost immediately. When brewing continuously in this fashion, occasionally remove some of the beer yeast or eventually it will fill the container. If the bed of beer yeast starts to look littered with the residue of hops and grain, or smells unpleasant, throw it away.

4. Capping

a) Beer bottles

   When you have filled your beer bottles, firmly fasten the special

caps with your capping tool.

b) Pressure barrels

   Simply screw the cap on tightly.

*TIP

Moving heavy bins and barrels

   Five gallons (23 litres) of beer weighs about 50 lbs (23 kgs). Easier moving is achieved by using a trolley.

   A trolley is easily made by screwing four castors to a thick wooden board.

5. Storage

a) Wipe clean, clearly label and store your bottled or barrelled brew somewhere fairly warm, about 18°C (64°F) for 7 days, to encourage fermentation of priming malt (maltose) or granulated sugar (sucrose), and formation of carbon dioxide gas.

b) After 7 days move your bottles or barrel to a cooler place, about 10°C (50°F) for 4–5 weeks to help it clear. All brews will clear naturally, assisted by the addition during brewing of tea (tannin) and pure lemon juice (citric acid) as detailed in recipes.

   For the best development of your brew's fullness and flavour store it somewhere cool, round 10°C (50°F) to 13°C (55°F) and away from direct sunlight.

6. Ready to drink

Recipes give you an idea of when to expect your brew to be ready for enjoyable drinking.

Your home brew should maintain its high quality for several months after being bottled or barrelled and high alcohol brews often remain in superb condition for up to a year – if you can bear to leave them that long.

11

CHEMICAL-FREE BREWS

All sorts of chemical aids are commercially available to home brewers. They include such items as crystals to adjust tap water for brewing ale; vitamin tablets to hurry fermentation and beer finings to clear brews before being bottled or barrelled. You may choose to experiment with these, but by using pure, natural ingredients it is possible to brew excellent ale, beer, lager and stout without adding chemicals to your brew, as our ancestors did.

Sodium metabisulphite

Mixed with water (see page 32) sodium metabisulphite makes an effective sterilising agent called *sulphite solution* that destroys bacteria on equipment and prevents possible infection of your brew. It is advisable to sterilise all your equipment with sulphite solution before brewing. But make sure you *rinse away* all traces of the solution with warm water before using items of equipment.

Epsom salts

A ¼ teaspoon of Epsom salts (magnesium sulphate) can be used to harden one gallon (4½ litres) of tap water for brewing light ales and bitter beers, but its use is entirely optional.

Salt

Up to ½ level (5 ml) teaspoon of salt (sodium chloride) may be added to soften one gallon (4½ litres) of tap water when brewing mild ale and stout. Its use is, however, a matter of choice.

Full instructions for the optional use of Epsom salts and salt are included in appropriate recipes.

12

WHAT GOES WRONG WITH BEER

Not a lot.

Beer is simple to make and little can go wrong.

But here is a list of things unlikely to happen, but which might, just to try your patience.

Burst beer bottles:

Naughty!

You have either:

a) Bottled too soon, before fermentation finished.

b) Primed with too much pure malt extract (maltose) or granulated sugar (sucrose).

c) Used chipped or cracked home brew beer bottles.

d) Collected bottles not designed for home brew and unsuitable for holding beer under pressure (see page 30).

Remedy:

Work out what went wrong and take precautions to prevent it happening again. Bursting bottles can cause serious injury and always create mess.

Flatness:

Your beer has no sparkle. Not the end of the world. If you followed the recipe it tastes good.

You have either:

a) Forgotten to prime your brew with pure malt extract (maltose) or granulated sugar (sucrose).

b) Used beer bottles chipped at the mouth, or improperly sealed.

Remedy:
Bottled beer
a) Replace any beer bottles with chipped mouths.
b) Reprime each one pint (½ litre) bottle of flat beer with a heaped teaspoon (5 mls) of pure malt extract syrup (maltose) **OR** a level teaspoon (5 mls) of pure malt extract dried powder (maltose) **OR** a level teaspoon (5 mls) of granulated sugar (sucrose). Dissolve the pure malt extract or granulated sugar in a small amount of the bottled brew warmed in a sterilised, rinsed saucepan. Remember to keep the bottle covered while you are doing this. Cover the saucepan and allow the primed brew to cool before pouring it back into the bottle through a sterilised, rinsed polythene funnel.
c) Re-cap the bottle. It is advisable to use a new cap.
d) Check caps on other bottles for cracks. Replace any damaged ones after repriming the flat brew.
e) Listen for the hiss of escaping carbon dioxide gas from leaking caps and fasten them securely. Replace where necessary.
Barrelled beer
a) Reprime your flat brew by dissolving 2 level tablespoons of pure malt extract syrup (maltose) or 1½ level tablespoons of pure malt extract dried powder (maltose) or 1½ level tablespoons of granulated sugar (sucrose) for each gallon (4½ litres) of barrelled beer in a few cupfuls of the flat brew, warmed in a sterilised, rinsed saucepan. Cover and allow to cool. When cool, pour the reprimed beer back into your plastic pressure barrel and screw the cap on securely.
b) Check your barrel cap is properly screwed down. You can put a sterilised, rinsed square of polythene inside the cap for a better seal. It may need a new rubber sealing ring. These are stocked by homebrew specialists.

No head on poured beer:
Either the brew is flat (see Flatness), or you have traces of detergent or grease in your tankard or glass inhibiting head formation and retention.
Remedy:
Wash tankard or glass in warm water and detergent. Rinse thoroughly with cold water. Pour yourself another pint. Cheers!

Foaming and frothing of poured beer:

The beer settles, given time.

You have either:

a) Primed with too much pure malt extract (maltose) or granulated sugar (sucrose).

b) Bottled or barrelled before fermentation ceased.

Remedy:

Overcome this annoying hindrance to quaffing your brew by storing beer bottles in a cool place. Chill before serving. Barrels sort themselves out after a few pints have been drawn off.

Check to make sure you left 1 inch (25 mm) air space between bottle cap and beer to accommodate carbon dioxide gas, or filled your barrel only to its shoulder. If you did not leave this minimum space, never mind. Remember next time.

Tastes peculiar:

Your brew may be infected by bacteria because the bottle or barrel was not sterilised with sulphite solution and rinsed with water before being filled. It is also possible that not all the sulphite solution was rinsed away with water and your beer's flavour is tainted.

Decide for yourself whether to throw away your brew or chalk it down to experience and drink up regardless.

13

SERVING BEER

Let your beer mature for at least the minimum time suggested in the recipe.

Wash glasses or tankards in detergent to remove any grease spots, which can prevent an attractive head forming.

Rinse away detergent with cold water to cool your drinking vessel.

Dry only the outside of the glass or tankard, in case bits of cloth stick to the inside.

Flick out droplets of water.

Pewter tankards keep beer cool, enhancing its taste.

Traditional pewter tankards often have a glass bottom so that you can see what your companions are up to when it is fully raised!

Solid based tankards create a blind spot when held to the lips and in the good old days the drinker was, at this moment, vulnerable to attack – hence the glass bottom.

A straight glass or glass mug gives paranoid drinkers all round vision and allows enjoyment of the beer's colour and bubbly effervescence.

Serve light ales and lager chilled, to crisp their tangy flavour.

Other ales, bitter and stout taste best cool, not cold.

Open bottles carefully and steadily to avoid disturbing sediment.

Reduce frothing by pouring beer gently along the inside of your tankard or glass.

Keep the bottle at an angle and stop pouring when dregs appear. Store dregs in a large lightly stoppered sterilised, rinsed bottle for cooking.

In the summer enjoy long, thirst quenching draughts of chilled light ale and lager.

Winter beers should be strong, full bodied, nourishing and warming.

Stout makes an excellent nightcap, as does mulled or heated spiced ale.

Beware of quaffing strong home brew by the pint. Remember its potency is greater than that of commercial beer.

Drink high alcohol beers by the half pint.

Recipes give you an idea of alcohol content.

Very strong beer can be sipped from a brandy glass.

All ales and beers go well with crusty wholemeal rolls and cheese or salad.

Light ale and lager complement curries, highly spiced food, fish and white meat dishes.

Strong ale and bitter beer taste best with red meat dishes or fish and chips.

14

BEER COOKERY

Terrific tastes and fabulous flavours are bestowed on ordinary dishes by using ale, beer or lager in exactly the same way cordon bleu chefs use wine.

Try some of these dishes and then move on to devise your own exciting, mouth-watering recipes.

For best results use ingredients uncontaminated by chemical additives.

Ale cake
Ingredients
Ale or beer – ¼ pint (142 mls)
Currants – 12 oz (340 gms)
Free range eggs – 2
Wholemeal flour – 8 oz (227 gms)
Soft vegetable margarine – 4 oz (113 gms)
Ground mixed spice – ¼ teaspoon
Pure honey – 2 level tablespoons
Method
Mix together margarine, honey, eggs and ale or beer. Mix in all other ingredients until well blended. Put into greased cake tin and bake in moderate oven, gas no. 4 (350° F) for about 1½ hours. After removing cake tin from oven, leave cake in tin for ten minutes; then turn out onto cooling rack. When cold, store in air-tight container for 24 hours before cutting.

Brown onion soup
Ingredients – serves 4
Bitter beer – ½ pint (284 mls)

Lean bacon – 1 slice, chopped
Wholemeal bread roll, or slice of stale wholemeal bread – 1
Soft vegetable margarine – 2 oz (56 gms)
Onions – 1½ lbs (680 gms), chopped
Freshly ground black pepper – to taste
Vegetable stock (liquid collected from cooked vegetables) – ½ pint (284 mls)

Method

Melt margarine in pan. Add chopped onions and fry until well browned. Cover and cook on a slow heat for 30 minutes. Add stock, beer, chopped bacon and bread broken in pieces. Pepper to taste. Cover and simmer for about 1 hour. Then rub through a sieve and serve with cheese croûtons or toast cut into small squares.

Casserole of beef

Ingredients – serves 4

Ale or beer – ½ pint (284 mls)
Bay leaves – 2
Carrots – ½ lb (227 gms), sliced
Pure vegetable oil – sufficient for frying
Wholemeal flour – 1 oz (28 gms)
Onions – ½ lb (227 gms), chopped
Sea salt and freshly ground black pepper – to taste
Stewing steak – 1 lb (½ kg)

Method

Season meat with salt and pepper and coat with flour. Fry in oil with chopped onions. Put in casserole with sliced carrots and bay leaves. Cover with ale or beer and cook in slow oven, gas no. 2 (300° F) for about 1½ hours. Remove bay leaves. Serve with boiled potatoes.

Cheesey smoked haddock

Ingredients – serves 2

Bitter beer – ½ pint (284 mls)
Grated cheese – 4 oz (113 gms)
Wholewheat flour – 1 oz (28 gms)
Milk – ¼ pint (142 mls)
English mustard powder – ¼ teaspoon
Smoked fillets of haddock – 2

Method

Wash and dry fish and poach for 10–15 minutes in beer. Remove fish from pan and put in oven proof dish. Make cheese sauce by mixing flour, milk, cheese and mustard over low heat till thick. Pour over fish and brown for about 15 minutes in hot oven, gas no. 6 (400°F) or under grill. Serve on mashed potato.

Chicken soup

Ingredients – serves 4–5
Lager or light ale – ½ pint (284 mls)
Carrot – 1 medium size
Minced chicken – 2 heaped tablespoons
Turnip – 1
Fresh parsley – 1 sprig
  or dried – ¼ teaspoon
Fresh thyme – 1 sprig
  or dried – ¼ teaspoon
Stock, made from chicken bones and trimmings – 1 pint (½ litre)
Method

Prepare and slice vegetables. Put into stewpan with stock and other ingredients. Bring to boiling point and simmer for 30 minutes, or until tender. Then serve.

*TIP
Fritters

Use ale or beer in place of milk when making fritter batter – no eggs required.

Goulash

Ingredients – serves 2
Ale – ½ pint (284 mls)
Bouquet garni
Sliced carrots – 2
Wholemeal flour – 1 oz (28 gms)
Pure vegetable oil – sufficient for frying
Sliced onions – ½ lb (227 gms)
Sliced parsnip – 1 medium size
Sea salt and freshly ground black pepper – to your taste
Stewing beef – 1 lb (½ kg)
Stock (stock cube) – ¼ pint (142 mls)

Method

Brown prepared vegetables by frying in oil. Cut meat into pieces and roll them in flour seasoned with salt and pepper. Add meat to vegetables and brown. Pour in ale. Let it reduce a little. Sprinkle any remaining flour over meat. Put in oven proof casserole dish. Add enough stock to cover and the bouquet garni. Cover with lid and cook in a slow oven, gas no. 3 (325° F) for about 2 hours. Then serve.

Lamb stew

Ingredients – serves 4
Lager – ¼ pint (142 mls)
Carrots – 1 lb (½ kg)
Dried mixed herbs – 1 level teaspoon
Neck of lamb – 2 lbs (1 kg)
Onions – 2
Sea salt and freshly ground black pepper – to your taste
Method

Cut meat into small joints and slice vegetables. Arrange in layers in an oven proof casserole dish. Sprinkle on mixed herbs, salt and pepper, to taste. Add lager. Cook in a slow oven, gas no. 3 (325° F) for about 2 hours. Serve with large potatoes, scrubbed and baked in their jackets. These can be cooked in the oven on a baking tray at the same time as the casserole.

*TIP
Sausages

Poach sausages in beer before adding them to batter for toad in the hole.

*TIP
Welsh rarebit

Add a tablespoon of bitter beer when making welsh rarebit and a dash of Worcester sauce.

15

MAKE MALT VINEGAR

Making your own malt vinegar is easy.

Try using vinegar made from home brewed honey, herb, flower and fruit ales as healthy and appetizing alternatives to commercial-style malt vinegar.

Vinegar improves salad dressings and marinades; tenderises meat and uniquely flavours cooked dishes and natural foods.

Wait until the ale or beer of your choice finishes fermenting, remove the quantity you wish to turn into vinegar and dilute each pint ($\frac{1}{2}$ litre) with $\frac{1}{4}$ pint (142 mls) of water; add $\frac{1}{2}$ pint (284 mls) of commercial malt vinegar.

Mix well and half fill sterilised, rinsed bottles or a large narrow necked vessel.

Plug with cotton wool and store somewhere warm for about eight weeks.

First a haze forms, then a wrinkled surface skin develops. When transformation into vinegar is complete, the liquid is clear.

When clear and bright, syphon the vinegar off its sediment and fill clean, sterilised and rinsed bottles to within $2\frac{1}{4}$ inches (57 mm) of the top of the bottle. Lightly stopper, or plug bottles with cotton wool and pasteurise the vinegar by standing the bottles on a cloth, wooden board or folded newspaper in a large saucepan of hot – not boiling – water. Maintain heat *below* boiling for thirty minutes. Then carefully remove bottles and fasten sterilised, rinsed cork or plastic stoppers.

Label and store for two months to mature.

Keep well away from stocks of beer to prevent absorption of vinegar odour.

Sterilise and rinse all equipment used.

16

ALE CUPS

Winter cups

In the freezing, dark winter days before central heating and electric lights, our ancestors warmed themselves with a tankard of hot ale or beer laced with health promoting herbs and spices to keep away colds and influenza – and it really does work. Try for yourself and see.

*Adjust the quantity of ingredients in these recipes according to the amount you or your guests wish to drink.

Winter punch

This once popular English tonic glows with nourishment and powerful vitamins.

Ingredients: To make 1¼ pints (¾ litre)

Ale or beer – 1 pint (½ litre)

Cloves – 3

Ground ginger – 1 level teaspoon

Pure honey – 1 level tablespoon

Pure lemon juice – 1 level tablespoon

Ground mixed spice – ¼ teaspoon

Water – ¼ pint (142 mls)

Method

Place all ingredients in a large saucepan and warm until simmering. Then remove from heat, cover and allow to cool. When cool, reheat until simmering and strain into warmed tankards, glasses or cups and drink while hot. A thin slice of lemon floated on the surface of each drink looks attractive.

Caudle

Very popular pick-me-up in Elizabethan England. Full of flavour and goodness.

Ingredients: To make 1 pint (½ litre)

Ale or beer – 1 pint (½ litre)

Pure honey – 2 heaped tablespoons

Pure lemon juice – 1 level tablespoon

Oatmeal – 1 level tablespoon

Ground nutmeg – ¼ teaspoon

Method

Put all the ingredients in a large saucepan and warm until simmering. Then remove from heat, cover and allow to cool. When cool, reheat until simmering and strain into warmed tankards, glasses or cups and enjoy it while hot. A slice of lemon placed on the surface of each drink adds an appetizing touch.

Lambs wool

An ancient recipe which offers a wholesome snack as well as an invigorating drink.

Ingredients: To make 1 pint (½ litre)

Ale or beer – 1 pint (½ litre)

Cooking apples – 2 large ones

Pure honey – 2 level tablespoons

Ground nutmeg – 2 level teaspoons

Method

Wash and dry the cooking apples. Cut out and discard the cores. This is most easily done by cutting around and through the centre of the apples with a coring knife. However, any small knife will do, providing you take care not to cut yourself. Place the cored apples on an oven proof tray and fill each hole with 1 level tablespoon of pure honey. Sprinkle 1 level teaspoon of ground nutmeg over each apple and then bake in a preheated moderate oven, gas no. 4 (350° F) for about 30 minutes. Then remove the oven proof tray and baked apples and pour the juice into a large saucepan. Put the apples on a plate or plates and set aside to cool. Add 1 pint (½ litre) of ale or beer to the juice in your saucepan; stir and heat until simmering. Then strain into warmed tankards, glasses or cups and drink while hot, taking a mouthful or spoonful of the delicious baked apple between sips.

17

CHEERS!

What's yours?

The following recipes offer a guide to help you brew quality ale, beer, lager and stout. Try them in 1 gallon (4½ litre) quantities to begin with and when you have completed the pleasurable task of sampling different brews you may like to make your favourites in larger batches.

Equipment and ingredients

All the items of equipment you need and ingredients specified in recipes are stocked by your local homebrew and/or health food stockist. The friendly, specialist staff are always pleased to help and advise you.

Special brews

Remember, the key to progressive home brewing is experiment. Once you have mastered the basics of brewing, begin to develop your own special brews. Keep a careful record of your recipes – the successful AND not quite so successful ones, and you will soon find yourself learning from experience. This is the only way to learn.

Caution

Please treat all the brews in this book with the respect their alcohol content demands.

CHEERS!

18

QUICK INDEX
TO BREWING PRINCIPLES AND METHODS

19

BEER AND ALE RECIPES

BEST BITTERS

Best Bitter Beer

Delicious bitter brew. Lovely blend of ingredients. Medium strength. Enjoyable 6 weeks after being bottled or barrelled.

Alcohol content about 4% alcohol by volume (7% proof).

Ingredients: To make 1 gallon (4½ litres)

Modern, economy recipe

Pure malt extract syrup – 8 oz (227 gms)
   or dried powder – 6 oz (170 gms)
Granulated sugar – 6 oz (170 gms)

Modern, sugar-free recipe
Pure malt extract syrup – 1 lb (454 gms)
   or dried powder – 12 oz (340 gms)

Both recipes
Dried hops – 1½ oz (42 gms)
Cracked crystal malt grains – 2 oz (56 gms)
Epsom salts *(optional)* – ¼ (5 ml) teaspoon
Brewed tea, strong – 1 level tablespoon
Pure lemon juice – 1 level teaspoon (5 mls)
Beer yeast starter bottle
and
Water to 1 gallon (4½ litres)

Things to do before you begin brewing

a) *Beer yeast starter bottle*

Activate the quantity of beer yeast recommended by the

manufacturer in a starter bottle (see page 33) at least an hour before preparing ingredients for brewing.

b) If you have not bought ready-cracked crystal malt grains, soak the uncracked grains for an hour in warm water and then crack them with a rolling pin.

c) Make a cup of fresh tea. Cover and allow to cool, or use cold tea from an earlier brew.

d) Extract required amount of juice from lemon and store in a covered, sterilised and rinsed cup until needed.

Method

When your beer yeast starter bottle is active and beginning to froth, simmer about 5 pints (3 litres) of water in a large saucepan and stir in malt extract (and granulated sugar and Epsom salts, *if you are using them*). Keep stirring until dissolved. Then add cracked crystal malt grains and ½ total measure of dried hops. Cover and simmer gently for 15 minutes. Then add remaining ½ of dried hops. Cover and simmer for 10 minutes. Then switch off heat and allow to cool. *When cool*, strain your brew into a bucket or brewing bin and cover. Discard solids. Add the activated beer yeast from your starter bottle to the brew and strained cold tea and pure lemon juice. Add enough cold water to bring the total amount of liquid to the quantity of beer you require. Allow at least 2 inches (51 mm)–4 inches (102 mm) head space at the top of your bucket or bin for frothing and foaming. Cover and place somewhere warm to ferment, about 18°C (64°F) is ideal. Leave 6–10 days to finish fermenting and then bottle or barrel.

Your best bitter beer remains in excellent condition in bottles for up to 7 months, after which its quality starts to decline.

When stored in a plastic pressure barrel your best bitter beer should stay in good condition for about 4 months, although its quality may begin a slow decline once the first few pints have been drawn off.

Extra Special Bitter Beer

Beer for the connoisseur. Strong, nourishing, well hopped and full flavoured bitter. Ready to drink 8 weeks after being bottled or barrelled.

Alcohol content about 6% alcohol by volume (10.5% proof).

Ingredients: To make 1 gallon (4½ litres)

Modern, economy recipe

Pure malt extract syrup – 12 oz (340 gms)
  or dried powder – 9 oz (255 gms)

Granulated sugar – 11 oz (312 gms)

Modern, sugar-free recipe

Pure malt extract syrup – 1½ lbs (680 gms)
  or dried powder – 1¼ lbs (567 gms)

Both recipes

Dried hops – 1½ oz (42 gms)

Cracked crystal malt grains – 3 oz (85 gms)

Epsom salts *(optional)* – ¼ (5 ml) teaspoon

Brewed tea, strong – 1 level tablespoon

Pure lemon juice – 1 level teaspoon (5 mls)

Beer yeast starter bottle

and

Water to 1 gallon (4½ litres)

Things to do before you begin brewing

a) *Beer yeast starter bottle*

Activate the quantity of beer yeast recommended by the manufacturer in a starter bottle (see page 33) at least an hour before preparing ingredients for brewing.

b) If you have not bought ready-cracked crystal malt grains, soak the uncracked grains for an hour in warm water and then crack them with a rolling pin.

c) Make a cup of fresh tea. Cover and allow to cool, or use cold tea from an earlier brew.

d) Extract required amount of juice from lemon and store in a covered, sterilised and rinsed cup until needed.

Method

When your beer yeast starter bottle is active and beginning to froth, simmer about 5 pints (3 litres) of water in a large saucepan and stir in malt extract (and granulated sugar and Epsom salts, *if you are using them*). Keep stirring until dissolved. Then add cracked crystal malt grains and ½ total measure of dried hops. Cover and simmer gently for 15 minutes. Then add remaining ½ of dried hops. Cover and simmer for 10 minutes. Then switch off heat and allow to cool. *When cool*, strain your brew into a bucket or brewing bin and cover. Discard solids. Add the activated beer yeast from your starter bottle to the brew and strained cold tea and pure lemon juice. Add enough cold water to bring the total amount of liquid to the quantity of beer you require. Allow at least 2 inches (51 mm)–4 inches (102 mm) head space at the top of your bucket or bin for frothing and foaming. Cover and place somewhere warm to ferment, about 18°C (64°F) is ideal. Leave for 7–12 days to finish fermenting and then bottle or barrel.

Your extra special bitter beer remains in excellent condition in bottles for up to 9 months, after which its quality starts to decline.

When stored in a plastic pressure barrel your extra special bitter beer should stay in good condition for about 6 months, although its quality may begin a slow decline once the first few pints have been drawn off.

TRADITIONAL COUNTRY ALES

Apple Ale

Fruity light ale. Invigorating, refreshing and exciting drink. Sparkles with life and vitality. Once commonly enjoyed by country folk.

*Any pure fruit juice, bought from your local health food stockist, may be used in place of pure apple juice to produce an authentic traditional country-style fruit ale.

Ready to sample 6 weeks after the ale has been bottled or barrelled.

Alcohol content about 4% alcohol by volume (7% proof).

*Use only pure juice bought from your health food stockist.

Ingredients: To make 1 gallon (4½ litres)
Country recipe
Pure malt extract syrup – 8 oz (227 gms)
 or dried powder – 6 oz (170 gms)
Granulated sugar – 6 oz (170 gms)

Natural, sugar-free recipe
Pure malt extract syrup – 1 lb (454 gms)
 or dried powder – 12 oz (340 gms)

Both recipes
Pure apple juice – 1 pint (½ litre)
Cracked crystal malt grains – 1 oz (28 gms)
Brewed tea, strong – 1 level tablespoon
Pure lemon juice – 1 level teaspoon (5 mls)
Beer yeast starter bottle
and
Water to 1 gallon (4½ litres)
Things to do before you begin brewing
a) *Beer yeast starter bottle*
   Activate the quantity of beer yeast recommended by the manufacturer in a starter bottle (see page 33) at least an hour before preparing ingredients for brewing.
b) If you have not bought ready-cracked crystal malt grains, soak the uncracked grains for an hour in warm water and then crack them with a rolling pin.
c) Make a cup of fresh tea. Cover and allow to cool, or use cold tea from an earlier brew.
d) Extract required amount of juice from lemon and store in a covered, sterilised and rinsed cup until needed.
Method
   When your beer yeast starter bottle is active and beginning to froth, simmer about 5 pints (3 litres) of water in a large saucepan and stir in malt extract (and granulated sugar, *if you are using it*). Keep stirring until dissolved. Then add cracked crystal malt grains. Cover and simmer gently for 25 minutes. Then switch off heat. Cover and allow to cool. *When cool*, strain your brew into a bucket or brewing bin; add apple juice and cover. Discard solids. Add the activated beer yeast from your starter bottle to the brew and strained cold tea and pure lemon juice. Add enough cold water to bring the total amount of liquid to the quantity of ale you require. Allow at least 2 inches (51 mm)–4 inches (102 mm) head space at the top of your bucket or bin for frothing and foaming. Cover and place somewhere warm to ferment, about 18°C (64°F) is ideal. Leave for 6–10 days to finish fermenting and then bottle or barrel.
   Your apple ale remains in excellent condition in bottles for up to 7 months, after which its quality starts to decline.
   When stored in a plastic pressure barrel your apple ale should stay in good condition for about 4 months, although its quality may

begin a slow decline once the first few pints have been drawn off.

Elizabethan Herb Ale

Flavourful and enjoyable ale. Full of goodness. Ready for drinking 8 weeks after being bottled or barrelled.

Alcohol content about 6% alcohol by volume (10.5% proof).

You may replace the herbs recommended in this recipe with a similar measure of herbs of your choice. They will impart their flavour and medicinal and health-giving properties to the ale. Favourite country herb ales include agrimony, borage, mint, parsley and thyme.

Tudor and Elizabethan ales were often highly spiced and reflect the excitement, zest for life, experiment and spirit of discovery characteristic of the age.

You can replace the herbs in the specimen recipe below with an equal quantity of spices. Popular spiced ales include balm, carraway seeds, cloves, marjoram and nutmeg.

Ingredients: To make 1 gallon (4½ litres)
Country, sugar-free recipe
Pure malt extract syrup – 1 lb (454 gms)
　or dried powder – 12 oz (340 gms)
Fresh bay leaves – 2 oz (56 gms)
　or dried – ½ oz (14 gms)
Fresh comfrey leaves – 2 oz (56 gms)
　or dried – ½ level (5 ml) teaspoon
Fresh rosemary leaves – 2 oz (56 gms)
　or dried – ½ level (5 ml) teaspoon
Pure honey – 8 oz (227 gms)
Cracked crystal malt grains – 1 oz (28 gms)
Brewed tea, strong – 1 level tablespoon
Pure lemon juice – 1 level teaspoon (5 mls)
Beer yeast starter bottle
and
Water to 1 gallon (4½ litres)
Things to do before you begin brewing
a) *Beer yeast starter bottle*

Activate the quantity of beer yeast recommended by the manufacturer in a starter bottle (see page 33) at least an hour before preparing ingredients for brewing.

b) If you have not bought ready-cracked crystal malt grains, soak the uncracked grains for an hour in warm water and then crack them with a rolling pin.

c) Make a cup of fresh tea. Cover and allow to cool, or use cold tea from an earlier brew.

d) Extract required amount of juice from lemon and store in a covered, sterilised and rinsed cup until needed.

e) If you are using fresh herbs, rinse the leaves in cold water.

Method

When your beer yeast starter bottle is active and beginning to froth, simmer about 5 pints (3 litres) of water in a large saucepan and stir in malt extract. Keep stirring until dissolved. Then add cracked crystal malt grains and ½ total measure of each herb. Cover and simmer gently for 15 minutes. Then add remaining ½ of herbs and all the pure honey; stir until dissolved. Cover and simmer for 10 minutes. Then switch off heat and allow to cool. *When cool*, strain your brew into a bucket or brewing bin and cover. Discard solids. Add the activated beer yeast from your starter bottle to the brew and strained cold tea and pure lemon juice. Add enough cold water to bring the total amount of liquid to the quantity of ale you require. Allow at least 2 inches (51 mm)–4 inches (102 mm) head space at the top of your bucket or bin for frothing and foaming. Cover and place somewhere warm to ferment, about 18° C (64° F) is ideal. Leave for 7–12 days to finish fermenting and then bottle or barrel.

Your herb ale remains in excellent condition in bottles for up to 9 months, after which its quality starts to decline.

When stored in a plastic pressure barrel your herb ale should stay in good condition for about 6 months, although its quality may begin a slow decline once the first few pints have been drawn off.

Ginger Ale

Strong, warming and full bodied ale. Marvellous tonic when feeling jaded. Drinkable 8 weeks after being bottled or barrelled.

Alcohol content about 6% alcohol by volume (10.5% proof). This is nothing like commercial "ginger ale" which is non-alcoholic.

Ingredients: To make 1 gallon (4½ litres)
Country recipe
Pure malt extract syrup – 8 oz (227 gms)
  or dried powder – 6 oz (170 gms)
Granulated sugar – 6 oz (170 gms)

Natural, sugar-free recipe
    Pure malt extract syrup – 1 lb (454 gms)
      or dried powder – 12 oz (340 gms)

Both recipes
Pure honey – 8 oz (227 gms)
Root ginger – 2 oz (56 gms)
Cracked crystal malt grains – 1 oz (28 gms)
Brewed tea, strong – 1 level tablespoon
Pure lemon juice – 3 level teaspoons (15 mls)
Beer yeast starter bottle
and
Water to 1 gallon (4½ litres)
Things to do before you begin brewing
a) *Beer yeast starter bottle*
  Activate the quantity of beer yeast recommended by the manufacturer in a starter bottle (see page 33) at least an hour before preparing ingredients for brewing.
b) If you have not bought ready-cracked crystal malt grains, soak the uncracked grains for an hour in warm water and then crack them with a rolling pin.
c) Make a cup of fresh tea. Cover and allow to cool, or use cold tea from an earlier brew.
d) Extract required amount of juice from lemon and store in a covered, sterilised and rinsed cup until needed.
e) Bruise root ginger by crushing it with a rolling pin or hammer.
Method
  When your beer yeast starter bottle is active and beginning to froth, simmer about 5 pints (3 litres) of water in a large saucepan and stir in malt extract (and granulated sugar, *if you are using it*). Keep stirring until dissolved. Then add cracked crystal malt grains and all the bruised ginger. Cover and simmer gently for 15 minutes. Then add the pure honey; stir until dissolved. Cover and simmer for

10 minutes. Then switch off heat and allow to cool. *When cool*, strain your brew into a bucket or brewing bin and cover. Discard solids. Add the activated beer yeast from your starter bottle to the brew and strained cold tea and pure lemon juice. Add enough cold water to bring the total amount of liquid to the quantity of ale you require. Allow at least 2 inches (51 mm)–4 inches (102 mm) head space at the top of your bucket or bin for frothing and foaming. Cover and place somewhere warm to ferment, about 18°C(64°F) is ideal. Leave for 7–12 days to finish fermenting and then bottle or barrel.

Your ginger ale remains in excellent condition in bottles for up to 9 months, after which its quality starts to decline.

When stored in a plastic pressure barrel your ginger ale should stay in good condition for about 6 months, although its quality may begin a slow decline once the first few pints have been drawn off.

Nettle Ale

Popular English country ale. Biting, dry tang. A drink with a sting in its tail. Packed with vitamins. Enjoyable 8 weeks after being bottled or barrelled.

Alcohol content about 5% alcohol by volume (9% proof).

*Gather young nettle tops for best results.

Ingredients: To make 1 gallon (4½ litres)
Country recipe
Pure malt extract syrup – 8 oz (227 gms)
    or dried powder – 6 oz (170 gms)
Granulated sugar – 6 oz (170 gms)

Natural, sugar-free recipe
    Pure malt extract syrup – 1 lb (454 gms)
        or dried powder – 12 oz (340 gms)

Both recipes
Nettle tops – 2 pints (1¼ litres)
Pure honey – 5 oz (142 gms)
Cracked crystal malt grains – 1 oz (28 gms)
Brewed tea, strong – 1 level tablespoon
Pure lemon juice – 3 level teaspoons (15 mls)

Beer yeast starter bottle
and
Water to 1 gallon (4½ litres)
Things to do before you begin brewing
a) *Beer yeast starter bottle*

Activate the quantity of beer yeast recommended by the manufacturer in a starter bottle (see page 33) at least an hour before preparing ingredients for brewing.

b) If you have not bought ready-cracked crystal malt grains, soak the uncracked grains for an hour in warm water and then crack them with a rolling pin.

c) Make a cup of fresh tea. Cover and allow to cool, or use cold tea from an earlier brew.

d) Extract required amount of juice from lemon and store in a covered, sterilised and rinsed cup until needed.

e) To measure young nettle tops, cut off and discard stalks and gently press tops in measuring jug. Then rinse them in cold water.
Method

When your beer yeast starter bottle is active and beginning to froth, simmer about 5 pints (3 litres) of water in a large saucepan and stir in malt extract (and granulated sugar *if you are using it*). Keep stirring until dissolved. Then add cracked crystal malt grains and ½ total measure of nettle tops. Cover and simmer gently for 15 minutes. Then add remaining ½ of nettle tops and all the pure honey; stir until dissolved. Cover and simmer for 10 minutes. Then switch off heat and allow to cool. *When cool*, strain your brew into a bucket or brewing bin, and cover. Discard solids. Add the activated beer yeast from your starter bottle to the brew and strained cold tea and pure lemon juice. Add enough cold water to bring the total amount of liquid to the quantity of ale you require. Allow at least 2 inches (51 mm)–4 inches (102 mm) head space at the top of your bucket or bin for frothing and foaming. Cover and place somewhere warm to ferment, about 18°C (64°F) is ideal. Leave for 7–12 days to finish fermenting and then bottle or barrel.

Your nettle ale remains in excellent condition in bottles for up to 9 months, after which its quality starts to decline.

When stored in a plastic pressure barrel your nettle ale should stay in good condition for about 6 months, although its quality may begin a slow decline once the first few pints have been drawn off.

Sack

Shakespeare's Sir Toby Belch thrived on a beverage similar to this one. Excellent drink. Full of flavour and nourishment. It helped put the merriment into Merrie England. Ready to enjoy 8 weeks after being bottled or barrelled.

Alcohol content about 6% alcohol by volume (10.5% proof).

Ingredients: To make 1 gallon (4½ litres)

Country, sugar-free recipe

Pure malt extract syrup – 1 lb (454 gms)
   or dried powder – 12 oz (340 gms)
Dried fennel seeds – 1 oz (28 gms)
Fresh rue sprays – 4
   or dried rue – ½ oz (14 gms)
Pure honey – 8 oz (227 gms)
Cracked crystal malt grains – 1 oz (28 gms)
Brewed tea, strong – 1 level tablespoon
Pure lemon juice – 1 level teaspoon (5 mls)
Beer yeast starter bottle
and
Water to 1 gallon (4½ litres)

Things to do before you begin brewing

a) *Beer yeast starter bottle*

Activate the quantity of beer yeast recommended by the manufacturer in a starter bottle (see page 33) at least an hour before preparing ingredients for brewing.

b) If you have not bought ready-cracked crystal malt grains, soak the uncracked grains for an hour in warm water and then crack them with a rolling pin.

c) Make a cup of fresh tea. Cover and allow to cool, or use cold tea from an earlier brew.

d) Extract required amount of juice from lemon and store in a covered, sterilised and rinsed cup until needed.

e) Rinse fresh rue sprays in cold water.

Method

When your beer yeast starter bottle is active and beginning to froth, simmer about 5 pints (3 litres) of water in a large saucepan and stir in malt extract. Keep stirring until dissolved. Then add cracked crystal malt grains and ½ total measure of rue and fennel seeds. Cover and simmer gently for 15 minutes. Then add remaining ½ of rue and fennel seeds and all the pure honey; stir until dissolved. Cover and simmer for 10 minutes. Then switch off heat and allow to cool. *When cool*, strain your brew into a bucket or brewing bin and cover. Discard solids. Add the activated beer yeast from your starter bottle to the brew and strained cold tea and pure lemon juice. Add enough cold water to bring the total amount of liquid to the quantity of sack you require. Allow at least 2 inches (51 mm)–4 inches (102 mm) head space at the top of your bucket or bin for frothing and foaming. Cover and place somewhere warm to ferment, about 18°C (64°F) is ideal. Leave for 7–12 days to finish fermenting and then bottle or barrel.

Your sack remains in excellent condition in bottles for up to 9 months, after which its quality starts to decline.

When stored in a plastic pressure barrel your sack should stay in good condition for about 6 months, although its quality may begin a slow decline once the first few pints have been drawn off.

Saxon Honey Ale

This style of ale was enjoyed in Saxon England. Drink some and know why King Alfred forgot those cakes. A rich, powerful ale. Drinkable 8 weeks after being bottled or barrelled.

Alcohol content about 7% alcohol by volume (12% proof).
Ingredients: To make 1 gallon (4½ litres)
Country, sugar-free recipe
Pure malt extract syrup – 8 oz (227 gms)
   or dried powder – 6 oz (170 gms)
Pure honey – 1 lb (454 gms)
Cracked crystal malt grains – 1 oz (28 gms)
Brewed tea, strong – 1 level tablespoon
Pure lemon juice – 3 level teaspoons (15 mls)
Beer yeast starter bottle
and
Water to 1 gallon (4½ litres)
Things to do before you begin brewing
a) *Beer yeast starter bottle*

Activate the quantity of beer yeast recommended by the manufacturer in a starter bottle (see page 33) at least an hour before preparing ingredients for brewing.

b) If you have not bought ready-cracked crystal malt grains, soak the uncracked grains for an hour in warm water and then crack them with a rolling pin.

c) Make a cup of fresh tea. Cover and allow to cool, or use cold tea from an earlier brew.

d) Extract required amount of juice from lemon and store in a covered, sterilised and rinsed cup until needed.

Method

When your beer yeast starter bottle is active and beginning to froth, simmer about 5 pints (3 litres) of water in a large saucepan and stir in malt extract. Keep stirring until dissolved. Then add cracked crystal malt grains. Cover and simmer gently for 15 minutes. Then add all the pure honey; stir until dissolved. Cover and simmer for 10 minutes. Then switch off heat and allow to cool. *When cool*, strain your brew into a bucket or brewing bin and cover. Discard solids. Add the activated beer yeast from your starter bottle to the brew and strained cold tea and pure lemon juice. Add enough cold water to bring the total amount of liquid to the quantity of ale you require. Allow at least 2 inches (51 mm)–4 inches (102 mm) head space at the top of your bucket or bin for frothing and foaming. Cover and place somewhere warm to ferment, about 18°C (64°F) is ideal. Leave for 7–12 days to finish fermenting and then bottle or barrel.

Your honey ale remains in excellent condition in bottles for up to 12 months, after which its quality starts to decline.

When stored in a plastic pressure barrel your honey ale should stay in good condition for about 7 months, although its quality may begin a slow decline once the first few pints have been drawn off.

Woodruff Ale

Delicious ale. An old English favourite, but you won't find it on draught in the saloon bar of the Dog and Duck. Ready to drink 6 weeks after being bottled or barrelled.

Alcohol content about 4% alcohol by volume (7% proof).

*You can replace the woodruff leaves in this recipe with a similar measure of any of the traditional English flower and herb ale flavourings like: dandelion *heads*, coltsfoot *heads*, elderflower *florets*, and sweet gale *leaves*.

Ingredients: To make 1 gallon (4½ litres)
Country recipe
Pure malt extract syrup – 8 oz (227 gms)
  or dried powder – 6 oz (170 gms)
Granulated sugar – 6 oz (170 gms)

Natural, sugar-free recipe
Pure malt extract syrup – 1 lb (454 gms)
  or dried powder – 12 oz (340 gms)

Both recipes
Fresh woodruff leaves – 4 oz (113 gms)
  or dried leaves – 1 oz (28 gms)
Cracked crystal malt grains – 1 oz (28 gms)
Brewed tea, strong – 1 level tablespoon
Pure lemon juice – 1 level teaspoon (5 mls)
Beer yeast starter bottle
and
Water to 1 gallon (4½ litres)

Things to do before you begin brewing
a) *Beer yeast starter bottle*
   Activate the quantity of beer yeast recommended by the manufacturer in a starter bottle (see page 33) at least an hour before preparing ingredients for brewing.
b) If you have not bought ready-cracked crystal malt grains, soak the uncracked grains for an hour in warm water and then crack them with a rolling pin.
c) Make a cup of fresh tea. Cover and allow to cool, or use cold tea from an earlier brew.
d) Extract required amount of juice from lemon and store in a covered, sterilised and rinsed cup until needed.
e) If you are using fresh woodruff leaves, rinse them in cold water.
Method
   When your beer yeast starter bottle is active and beginning to froth, simmer about 5 pints (3 litres) of water in a large saucepan

and stir in malt extract (and granulated sugar *if you are using it*). Keep stirring until dissolved. Then add cracked crystal malt grains and ½ total measure of woodruff leaves. Cover and simmer gently for 15 minutes. Then add remaining ½ of woodruff leaves. Cover and simmer for 10 minutes. Then switch off heat and allow to cool. *When cool*, strain your brew into a bucket or brewing bin and cover. Discard solids. Add the activated beer yeast from your starter bottle to the brew and strained cold tea and pure lemon juice. Add enough cold water to bring the total amount of liquid to the quantity of ale you require. Allow at least 2 inches (51 mm) – 4 inches (102 mm) head space at the top of your bucket or bin for frothing and foaming. Cover and place somewhere warm to ferment, about 18°C (64°F) is ideal. Leave for 6–10 days to finish fermenting and then bottle or barrel.

Your woodruff ale remains in excellent condition in bottles for up to 7 months, after which its quality starts to decline.

When stored in a plastic pressure barrel your woodruff ale should stay in good condition for about 4 months, although its quality may begin a slow decline once the first few pints have been drawn off.

VICTORIAN ALES
Victorian Old Ale

Strong, rich, golden ale. Old ale or India Pale Ale (I.P.A.) was originally brewed for British troops serving in India. There were riots when its alcohol content was reduced from about 10.5%

alcohol by volume (18.5% proof) to 6.5% alcohol by volume (11% proof). Imagine what those troops would think of our average commercial ale, at about 3.5% alcohol by volume (6% proof)!

This recipe brews an ale ready for drinking 8 weeks after being bottled or barrelled.

Alcohol content about 6% alcohol by volume (10.5% proof).

No riots, please.

Ingredients: To make 1 gallon (4½ litres)

Victorian, sugar-free recipe

Pure malt extract syrup – 1 lb (454 gms)
   or dried powder – 12 oz (340 gms)

Dried hops – 1 oz (28 gms)

Pure honey – 8 oz (227 gms)

Cracked crystal malt grains – 1 oz (28 gms)

Flaked barley – 1 oz (28 gms)

Black malt grains – 1 oz (28 gms)

Bran – 2 oz (56 gms)

Brewed tea, strong – 1 level tablespoon

Pure lemon juice – 1 level teaspoon (5 mls)

Beer yeast starter bottle

and

Water to 1 gallon (4½ litres)

Things to do before you begin brewing

a) *Beer yeast starter bottle*

Activate the quantity of beer yeast recommended by the manufacturer in a starter bottle (see page 33) at least an hour before preparing ingredients for brewing.

b) If you have not bought ready-cracked crystal malt grains, soak the uncracked grains for an hour in warm water and then crack them with a rolling pin.

c) DO NOT crack the black malt grains, use them as they are. If cracked, their flavour in your brew will be too strong. The flaked barley may be used as it is.

d) Make a cup of fresh tea. Cover and allow to cool, or use cold tea from an earlier brew.

e) Extract required amount of juice from lemon and store in a covered, sterilised and rinsed cup until needed.

Method

When your beer yeast starter bottle is active and beginning to froth, simmer about 6 pints (3½ litres) of water in a large saucepan and stir in malt extract. Keep stirring until dissolved. Then add cracked crystal malt grains, flaked barley, black malt grains and bran and ½ total measure of dried hops. Cover and simmer gently for 15 minutes. Then add remaining ½ of dried hops and all the pure honey; stir until dissolved. Cover and simmer for 10 minutes. Then switch off heat and allow to cool. *When cool*, strain your brew into a bucket or brewing bin and cover. Discard solids. Add the activated beer yeast from your starter bottle to the brew and strained cold tea and pure lemon juice. Add enough cold water to bring the total amount of liquid to the quantity of ale you require. Allow at least 2 inches (51 mm)–4 inches (102 mm) head space at the top of your bucket or bin for frothing and foaming. Cover and place somewhere warm to ferment, about 18°C (64°F) is ideal. Leave for 7–12 days to finish fermenting and then bottle or barrel.

Your Victorian old ale remains in excellent condition in bottles for up to 9 months, after which its quality starts to decline.

When stored in a plastic pressure barrel your Victorian old ale should stay in good condition for about 6 months, although its quality may begin a slow decline once the first few pints have been drawn off.

Porter

Originally, a mixture of ale and beer, coloured by roasted cereal grains and favoured by market porters in London. A working-class breakfast beverage in Victorian England – fortified the drinker in preparation for the long, hard day's labour ahead.

Strong, full bodied ale. Enjoyable 8 weeks after being bottled or barrelled.

Alcohol content about 6% alcohol by volume (10.5% proof).

Ingredients: To make 1 gallon (4½ litres)

Victorian, economy recipe

Pure malt extract syrup – 12 oz (340 gms)
  or dried powder – 9 oz (255 gms)
Granulated sugar – 11 oz (312 gms)

Victorian, sugar-free recipe
Pure malt extract syrup – 1½ lbs (680 gms)
  or dried powder – 1¼ lbs (567 gms)

Both recipes
Dried hops – 1 oz (28 gms)
Flaked barley – 1 oz (28 gms)
Black malt grains – 2 oz (56 gms)
Brewed tea, strong – 1 level tablespoon
Pure lemon juice – 1 level teaspoon (5 mls)
Beer yeast starter bottle
and
Water to 1 gallon (4½ litres)

Things to do before you begin brewing

a) *Beer yeast starter bottle*

Activate the quantity of beer yeast recommended by the manufacturer in a starter bottle (see page 33) at least an hour before preparing ingredients for brewing.

b) DO NOT crack the black malt grains, use them as they are. If cracked, their flavour in your brew will be too strong. The flaked barley may be used as it is.

c) Make a cup of fresh tea. Cover and allow to cool, or use cold tea from an earlier brew.

d) Extract required amount of juice from lemon and store in a covered, sterilised and rinsed cup until needed.

Method

When your beer yeast starter bottle is active and beginning to froth, simmer about 5 pints (3 litres) of water in a large saucepan and stir in malt extract (and granulated sugar, *if you are using it*). Keep stirring until dissolved. Then add flaked barley, black malt grains and ½ total measure of dried hops. Cover and simmer gently for 15 minutes. Then add remaining ½ of dried hops. Cover and simmer for 10 minutes. Then switch off heat and allow to cool. *When cool*, strain your brew into a bucket or brewing bin and cover. Discard solids. Add the activated beer yeast from your starter bottle to the brew and strained cold tea and pure lemon juice. Add enough cold water to bring the total amount of liquid to the quantity of ale you require. Allow at least 2 inches (51 mm)–4 inches (102 mm) head space at the top of your bucket or bin for frothing and foaming. Cover and place somewhere warm to ferment, about 18°C (64°F) is ideal. Leave for 7–12 days to finish fermenting and then bottle or barrel.

Your porter remains in excellent condition in bottles for up to 9 months, after which its quality starts to decline.

When stored in a plastic pressure barrel your porter should stay in good condition for about 6 months, although its quality may begin a slow decline once the first few pints have been drawn off.

MODERN ALES
Forest Brown Ale
Glorious brown ale. Appetising flavour and inviting colour. Enjoyable 6 weeks after being bottled or barrelled.

Alcohol content about 4% alcohol by volume (7% proof).
Ingredients: To make 1 gallon (4½ litres)
Modern, economy recipe
Pure malt extract syrup – 8 oz (227 gms)
   or dried powder – 6 oz (170 gms)
Granulated sugar – 6 oz (170 gms)

Modern, sugar-free recipe
Pure malt extract syrup – 1 lb (454 gms)
   or dried powder – 12 oz (340 gms)

Both recipes
Dried hops – 1 oz (28 gms)
Cracked crystal malt grains – 1 oz (28 gms)

Black malt grains – 2½ oz (71 gms)
Salt *(optional)* – ½ (5 ml) teaspoon
Brewed tea, strong – 1 level tablespoon
Pure lemon juice – 1 level teaspoon (5 mls)
Beer yeast starter bottle
and
Water to 1 gallon (4½ litres)
Things to do before you begin brewing
a) *Beer yeast starter bottle*

Activate the quantity of beer yeast recommended by the manufacturer in a starter bottle (see page 33) at least an hour before preparing ingredients for brewing.

b) If you have not bought ready-cracked crystal malt grains, soak the uncracked grains for an hour in warm water and then crack them with a rolling pin.

c) DO NOT crack the black malt grains, use them as they are. If cracked, their flavour in your brew will be too strong.

d) Make a cup of fresh tea. Cover and allow to cool, or use cold tea from an earlier brew.

e) Extract required amount of juice from lemon and store in a covered, sterilised and rinsed cup until needed.

Method

When your beer yeast starter bottle is active and beginning to froth, simmer about 5 pints (3 litres) of water in a large saucepan and stir in malt extract (and granulated sugar and salt, *if you are using them*). Keep stirring until dissolved. Then add cracked crystal malt grains, black malt grains and ½ total measure of dried hops. Cover and simmer gently for 15 minutes. Then add remaining ½ of dried hops. Cover and simmer for 10 minutes. Then switch off heat and allow to cool. *When cool*, strain your brew into a bucket or brewing bin and cover. Discard solids. Add the activated beer yeast from your starter bottle to the brew and strained cold tea and pure lemon juice. Add enough cold water to bring the total amount of liquid to the quantity of ale you require. Allow at least 2 inches (51 mm)–4 inches (102 mm) head space at the top of your bucket or bin for frothing and foaming. Cover and place somewhere warm to ferment, about 18°C (64°F) is ideal. Leave for 6–10 days to finish fermenting and then bottle or barrel.

Your Forest brown ale remains in excellent condition in bottles for up to 7 months, after which its quality starts to decline.

When stored in a plastic pressure barrel your Forest brown ale should stay in good condition for about 4 months, although its quality may begin a slow decline once the first few pints have been drawn off.

John's College Old Ale

Excellent, tasty ale. Beautifully smooth and refreshing drink. Ready to drink 6 weeks after being bottled or barrelled.

Alcohol content about 4% alcohol by volume (7% proof).

Ingredients: To make 1 gallon (4½ litres)

Modern, economy recipe

Pure malt extract syrup – 8 oz (227 gms)
   or dried powder – 6 oz (170 gms)
Granulated sugar – 6 oz (170 gms)

Modern, sugar-free recipe
Pure malt extract syrup – 1 lb (454 gms)
   or dried powder – 12 oz (340 gms)

Both recipes
Dried hops – 1 oz (28 gms)
Flaked maize – 1 oz (28 gms)
Flaked barley – 2 oz (56 gms)
Epsom salts *(optional)* – ¼ (5 ml) teaspoon
Brewed tea, strong – 1 level tablespoon
Pure lemon juice – 1 level teaspoon (5 mls)
Beer yeast starter bottle
and
Water to 1 gallon (4½ litres)

Things to do before you begin brewing

a) *Beer yeast starter bottle*

Activate the quantity of beer yeast recommended by the manufacturer in a starter bottle (see page 33) at least an hour before preparing ingredients for brewing.

b) Make a cup of fresh tea. Cover and allow to cool, or use cold tea from an earlier brew.

c) Extract required amount of juice from lemon and store in a covered, sterilised and rinsed cup until needed.

Method

When your beer yeast starter bottle is active and beginning to froth, simmer about 5 pints (3 litres) of water in a large saucepan and stir in malt extract (and granulated sugar and Epsom salts, *if you are using them*). Keep stirring until dissolved. Then add flaked maize, flaked barley and ½ total measure of dried hops. Cover and simmer gently for 15 minutes. Then add remaining ½ of dried hops. Cover and simmer for 10 minutes. Then switch off heat and allow to cool. *When cool*, strain your brew into a bucket or brewing bin and cover. Discard solids. Add the activated beer yeast from your starter bottle to the brew and strained cold tea and pure lemon juice. Add enough cold water to bring the total amount of liquid to the quantity of ale you require. Allow at least 2 inches (51 mm)–4 inches (102 mm) head space at the top of your bucket or bin for frothing and foaming. Cover and place somewhere warm to ferment, about 18°C (64°F) is ideal. Leave for 6–10 days to finish fermenting and then bottle or barrel.

Your John's College old ale remains in excellent condition in bottles for up to 7 months, after which its quality starts to decline.

When stored in a plastic pressure barrel your John's College old ale should stay in good condition for about 4 months, although its quality may begin a slow decline once the first few pints have been drawn off.

Shire Light Ale

Light, fresh, tangy ale. Nice long drink. Ready to enjoy 6 weeks after being bottled or barrelled.

Alcohol content about 4% alcohol by volume (7% proof).

Ingredients: To make 1 gallon (4½ litres)

Modern, economy recipe

Pure malt extract syrup – 8 oz (227 gms)
  or dried powder – 6 oz (170 gms)

Granulated sugar – 6 oz (170 gms)

Modern, sugar-free recipe

Pure malt extract syrup – 1 lb (454 gms)
  or dried powder – 12 oz (340 gms)

Both recipes
Dried hops – 1 oz (28 gms)
Cracked crystal malt grains – 1 oz (28 gms)
Flaked barley – 1 oz (28 gms)
Epsom salts *(optional)* – ¼ (5 ml) teaspoon
Brewed tea, strong – 1 level tablespoon
Pure lemon juice – 1 level teaspoon (5 mls)
Beer yeast starter bottle
and
Water to 1 gallon (4½ litres)

Things to do before you begin brewing

a) *Beer yeast starter bottle*

Activate the quantity of beer yeast recommended by the manufacturer in a starter bottle (see page 33) at least an hour before preparing ingredients for brewing.

b) If you have not bought ready-cracked crystal malt grains, soak the uncracked grains for an hour in warm water and then crack them with a rolling pin. The flaked barley may be used as it is.

c) Make a cup of fresh tea. Cover and allow to cool, or use cold tea from an earlier brew.

d) Extract required amount of juice from lemon and store in a covered, sterilised and rinsed cup until needed.

Method

When your beer yeast starter bottle is active and beginning to froth, simmer about 5 pints (3 litres) of water in a large saucepan and stir in malt extract (and granulated sugar and Epsom salts, *if you are using them*). Keep stirring until dissolved. Then add cracked crystal malt grains, flaked barley and ½ total measure of dried hops. Cover and simmer gently for 15 minutes. Then add remaining ½ of dried hops. Cover and simmer for 10 minutes. Then switch off heat and allow to cool. *When cool*, strain your brew into a bucket or brewing bin and cover. Discard solids. Add the activated beer yeast from your starter bottle to the brew and strained cold tea and pure lemon juice. Add enough cold water to bring the total amount of liquid to the quantity of ale you require. Allow at least 2 inches (51 mm)–4 inches (102 mm) head space at the top of your bucket or bin for frothing and foaming. Cover and place somewhere warm to ferment, about 18°C (64°F) is ideal. Leave for 6 – 10 days to finish fermenting and then bottle or barrel.

Your Shire light ale remains in excellent condition in bottles for up to 7 months, after which its quality starts to decline.

When stored in a plastic pressure barrel your Shire light ale should stay in good condition for about 4 months, although its quality may begin a slow decline once the first few pints have been drawn off.

MODERN LAGERS
Munich Lager

German style lager. Superb quality. Strong, full bodied, smooth and golden. Savour every silken mouthful as you sip it down. For best results use a "lager" or light malt extract syrup or dried powder, see page 23. Ready to drink 8 weeks after being bottled or barrelled.

Alcohol content about 6% alcohol by volume (10.5% proof).

Ingredients: To make 1 gallon (4½ litres)

Modern, economy recipe

Pure malt extract syrup – 12 oz (340 gms)
  or dried powder – 9 oz (255 gms)
Granulated sugar – 11 oz (312 gms)

Modern, sugar-free recipe
  Pure malt extract syrup – 1½ lbs (680 gms)
    or dried powder – 1¼ lbs (567 gms)

Both recipes
Dried Hallertau hops – 1 oz (28 gms)
Cracked crystal malt grains – 1 oz (28 gms)
Flaked maize – 3 oz (85 gms)
Brewed tea, strong – 1 level tablespoon
Pure lemon juice – 1 level teaspoon (5 mls)
Lager yeast starter bottle
and
Water to 1 gallon (4½ litres)

Things to do before you begin brewing

a) *Lager yeast starter bottle*

Activate the quantity of lager yeast recommended by the manufacturer in a starter bottle (see page 33) at least an hour before preparing ingredients for brewing.

b) If you have not bought ready-cracked crystal malt grains, soak the uncracked grains for an hour in warm water and then crack them with a rolling pin.

c) Make a cup of fresh tea. Cover and allow to cool, or use cold tea from an earlier brew.

d) Extract required amount of juice from lemon and store in a covered, sterilised and rinsed cup until needed.

Method

When your lager yeast starter bottle is active and beginning to froth, simmer about 5 pints (3 litres) of water in a large saucepan and stir in malt extract (and granulated sugar, *if you are using it*). Keep stirring until dissolved. Then add cracked crystal malt grains, flaked maize and ½ total measure of dried hops. Cover and simmer gently for 15 minutes. Then add remaining ½ of dried hops. Cover and simmer for 10 minutes. Then switch off heat and allow to cool. *When cool*, strain your brew into a bucket or brewing bin and cover. Discard solids. Add the activated lager yeast from your starter bottle to the brew and strained cold tea and pure lemon juice. Add enough cold water to bring the total amount of liquid to the quantity of lager you require. Allow at least 2 inches (51 mm)–4 inches (102 mm) head space at the top of your bucket or bin for frothing and foaming. Cover and place somewhere warm to ferment, about 18°C (64°F) is ideal. Leave for 7–12 days to finish fermenting and then bottle or barrel.

Your Munich lager remains in excellent condition in bottles for up to 9 months, after which its quality starts to decline.

When stored in a plastic pressure barrel your Munich lager should stay in good condition for about 6 months, although its quality may begin a slow decline once the first few pints have been drawn off.

Scandinavian Lager

Rich, powerful lager. For best results, use a "lager" or light malt extract syrup or dried powder, see page 23. Ready to enjoy 6 weeks after being bottled or barrelled.

Alcohol content about 4.5% alcohol by volume (8% proof).

Ingredients: To make 1 gallon (4½ litres)
Modern, economy recipe
Pure malt extract syrup – 8 oz (227 gms)
   or dried powder – 6 oz (170 gms)
Granulated sugar – 6 oz (170 gms)

              Modern, sugar-free recipe
                 Pure malt extract syrup – 1 lb (454 gms)
                    or dried powder – 12 oz (340 gms)

Both recipes
Dried Hallertau hops – 1 oz (28 gms)
Pure honey – 2 heaped tablespoons
Cracked crystal malt grains – 1 oz (28 gms)
Flaked maize – 1 oz (28 gms)
Brewed tea, strong – 1 level tablespoon
Pure lemon juice – 1 level teaspoon (5 mls)
Lager yeast starter bottle
and
Water to 1 gallon (4½ litres)
Things to do before you begin brewing
a) *Lager yeast starter bottle*
   Activate the quantity of lager yeast recommended by the manufacturer in a starter bottle (see page 33) at least an hour before preparing ingredients for brewing.
b) If you have not bought ready-cracked crystal malt grains, soak the uncracked grains for an hour in warm water and then crack them with a rolling pin.
c) Make a cup of fresh tea. Cover and allow to cool, or use cold tea from an earlier brew.
d) Extract required amount of juice from lemon and store in a covered, sterilised and rinsed cup until needed.
Method
   When your lager yeast starter bottle is active and beginning to froth, simmer about 5 pints (3 litres) of water in a large saucepan and stir in malt extract (and granulated sugar, *if you are using it*). Keep stirring until dissolved. Then add cracked crystal malt grains, flaked maize and ½ total measure of dried hops. Cover and simmer gently for 15 minutes. Then add remaining ½ of dried hops and all

the pure honey; stir until dissolved. Cover and simmer for 10 minutes. Then switch off heat and allow to cool. *When cool*, strain your brew into a bucket or brewing bin and cover. Discard solids. Add the activated lager yeast from your starter bottle to the brew and strained cold tea and pure lemon juice. Add enough cold water to bring the total amount of liquid to the quantity of lager you require. Allow at least 2 inches (51 mm)–4 inches (102 mm) head space at the top of your bucket or bin for frothing and foaming. Cover and place somewhere warm to ferment, about 18°C (64°F) is ideal. Leave for 6–10 days to finish fermenting and then bottle or barrel.

Your Scandinavian lager remains in excellent condition in bottles for up to 7 months, after which its quality starts to decline.

When stored in a plastic pressure barrel your Scandinavian lager should stay in good condition for about 4 months, although its quality may begin a slow decline once the first few pints have been drawn off.

OTHER ALES
Barley Wine

Strong, full bodied beverage. Lots of flavour. Ready to drink 8 weeks after being bottled or barrelled.

Alcohol content about 8.5% by volume (14.5% proof).

Ingredients: To make 1 gallon (4½ litres)

Barley wine, economy recipe
Pure malt extract syrup – 12 oz (340 gms)
  or dried powder – 9 oz (255 gms)
Granulated sugar – 11 oz (312 gms)

Barley wine, sugar-free recipe
  Pure malt extract syrup – 1½ lbs (680 gms)
  or dried powder – 1¼ lbs (567 gms)

Both recipes
Dried hops – 1 oz (28 gms)
Pure honey – 8 oz (227 gms)
Cracked crystal malt grains – 4 oz (113 gms)
Black malt grains – 2½ oz (71 gms)
Flaked barley – 3 oz (85 gms)

Brewed tea, strong – 1 level tablespoon
Pure lemon juice – 3 level teaspoons (15 mls)
Beer yeast starter bottle
and
Water to 1 gallon (4½ litres)
Things to do before you begin brewing
a) *Beer yeast starter bottle*

Activate the quantity of beer yeast recommended by the manufacturer in a starter bottle (see page 33) at least an hour before preparing ingredients for brewing.

b) If you have not bought ready-cracked crystal malt grains, soak the uncracked grains for an hour in warm water and then crack them with a rolling pin.

c) DO NOT crack the black malt grains, use them as they are. If cracked, their flavour in your brew will be too strong. The flaked barley may be used as it is.

d) Make a cup of fresh tea. Cover and allow to cool, or use cold tea from an earlier brew.

e) Extract required amount of juice from lemon and store in a covered, sterilised and rinsed cup until needed.

Method

When your beer yeast starter bottle is active and beginning to froth, simmer about 6 pints (3½ litres) of water in a large saucepan and stir in malt extract (and granulated sugar, *if you are using it*). Keep stirring until dissolved. Then add cracked crystal malt grains, flaked barley, black malt grains and ½ total measure of dried hops. Cover and simmer gently for 15 minutes. Then add remaining ½ of dried hops and all the pure honey; stir until dissolved. Cover and simmer for 10 minutes. Then switch off heat and allow to cool. *When cool*, strain your brew into a bucket or brewing bin and cover. Discard solids. Add the activated beer yeast from your starter bottle to the brew and strained cold tea and pure lemon juice. Add enough cold water to bring the total amount of liquid to the quantity of barley wine you require. Allow at least 2 inches (51 mm) – 4 inches (102 mm) head space at the top of your bucket or bin for frothing and foaming. Cover and place somewhere warm to ferment, about 18°C (64°F) is ideal. Leave for 9–14 days to finish fermenting and then bottle or barrel.

Your barley wine remains in excellent condition in bottles for up to 12 months, after which its quality starts to decline.

When stored in a plastic pressure barrel your barley wine should stay in good condition for about 7 months, although its quality may begin a slow decline once the first few pints have been drawn off.

Stout

Vitalizing, wholesome brew. Feel it doing you good as it slips down. The first recipe for stout is commonly credited to eighteenth century Irishman, Arthur Guinness, who developed his brew while experimenting with roasted grains in beer. You see, there is the chance of an exciting discovery for us all. Ready to drink 8 weeks after being bottled or barrelled.

Alcohol content about 6% by volume (10.5% proof).

Ingredients: To make 1 gallon (4½ litres)

Stout, economy recipe

Pure malt extract syrup – 12 oz (340 gms)

   or dried powder – 9 oz (255 gms)

Granulated sugar – 11 oz (312 gms)

Stout, sugar-free recipe

Pure malt extract syrup – 1½ lbs (680 gms)

   or dried powder – 1¼ lbs (567 gms)

Both recipes

Dried hops – 1 oz (28 gms)

Cracked crystal malt grains – 3 oz (85 gms)

Black malt grains – 5 oz (142 gms)

Brown rice – 1 oz (28 gms)

Salt *(optional)* – ½ level (5 ml) teaspoon

Brewed tea, strong – 1 level tablespoon

Pure lemon juice – 2 level teaspoons (10 mls)

Beer yeast starter bottle

and

Water to 1 gallon (4½ litres)

Things to do before you begin brewing

a) *Beer yeast starter bottle*

Activate the quantity of beer yeast recommended by the manufacturer in a starter bottle (see page 33) at least an hour before preparing ingredients for brewing.

b) If you have not bought ready-cracked crystal malt grains, soak the uncracked grains for an hour in warm water and then crack them with a rolling pin.

c) DO NOT crack the black malt grains, use them as they are. If cracked, their flavour in your brew will be too strong. The brown rice may be used as it is.

d) Make a cup of fresh tea. Cover and allow to cool, or use cold tea from an earlier brew.

e) Extract required amount of juice from lemon and store in a covered, sterilised and rinsed cup until needed.

Method

When your beer yeast starter bottle is active and beginning to froth, simmer about 6 pints (3½ litres) of water in a large saucepan and stir in malt extract (and granulated sugar and salt, *if you are using them*). Keep stirring until dissolved. Then add cracked crystal malt grains, black malt grains, rice and ½ total measure of dried hops. Cover and simmer gently for 15 minutes. Then add remaining ½ of dried hops. Cover and simmer for 10 minutes. Then switch off heat and allow to cool. *When cool*, strain your brew into a bucket or brewing bin and cover. Discard solids. Add the activated beer yeast from your starter bottle to the brew and strained cold tea and pure lemon juice. Add enough cold water to bring the total amount of liquid to the quantity of stout you require. Allow at least 2 inches (51 mm)–4 inches (102 mm) head space at the top of your bucket or bin for frothing and foaming. Cover and place somewhere warm to ferment, about 18°C (64°F) is ideal. Leave for 7–12 days to finish fermenting and then bottle or barrel.

Your stout remains in excellent condition in bottles for up to 9 months, after which its quality starts to decline.

When stored in a plastic pressure barrel your stout should stay in good condition for about 6 months, although its quality may begin a slow decline once the first few pints have been drawn off.

20

CIDER, APPLES, LOVE
AND HEALTH

Ever since Eve gave Adam a bite of her fruit, the juicy, luscious apple has been linked with love, romance and vitality. The beautiful Greek goddess Juno gave Jupiter the golden apples of the Hesperides on their wedding day, and the wounded Celtic King Arthur was taken to the Vale of Avalon (Apple Vale) to be restored to full health. Numerous Greek, Roman, Scandinavian and Celtic legends refer to the magic power of apples in all matters concerning love and health.

These ancient stories do have a basis in fact, for the apple is full of nourishing goodness. Apples contain vitamins A, B, C and G (also known as B_2, riboflavin); protein, carbohydrates, calcium, iron, phosphorous and potassium.

A regular, moderate daily intake of apples, pure apple juice, or cider is said to prevent – or help cure: acne, anaemia, arthritis, asthma, catarrh, poor skin complexion and pyorrhea.

Apples, pure apple juice and cider are thought to stimulate all bodily functions, reduce emotional tension, headaches; aid digestion and prevent constipation.

21

CIDER: THE THINGS YOU NEED TO KNOW

Equipment

Equipment needed for making cider is much the same as equipment needed for brewing ale and beer. To save repeating all the information here, you may like to refer to Chapter 8, on page 28 in the brewing section of this book.

a) Food grade bucket or brewing bin, with lid.

b) Syphon tubing.

c) Polythene funnel.

d) Strainer.

e) Kitchen scales.

f) Measuring jug.

g) 1 pint (½ litre) home brew beer bottles.

h) Metal caps to fit home brew beer bottles.

i) Capping tool to fasten metal caps on home brew bottles.

j) A plastic pressure barrel, if you are making cider in large quantities and look forward to drinking it regularly.

k) A wire handled bottle brush for cleaning bottles and barrels.
In addition, you will require:

a) A kitchen mincer, either manual or electric.

b) A large wooden or plastic spoon for stirring.

c) One or more 1 gallon (4½ litre) narrow-necked glass or plastic
vessels, in which first to ferment and then store the cider to mature
before bottling or barrelling. These are sold by your local
homebrew stockist.

d) Cotton wool, or air locks and *bored* cork or rubber bungs to
plug into the tops of your 1 gallon (4½ litre) narrow-necked vessels
while the cider is fermenting.

e) Cork or rubber bungs to seal the tops of your 1 gallon (4½ litre)
narrow-necked vessels while the cider is maturing.

If you have access to lots of apples and wish to make your cider
entirely from pure pressed apple juice, about 20 lbs (9 kgs) of apples
is needed to make 1 gallon (4½ litres) of cider. This way, you will
have to use a fruit press. You may know someone who has one, or
you might like to buy a small purpose-made fruit press from your
local homebrew stockist. If you are an accomplished D.I.Y.
enthusiast you can make one using a car jack temporarily fitted into
a stout wooden fame.

Super cider can be made using much smaller quantities of apples,
combined with pure apple juice bought from your health food
stockist and pure honey OR granulated sugar. Full details are given
in recipes.

Cleanliness

Before use, sterilise ALL your equipment with sulphite solution
(sodium metabisulphite mixed with water, see page 32) and then
rinse away traces of the solution with warm water.

Ingredients

Commercial cider makers use a blend of cider apples to produce
the final rich, smooth, golden bottled cider.

Their secret lies in extracting and mixing juice from sweet and
bitter tasting apples. You will achieve best results by following their
example and fermenting juice from a selection of apples chosen for
their varying sweet and bitter flavours. A half sweet and half bitter
mix gives superb results. However, you can make excellent cider
using whichever types of apple are most readily available to you.
Windfalls are ideal and pears may be used successfully in place of

up to ½ the total measure of apples required for each recipe.
Perry

If you have access to large numbers of pears, you can make *perry*, a light cider-like drink, by substituting pears for the *entire* quantity of apples suggested in cider recipes in this book.

True perry is fermented from pure pressed pear juice. However, cider-perry is a gorgeous drink made from a combination of pears and apples.
Pure perry

To make pure perry, follow the Celtic cider recipe. You will need about 20 lbs (9 kgs) of pears to replace the whole quantity of apples and produce 1 gallon (4½ litres) of pure pear juice.
Cider-perry

Replace apples in each of the cider recipes except Celtic cider (see above) with an identical measure of pears. In addition use pure apple juice, bought from your health food stockist, as directed in recipes.

Prepare, ferment, mature, bottle or barrel and serve your perry in exactly the same way as cider.

22

MAKING CIDER

Fermenting cider

To ferment the natural sugar (fructose and glucose) content of pure apple juice and pure honey, and any granulated sugar (sucrose) you choose to add to your recipe in place of pure honey, use all-purpose wine yeast (saccharomyces ellipsoideus). During fermentation, wine yeast turns the natural sugar (fructose and glucose) and any granulated sugar (sucrose) into alcohol.

Forms of wine yeast

All-purpose wine yeast is available from your homebrew stockist and is marketed in dry granular form in tubs, sachets; as tablets in tubes and also as a pure, natural strain in a liquid or jelly medium in a phial.

Dried wine yeast compounds

Some dried wine yeast compounds contain tiny amounts of sugar (sucrose) and chemicals like ammonium chloride and ammonium phosphate dibasic. If you wish to make your cider completely free of sugar (sucrose) and chemicals, check the list of contents carefully before buying.

Wine yeast starter bottle

Wine yeast can be added directly to your cider ingredients, but, for an express start to fermentation, prepare a wine yeast starter bottle about 48 hours before you plan to start making your cider.

Method

a) Sterilise with sulphite solution (sodium metabisulphite mixed with water, see page 32) and *rinse* with warm water, a 1 pint (½ litre) bottle and polythene funnel.

b) Put the funnel in the mouth of your bottle and following the manufacturer's instructions, measure sufficient wine yeast to ferment 1 gallon (4½ litres) into the bottle.

c) Pour in ¾ pint (426 mls) of pure apple juice previously pressed from apples or bought from your health food stockist. You can count this ¾ pint (426 mls) of pure apple juice as part of the total quantity of apple juice required to make your cider. Cover the bottle with a 4 inch (102 mm) square of sterilised, rinsed polythene smoothed over the bottle mouth and secured around the neck with an elastic band, string or strong thread.

d) Keep the bottle in a warm place. The wine yeast multiplies in the pure apple juice and within 48 hours should be active and ready to start fermenting your cider.

Storage

After it has finished fermenting, all cider benefits from a period of storage in 1 gallon (4½ litre) narrow-necked glass or plastic vessels before being bottled or barrelled. During storage the cider flavour develops and matures and the initially rough texture rounds into a rich, velvet smoothness.

Recommended periods of storage for your cider, before bottling or barrelling and serving, are given in recipes.

Clearing

Your cider should clear naturally, during storage. Tannin in the tea and citric acid in the pure lemon juice added to recipes in this book assist your cider's clearing. However, if the cider has not cleared completely by the time you are ready to bottle or barrel it, try this trick:

For each gallon (4½ litres) of cider you wish to clear:

a) Pour or syphon ½ cup of cloudy cider into a sterilised, rinsed cup.

b) Add the white of 1 egg + 1 level tablespoon of strained, cold tea.

c) Mix ingredients thoroughly and pour back into the vessel of cloudy cider.

d) Sterilise, rinse and refit the cork or rubber bung and store cider in a cool place.

Your cider should clear within 3–5 weeks.

If you prefer, you can buy all sorts of commercial clearing compounds from your local homebrew stockist.

Still or sparkling?

Sparkling cider

Sparkling cider is simply cider matured for the length of time suggested in the recipe, which has pure honey OR granulated sugar added to it before being bottled or barrelled. A secondary fermentation of the pure honey or granulated sugar takes place in the bottle or barrel, giving the cider natural life and sparkle and providing a protective covering of carbon dioxide gas, that keeps the sparkling cider in super condition longer than still cider. Refer to page 96 and recipes for details.

Still cider

Is mature, ready-for-bottling cider which is syphoned straight into bottles without the addition of pure honey or granulated sugar. Still cider does not sparkle and because there is no protective blanket of carbon dioxide gas it is unsuitable for barrelling and will not keep in bottles for as long as sparkling cider. See page 96 and recipes for full details.

Bottles

Some home cider makers bottle their sparkling cider in screw-top lemonade or commercial cider bottles. Such bottles are not designed to withstand the comparatively high pressure of carbon dioxide gas which can develop in your home made bottled cider and may explode!

For *safety's sake* use only specially manufactured 1 pint (½ litre) home brew beer bottles and bottle caps sold by your homebrew stockist, see page 30. Flying glass from burst bottles can cause serious physical injury – DO NOT TAKE RISKS.

This warning ALSO applies to your home made still cider. A chance secondary fermentation of any residual natural sugar (fructose and glucose) or granulated sugar (sucrose) in still cider stored in an unsuitable bottle could cause the bottle to *explode*.

Use home brew beer bottles for your sparkling AND still cider.

Plastic pressure barrels

May be used for storing and dispensing sparkling cider in the same way they are used for beer, see page 29.

Bottling or barrelling

Whether you have decided to bottle or barrel your cider, begin your bottling or barrelling this way:

1. *Sterilise and rinse:*
a) Syphon tubing
b) Plastic (food grade) bucket or brewing bin and lid.
c) Polythene funnel
2. Place your 1 gallon (4½ litre) narrow-necked vessel of clear, mature cider on a surface at a higher level than the bucket or brewing bin. Put one end of the syphon tubing in the cider so it rests just above the sediment. Suck some cider into the tube and place the open end in your bucket or brewing bin. Cider will flow from the vessel into your bucket or brewing bin. When only sediment remains in the vessel; cover the bucket or brewing bin and wash out, sterilise and rinse your 1 gallon (4½ litre) narrow-necked vessel. Store it away, ready for your next cider making session.

Bottling still cider

To bottle still cider scoop the cider from your bucket or brewing bin in a sterilised, rinsed jug, mug or cup and pour through the polythene funnel into sterilised, rinsed home brew beer bottles. Fill each bottle to within 1 inch (25 mm) of the top of the bottle. Then fasten a sterilised, rinsed metal cap with your capping tool, see page 40. When bottling *still cider only*, you may choose to use sterilised, rinsed reusable plastic caps.

Putting sparkle into cider

For each gallon (4½ litres) of cider you wish to make sparkle:
a) Take two or three cupfuls of cider from your bucket or brewing bin and pour into a sterilised, rinsed saucepan.
b) Heat the cider in your saucepan until simmering; then dissolve 2 level tablespoons of pure honey OR 1½ level tablespoons of granulated sugar. Cover and allow to cool.
WARNING – Never exceed the recommended measure of pure honey or granulated sugar, or your bottles may explode!
c) *When cool*, pour the sweetened cider from the saucepan into your bucket or brewing bin of cider. Stir vigorously. Cover and leave for about 10 minutes to blend and mix thoroughly.

Bottling sparkling cider

Fill your home brew beer bottles with sparkling cider in exactly the same way as you would still cider, see above. You should secure *metal caps only* on bottles of sparkling cider. To do this you will need a capping tool, see page 30. Re-usable plastic caps are often blown off by the force of carbon dioxide gas in sparkling cider and cannot be recommended.

Barrelling sparkling cider

Fill your plastic pressure barrel to its shoulder with sparkling cider, allowing 2–3 inches (51–76 mm) air space between its cap and the surface of your cider. Screw the cap on tightly.

Development in bottles or barrel

Your still and sparkling cider continues to develop and mature for several weeks after being bottled or barrelled. The recipes suggest when your cider should be ready to serve.

Serving cider

Cider tastes best if chilled in your fridge or a bowl of cold water, before being served.

Chilled sparkling or still cider complements salads, fish and white meat dishes and goes well with the traditional countryman's lunch of crusty wholemeal bread, cheese and pickles.

Sweetening cider

To sweeten one pint (½ litre) of cider, vigorously stir and dissolve one heaped tablespoon of pure honey OR one level tablespoon of caster sugar in the poured cider immediately before serving. Of course, you may vary the amount of pure honey or caster sugar to suit your taste, or the preference of guests.

23

CIDER VINEGAR FOR HEALTH AND FITNESS

Cider vinegar is becoming increasingly popular with health conscious people. It enhances nourishing, gourmet whole food meals AND is a marvellous aid to slim, trim healthiness.

For good health

There is considerable evidence to suggest that 2 level teaspoons (10 mls) of cider vinegar, mixed with 1 level teaspoon of pure honey in a glass of cold or warm water, taken three times a day after meals, will help slimmers to achieve their target weight and greatly benefit people suffering from arthritis, asthma, insomnia and rheumatism. It is also an excellent guard against the common cold.

For cooking

Many cordon bleu chefs use cider vinegar in preference to wine or malt vinegar. When you prepare a meal from organically raised, natural whole foods you will find the quality of most dishes improved by the addition of some cider vinegar. It also gives extra appeal to gravies, sauces, salad dressings and makes superb chutney and pickle.

Make your own

You may convert to vinegar any clear, mature cider which is ready for bottling. Simply follow these instructions:

a) Decide how much cider vinegar you wish to make and then dilute each pint ($\frac{1}{2}$ litre) of mature cider with $\frac{1}{4}$ pint (142 mls) of cold water and add $\frac{1}{2}$ pint (284 mls) of commercial cider vinegar.

b) Half fill sterilised, rinsed bottles or a large narrow-necked vessel with the mixture and plug the top with cotton wool.

c) Keep it in a warm place for about eight weeks. During this time the cider vinegar will cloud and a skin form on its surface. When transformation to vinegar is complete the cider vinegar clears.

d) When clear and bright, syphon the cider vinegar off its sediment into clean, sterilised bottles to within 2¼ inches (57 mm) of the top of each bottle. Lightly stopper the bottles with sterilised, rinsed cork or plastic stoppers, or plug with cotton wool.

e) Pasteurise the cider vinegar by standing the bottles on a wooden board, thick cloth or folded newspaper placed in a large saucepan partly filled with water. Heat until hot – NOT boiling. Keep the temperature just off boiling for thirty minutes; then switch off heat and fasten sterilised, rinsed cork or plastic stoppers securely into bottles.

f) Label clearly and store for eight weeks to mature. Your cider vinegar is then ready to use.

Please remember to keep your cider vinegar well away from stocks of wine, beer and cider. The cider vinegar aroma can taint them and if any cider vinegar comes into contact with them, they too may convert to vinegar.

Clean and sterilise all equipment used.

24

CIDER SNAGS

You should encounter few snags in your cider making. Here are some snags to watch for – and the action to take to put things right.

Snag 1

The fermenting or maturing cider smells like vinegar and tastes bitter.

Action:

Your cider has been infected by the tiny vinegar fly (Drosophila Melanogaster). Your only action must be to convert fully the cider to excellent, health promoting cider vinegar, see page 98.

This snag should not occur when the fermenting or maturing cider is kept securely covered at all times.

Snag 2

The surface of the maturing cider is being slowly covered by a film of tiny white flecks of powder.

Action:

The cider has been infected by a species of wild yeast. Immediate action is necessary to prevent the alcohol being gradually turned into carbon dioxide and water.

a) Strain your cider through a sterilised, rinsed, finely-meshed sieve, piece of muslin or tights trimmed into a square with scissors. Discard the white flecks. To kill the bacteria, to each gallon (4½ litres) of infected cider; add the juice of one or two lemons OR 1 level teaspoon (5 mls) of sulphite solution (sodium metabisulphite mixed with water, see page 32) OR one crushed Campden tablet (sodium metabisulphite).

Snag 3

The cider has been matured for the period suggested in the recipe and is ready for bottling or barrelling, but tastes insipid.

Action:

Add 1 level tablespoon of strained, brewed tea and the juice of one lemon OR one orange to each gallon (4½ litres) of cider before bottling or barrelling.

Snag 4

Your cider has been matured for the period suggested in the recipe and is ready for bottling or barrelling, but tastes too sharp and acidic.

Action:

Bottle or barrel the cider as it is. You may well find the acidity is balanced naturally by the time you wish to drink it, but if not add ½ level tablespoon of caster sugar OR 1 level tablespoon of pure honey to each 1 pint (½ litre) glass or tankard before serving. Pour the cider onto the caster sugar or pure honey and stir vigorously until dissolved. Then serve. The sweetness of the sugar or pure honey smooths and rounds the taste of your cider and removes its biting edge.

25

DRINK UP THEE ZIDER

Cider recipes in this book list ingredients required to make 1 gallon (4½ litres) of cider. Allowing for sediment discarded before bottling, this quantity will fill eight 1 pint (½ litre) home brew beer bottles.

Zider zeal

If you are a zealous cider maker, or intend to become one, and wish to make your cider in larger amounts than 1 gallon (4½ litres), you can buy brewing bins and narrow-necked glass and plastic vessels designed to hold up to 5½ gallons (25 litres) of fermenting or maturing home brew, see page 28.

Never be conservative

Do not get stuck in a rut with your cider making. Be adventurous and inventive – experiment!

You can add many single natural ingredients to enrich your cider's flavour and health enhancing properties. Pop an extra in while the cider ferments for 5 days in your bucket or brewing bin.

Among additives well worth trying separately are: fresh, rinsed rose petals – 4 oz (113 gms) or 1 oz (28 gms) dried; elderflower florets – 2 oz (56 gms) or ½ oz (14 gms) dried; dandelion heads – 4 oz (113 gms) or 1 oz (28 gms) dried; fresh, chopped peaches with stones discarded – 8 oz (227 gms); pure blackcurrant juice – 5 fl oz (142 mls); pure orange juice – 5 fl oz (142 mls); pure grapefruit juice – 5 fl oz (142 mls); pure passion fruit juice – 5 fl oz (142 mls) etc., etc.

All these items are available from your health food stockist.

Are you strong?

Be strong willed and resist the temptation to quaff your "real" cider too quickly. Remember its strength. Think of the morning after the night before!

GOOD HEALTH!

COOKING WITH CIDER

Bring your cooking to life with cider. Use your home-made cider to lend ordinary food extra health-giving goodness and appetizing appeal.

Think of the many ways you can employ cider to make your favourite meals even more exciting.

Here are a few ideas to get you started.

Cider ice cream

Make this delicious sweet by mixing your favourite ice cream with an equal amount of fresh whipped cream. Pour chilled cider over the mixed ice cream and whipped cream before serving.

Lentil soup – *serves 4*
Ingredients
Cider – ½ pint (284 mls)
Soft vegetable margarine – 1 oz (28 gms)
Carrot – 1
Onion – 1
Red lentils – ¼ pint (142 mls)
Sea salt and freshly ground black pepper – to your taste
Stock (stock cube) – ½ pint (284 mls)
Method

Melt margarine in saucepan. Add lentils and thinly sliced vegetables. Cook over low heat until margarine has been absorbed. Add cider and stock; salt and pepper. Simmer until vegetables and lentils are cooked. Then rub the soup through a finely meshed sieve and serve.

Liver and onion pudding – *serves 2–3*
Ingredients
Cider – 1 pint (½ litre)

Soft vegetable margarine – ¼ lb (113 gms)
Oats – 1 lb (454 gms)
Onion – 1
Pig's liver – ½ lb (227 gms)
Sea salt and freshly ground black pepper to your taste
Method

Put oats in mixing bowl and cover with cider. While the cider is being absorbed by the oats, mince liver and onion; season with salt and pepper to your taste and then mix well with oats and margarine. Turn mixture into greased basin. Cover top with cooking foil and place in a steamer. Steam for 2 hours. Serve with potatoes and peas.

*TIP

Mixed fruit dessert

Serve your favourite fresh fruit topped with a liberal measure of chilled cider. Add ice cream as an appetizing bonus.

*TIP

Poached fruit with cider

Keep cooked fruit whole by poaching in cider. Prepare fruit of your choice and place in an oven proof dish. Add some cider and cover. Poach in moderate oven, gas no. 4 (350° F). When cooked, serve sweetened with pure honey.

*TIP

Sausages and bacon

For fuller flavour poach sausages and lean bacon in cider instead of frying.

Tripe supper dish – *serves 2–3*
Ingredients
Cider – ½ pint (284 mls)
Dry crumbs from wholemeal bread – 1 cup (finely grated)
Free range egg – 1
Clove of garlic – 1
Green pepper – 1
Pure vegetable oil – sufficient for frying
Onions – 2
Tomatoes – 1 lb (½ kg)
Tripe – 1½ lbs (680 gms)
Sea salt and freshly ground black pepper – to your taste

Method

Simmer tripe for about 45 minutes in cider. Fry finely chopped onions, garlic and green pepper until onions are lightly browned. Then add sliced tomatoes and salt and pepper to your taste. Simmer for 10 minutes. Cut tripe into 2 inch (51 mm) squares; dip tripe squares in beaten egg, and roll in breadcrumbs. Fry in vegetable oil until golden brown. Serve with the onions, green pepper and tomatoes.

27

CIDER CUPS

Summer cups

Cider cups offer you and your friends a long, refreshing and revitalizing drink on sizzling hot summer's days.

A small measure of vodka can be added to any of these recipes if you desire a strong summer party punch.

Adjust the quantity of ingredients in these recipes to suit the amount you or your guests wish to drink.

Egg flip cider cup

Traditional, nourishing and satisfying cider cup. Also an ancient and popular remedy for unexpected summer colds or influenza.

Ingredients: To make 1 pint (½ litre)

Chilled cider – 1 pint (½ litre)

Free range eggs – 2

Pure honey – 2 level tablespoons

Method

Mix all ingredients briskly until the cider is frothy. Then serve in a chilled tankard or glass.

Fruit cider cup

Delightful, thirst quenching light drink.

*Use only pure orange juice bought from your health food stockist.

Ingredients: To make 2 pints (1¼ litres)

Chilled cider – 1 pint (½ litre)

Chilled mineral water – ½ pint (284 mls)
  or chilled soda water – ½ pint (284 mls)

Chilled pure orange juice – ½ pint (284 mls)

Raspberries – ½ lb (227 gms)
  or strawberries – ½ lb (227 gms)

Lemon – 6 thin slices
Cucumber – 6 thin slices
Ice – 6 cubes
Method

Wash fruit in cold water. Remove and discard stalks and any diseased parts. Place in a bowl and crush. Add all other ingredients and mix well. Cover and leave for 20 minutes; then serve in chilled tankards or glasses. Include some fruit in each serving.

Pineapple cider cup

Cooling, invigorating beverage. Ideal for a sultry summer's day.

*Use only pure pineapple juice bought from your health food stockist.

Ingredients: To make 2 pints (1¼ litres)
Chilled cider – 1 pint (½ litre)
Chilled mineral water – ½ pint (284 mls)
    or chilled soda water – ½ pint (284 mls)
Chilled pure pineapple juice – ½ pint (284 mls)
Pure honey – 2 level tablespoons
Method

Mix all ingredients together in a bowl and serve with ice cubes in chilled tankards or glasses.

Raspberry cider cup

Beautiful, decadent and welcome summer cider cup.

Ingredients: To make 2 pints (1¼ litres)
Chilled cider – 1 pint (½ litre)
Chilled white wine – 1 pint (½ litre)
    or chilled rosé wine – 1 pint (½ litre)
Raspberries – ½ lb (227 gms)
Pure honey – 2 heaped tablespoons
Ice cream – 1 heaped tablespoon per glass
Ice cubes – 6
Method

Wash raspberries in cold water. Remove and discard stalks and any diseased parts. Place in a bowl and crush. Add all other ingredients EXCEPT ice cream. Cover bowl and leave for 20 minutes; then serve in chilled large glasses. Include some raspberries in each serving and float a heaped tablespoon of ice cream on the surface of each drink.

28

QUICK INDEX TO CIDER MAKING PRINCIPLES AND METHODS

29

CIDER RECIPES

COUNTRY CIDER
Olde English Cider

Rich, wholesome cider. Unique, delicious flavour. Full of vitamins and goodness.

Ready to drink 8 weeks after being bottled or barrelled (about 5 months after it has finished fermenting).

Alcohol content about 7% alcohol by volume (12% proof).

*Use pure apple juice bought from your health food stockist.

Ingredients: To make 1 gallon (4½ litres)
Pure apple juice – 3½ pints (2 litres)
Mixed sweet and bitter apples – 3¼ lbs (1½ kgs)
Pears – 2¼ lbs (1 kg)
Root ginger – 1 oz (28 gms)
Pure honey – 9 oz (255 gms)
   or granulated sugar – 8 oz (227 gms)
Brewed tea, strong – 1 level tablespoon
Pure lemon juice – 1 level tablespoon
Pure orange juice – 2 level tablespoons
All-purpose wine yeast starter bottle (see page 93)
   or all-purpose dried wine yeast
   or all-purpose liquid natural wine yeast
and
Water to 1 gallon (4½ litres)
Method
a) Pour the pure apple juice bought from your health food stockist into a sterilised, rinsed plastic (food grade) bucket or brewing bin. Cover.

b) Wash apples and pears in warm water. Cut out and discard diseased parts. Chop the apples and pears into chunks. Do not remove skins, cores or pips as these contain much goodness and contribute considerably to this cider's full flavour.

c) Mince apple and pear chunks with your kitchen mincer. Let the juice and minced apple and pear pulp run into your bucket or bin. Cover.

d) Bruise root ginger by crushing with a rolling pin or hammer.

e) Simmer about 2 pints (1¼ litres) of water in a saucepan and add bruised ginger. Cover and simmer gently for 15 minutes. Then add the pure honey OR granulated sugar and stir until dissolved. Cover and allow to cool. When cool, remove and discard root ginger and add liquid to apple and pear juice and pulp in bucket or bin. Cover.

f) Make tea, strain and allow to cool, or use strained cold tea from an earlier brew. Discard leaves or bag. Then add to bucket or bin. Cover.

g) Extract juice from lemon and orange and pour into bucket or bin.

h) Add the activated wine yeast from your starter bottle, or the quantity recommended by the manufacturer of the dried wine yeast, or liquid natural wine yeast.

i) Top up with cold water to the total quantity of cider you require.

j) Check you have allowed at least 2 inches (51 mm) 4 inches (102 mm) at the top of your bucket or bin for frothing and foaming.

k) Cover and keep somewhere warm for 5 days, about 18°C (64°F) is ideal.

l) Stir juice and pulp twice daily.

After 5 days

a) Strain into a sterilised, rinsed 1 gallon (4½ litre) narrow-necked glass or plastic vessel. If necessary, top up to the neck with cold water.

b) Fit a sterilised, rinsed bored cork or rubber bung and an air lock filled with water, or preferably sulphite solution (sodium metabisulphite mixed with water, see page 32) OR plug the neck with cotton wool OR cover the mouth with a 7 inch (178 mm) square of sterilised, rinsed polythene; smoothed tightly over the top of the vessel and secured around the neck with an elastic band, string or strong thread.

Keep the cider in a warm place until it has finished fermenting.

This can take from 12–17 days.

Judging when fermentation has finished

a) Air locks

If you have fitted an air lock, bubbles of carbon dioxide gas pass up through the water or sulphite solution in the air lock while your cider is fermenting. As fermentation slows the bubbles become less frequent and eventually stop altogether. This is an indication that fermentation has ceased.

b) Cotton wool or covering square of polythene

Watch the surface of your cider. When bubbling has ceased and your cider is beginning to fall clear from the top downwards, your cider has probably finished fermenting.

Checks

Pour or syphon a little cider into a glass and take a sip to see if your cider tastes dry (non-sweet). If there is no hint of sweetness; no bubbles of carbon dioxide gas and the cider is not fizzy on your tongue, it has finished fermenting.

When you are satisfied your cider has finished fermenting:

a) Sterilise and rinse your plastic (food grade) bucket or brewing bin and syphon the cider from the 1 gallon (4½ litre) narrow-necked vessel into your bucket or bin. Cover.

b) Rinse the sediment from your 1 gallon (4½ litre) vessel. Sterilise and rinse the vessel and then pour the cider from your bucket or bin back into the 1 gallon (4½ litre) vessel through a sterilised, rinsed polythene funnel.

c) Top up to the neck with cold water or cider from a previously made batch.

d) Plug the neck with a sterilised, rinsed cork or rubber bung. Occasionally, a small fermentation of residual natural sugar (fructose and glucose) or granulated sugar (sucrose) in the cider takes place and forces up the cork or rubber bung. To guard against this possibility, cover the bung with a 7 inch (178 mm) square of sterilised, rinsed polythene; smoothed tightly over the bung and secured around the vessel's neck with two elastic bands (two in case one perishes and snaps). If a small fermentation does occur, the bung rises to release the carbon dioxide gas but does not fly off, exposing your cider to possible bacterial infection. Check bungs periodically and re-fasten where necessary. Store somewhere cool to clear and mature, about 10°C (50°F) to 13°C (55°F) is ideal.

Your olde English cider should be clear and ready for bottling or barrelling (see page 95) about 3 months after it has finished fermenting and been stored to clear and mature.

After being bottled or barrelled, your olde English still or sparkling cider should be allowed a further 8 weeks to develop and condition before being served.

Olde English still cider remains in excellent condition in bottles for up to 6 months. It is not suitable for barrelling.

Olde English sparkling cider remains in excellent condition in bottles for up to 10 months. When stored in a plastic pressure barrel it should stay in good condition for about 7 months, although its quality may begin a slow decline once the first few pints have been drawn off.

Rogue's Cider

If you want to make good quality cider without fuss and bother and with only a minimum of effort then you are a rogue, and this is the very cider for you.

Ready to drink 8 weeks after being bottled or barrelled (about 5 months after it has finished fermenting).

Alcohol content about 7% alcohol by volume (12% proof).

*Use pure apple juice bought from your health food stockist.

Ingredients: To make 1 gallon (4½ litres)

Pure apple juice – 3½ pints (2 litres)

Mixed sweet and bitter apples – 2¼ lbs (1 kg)

Pure honey – 11 oz (312 gms)

   or granulated sugar – 10 oz (283 gms)

Brewed tea, strong – 1 level tablespoon

Pure lemon juice – 1 level tablespoon

All-purpose wine yeast starter bottle (see page 93)

   or all-purpose dried wine yeast

   or all-purpose liquid natural wine yeast

and

Water to 1 gallon (4½ litres)

Method

a) Pour the pure apple juice bought from your health food stockist into a sterilised, rinsed plastic (food grade) bucket or brewing bin. Cover.

b) Wash apples in warm water. Cut out and discard diseased parts. Chop the apples into chunks. Do not remove skins, cores or pips as these contain much goodness and contribute considerably to this cider's full flavour.

c) Mince apple chunks with your kitchen mincer. Let the juice and minced apple pulp run into your bucket or bin. Cover.

d) Simmer 1 pint (½ litre) of water in a saucepan and dissolve the pure honey OR granulated sugar. Cover and allow to cool. When cool, add to apple juice and pulp in bucket or bin. Cover.

e) Make tea, strain and allow to cool, or use strained cold tea from an earlier brew. Discard leaves or bag. Then add to bucket or bin. Cover.

f) Extract juice from lemon and pour into bucket or bin.

g) Add the activated wine yeast from your starter bottle, or the quantity recommended by the manufacturer of the dried wine yeast, or liquid natural wine yeast.

h) Top up with cold water to the total quantity of cider you require.

i) Check you have allowed at least 2 inches (51 mm)–4 inches (102 mm) at the top of your bucket or bin for frothing and foaming.

j) Cover and keep somewhere warm for 5 days, about 18°C (64°F) is ideal.

k) Stir juice and pulp twice daily.

After 5 days

a) Strain into a sterilised, rinsed 1 gallon (4½ litre) narrow-necked glass or plastic vessel. If necessary, top up to the neck with cold water.

b) Fit a sterilised, rinsed bored cork or rubber bung and an air lock filled with water, or preferably sulphite solution (sodium metabisulphite mixed with water, see page 32) OR plug the neck with cotton wool OR cover the mouth with a 7 inch (178 mm) square of sterilised, rinsed polythene; smoothed tightly over the top of the vessel and secured around the neck with an elastic band, string or strong thread.

Keep the cider in a warm place until it has finished fermenting. This can take from 12–17 days.

Judging when fermentation has finished

a) Air locks

If you have fitted an air lock, bubbles of carbon dioxide gas pass up through the water or sulphite solution in the air lock while your cider is fermenting. As fermentation slows the bubbles become less frequent and eventually stop altogether. This is an indication that fermentation has ceased.

b) Cotton wool or covering square of polythene

Watch the surface of your cider. When bubbling has ceased and your cider is beginning to fall clear from the top downwards, your cider has probably finished fermenting.

Checks

Pour or syphon a little cider into a glass and take a sip to see if your cider tastes dry (non-sweet). If there is no hint of sweetness; no bubbles of carbon dioxide gas and the cider is not fizzy on your tongue, it has finished fermenting.

When you are satisfied your cider has finished fermenting:

a) Sterilise and rinse your plastic (food grade) bucket or brewing bin and syphon the cider from the 1 gallon (4½ litre) narrow-necked vessel into your bucket or bin. Cover.

b) Rinse the sediment from your 1 gallon (4½ litre) vessel. Sterilise and rinse the vessel and then pour the cider from your bucket or bin back into the 1 gallon (4½ litre) vessel through a sterilised, rinsed polythene funnel.

c) Top up to the neck with cold water or cider from a previously made batch.

d) Plug the neck with a sterilised, rinsed cork or rubber bung. Occasionally, a small fermentation of residual natural sugar (fructose and glucose) or granulated sugar (sucrose) in the cider takes place and forces up the cork or rubber bung. To guard against this possibility, cover the bung with a 7 inch (178 mm) square of sterilised, rinsed polythene; smoothed tightly over the bung and secured around the vessel's neck with two elastic bands (two in case one perishes and snaps). If a small fermentation does occur, the bung rises to release the carbon dioxide gas but does not fly off, exposing your cider to possible bacterial infection. Check bungs periodically and re-fasten where necessary. Store somewhere cool to clear and mature, about 10°C (50°F) to 13°C (55°F) is ideal.

Your rogue's cider should be clear and ready for bottling or barrelling (see page 95) about 3 months after it has finished fermenting and been stored to clear and mature.

After being bottled or barrelled, your rogue's still or sparkling cider should be allowed a further 8 weeks to develop and condition before being served.

Rogue's still cider remains in excellent condition in bottles for up to 6 months. It is not suitable for barrelling.

Rogue's sparkling cider remains in excellent condition in bottles for up to 10 months. When stored in a plastic pressure barrel it should stay in good condition for about 7 months, although its quality may begin a slow decline once the first few pints have been drawn off.

Celtic Cider

Real cider, made exclusively from pure apple juice. Full of rich apple goodness. Ready to drink 8 weeks after being bottled or barrelled (about 6 months after it has finished fermenting).

Alcohol content about 7% alcohol by volume (12% proof).

Please Note

For this recipe you need access to a fruit press. If you have a large supply of apples and wish to make cider for regular consumption, you may like to buy your own press. Small fruit presses are sold by your local homebrew stockist. As a sturdy press should last your lifetime, the cost is reasonable.

To make 1 gallon (4½ litres) of 100% natural cider from pure juice pressed from apples, you require about 20 lbs (9 kgs) of mixed sweet and bitter apples. The best combination is about 10 lbs (4½ kgs) of assorted sweet apples and about 10 lbs (4½ kgs) of assorted bitter apples, but you can successfully use any selection of sweet and bitter windfalls.

Ingredients: To make 1 gallon (4½ litres)

Natural, sugar-free recipe

Mixed sweet and bitter apples – about 20 lbs (9 kgs)

Brewed tea, strong – 1 level tablespoon

Pure lemon juice – 1 level tablespoon

All-purpose wine yeast starter bottle (see page 93)

    or all-purpose dried wine yeast

    or all-purpose liquid natural wine yeast

Method

a) Wash apples in warm water. Cut out and discard diseased parts. Chop the apples into chunks. There is no need to remove skins, cores or pips.

b) Extract juice from apples with your fruit press. Let the juice run into a sterilised, rinsed plastic (food grade) bucket or brewing bin. Cover. Discard apple pulp.

c) Make tea, strain and allow to cool, or use strained cold tea from an earlier brew. Discard leaves or bag. Then add to apple juice in bucket or bin. Cover.

d) Extract juice from lemon and pour into bucket or bin.

e) Add the activated wine yeast from your starter bottle, or the quantity recommended by the manufacturer of the dried wine yeast, or liquid natural wine yeast.

f) Top up with pure pressed apple juice to the total quantity of cider you require.

g) Check you have allowed at least 2 inches (51 mm)–4 inches (102 mm) at the top of your bucket or bin for frothing and foaming.

h) Cover and keep somewhere warm for 5 days, about 18°C (64°F) is ideal.

i) Stir juice twice daily.

After 5 days

a) Strain into a sterilised, rinsed 1 gallon (4½ litre) narrow-necked glass or plastic vessel. If necessary, top up to the neck with pure apple juice pressed from apples or bought from your health food stockist.

b) Fit a sterilised, rinsed bored cork or rubber bung and an air lock filled with water, or preferably sulphite solution (sodium metabisulphite mixed with water, see page 32) OR plug the neck with cotton wool OR cover the mouth with a 7 inch (178 mm) square of sterilised, rinsed polythene; smoothed tightly over the top of the vessel and secured around the neck with an elastic band, string or strong thread.

Keep the cider in a warm place until it has finished fermenting. This can take from 12–17 days.

Judging when fermentation has finished

a) Air locks

If you have fitted an air lock, bubbles of carbon dioxide gas pass up through the water or sulphite solution in the air lock while your cider is fermenting. As fermentation slows the bubbles become less frequent and eventually stop altogether. This is an indication that fermentation has ceased.

b) Cotton wool or covering square of polythene

Watch the surface of your cider. When bubbling has ceased and your cider is beginning to fall clear from the top downwards, your cider has probably finished fermenting.

Checks

Pour or syphon a little cider into a glass and take a sip to see if your cider tastes dry (non-sweet). If there is no hint of sweetness; no bubbles of carbon dioxide gas and the cider is not fizzy on your tongue, it has finished fermenting.

When you are satisfied your cider has finished fermenting:

a) Sterilise and rinse your plastic (food grade) bucket or brewing bin and syphon the cider from the 1 gallon ($4\frac{1}{2}$ litre) narrow-necked vessel into your bucket or bin. Cover.

b) Rinse the sediment from your 1 gallon ($4\frac{1}{2}$ litre) vessel. Sterilise and rinse the vessel and then pour the cider from your bucket or bin back into the 1 gallon ($4\frac{1}{2}$ litre) vessel through a sterilised, rinsed polythene funnel.

c) Top up to the neck with cold water or cider from a previously made batch.

d) Plug the neck with a sterilised, rinsed cork or rubber bung. Occasionally, a small fermentation of residual natural sugar (fructose and glucose) or granulated sugar (sucrose) in the cider takes place and forces up the cork or rubber bung. To guard against this possibility, cover the bung with a 7 inch (178 mm) square of sterilised, rinsed polythene; smoothed tightly over the bung and secured around the vessel's neck with two elastic bands (two in case one perishes and snaps). If a small fermentation does occur, the bung rises to release the carbon dioxide gas but does not fly off, exposing your cider to possible bacterial infection. Check bungs periodically and re-fasten where necessary. Store somewhere cool to clear and mature, about 10°C (50°F) to 13°C (55°F) is ideal.

Your Celtic cider should be clear and ready for bottling or barrelling (see page 95) about 4 months after it has finished fermenting and been stored to clear and mature.

After being bottled or barrelled, your Celtic still or sparkling cider should be allowed a further 8 weeks to develop and condition before being served.

Celtic still cider remains in excellent condition in bottles for up to

6 months. It is not suitable for barrelling.

Celtic sparkling cider remains in excellent condition in bottles for up to 10 months. When stored in a plastic pressure barrel it should stay in good condition for about 7 months, although its quality may begin a slow decline once the first few pints have been drawn off.

Golden Cider

Golden, glowing drink. Easily made cider, rewarding in its excellence. Ready to drink 8 weeks after being bottled or barrelled (about 5 months after it has finished fermenting).

Alcohol content about 7% alcohol by volume (12% proof).

*Use pure apple juice bought from your health food stockist.

Ingredients: To make 1 gallon (4½ litres)

Pure apple juice – 3½ pints (2 litres)

Mixed sweet and bitter apples – 5 lbs (2¼ kgs)

Pure honey – 9 oz (255 gms)

   or granulated sugar – 8 oz (227 gms)

Brewed tea, strong – 1 level tablespoon

Pure lemon juice – 1 level tablespoon

All-purpose wine yeast starter bottle (see page 93)

   or all-purpose dried wine yeast

   or all-purpose liquid natural wine yeast

and

Water to 1 gallon (4½ litres)

Method

a) Pour the pure apple juice bought from your health food stockist into a sterilised, rinsed plastic (food grade) bucket or brewing bin. Cover.

b) Wash apples in warm water. Cut out and discard diseased parts. Chop the apples into chunks. Do not remove skins, cores or pips as these contain much goodness and contribute considerably to this cider's full flavour.

c) Mince apple chunks with your kitchen mincer. Let the juice and minced apple pulp run into your bucket or bin. Cover.

d) Simmer 1 pint (½ litre) of water in a saucepan and dissolve the pure honey OR granulated sugar. Cover and allow to cool. When cool, add to apple juice and pulp in bucket or bin. Cover.

e) Make tea, strain and allow to cool, or use strained cold tea from an earlier brew. Discard leaves or bag. Then add to bucket or bin. Cover.

f) Extract juice from lemon and pour into bucket or bin.

g) Add the activated wine yeast from your starter bottle, or the quantity recommended by the manufacturer of the dried wine yeast, or liquid natural wine yeast.

h) Top up with cold water to the total quantity of cider you require.

i) Check you have allowed at least 2 inches (51 mm)–4 inches (102 mm) at the top of your bucket or bin for frothing and foaming.

j) Cover and keep somewhere warm for 5 days, about 18°C (64°F) is ideal.

k) Stir juice and pulp twice daily.

After 5 days

a) Strain into a sterilised, rinsed 1 gallon (4½ litre) narrow-necked glass or plastic vessel. If necessary, top up to the neck with cold water.

b) Fit a sterilised, rinsed bored cork or rubber bung and an air lock filled with water, or preferably sulphite solution (sodium metabisulphite mixed with water, see page 32) OR plug the neck with cotton wool OR cover the mouth with a 7 inch (178 mm) square of sterilised, rinsed polythene; smoothed tightly over the top of the vessel and secured around the neck with an elastic band, string or strong thread.

Keep the cider in a warm place until it has finished fermenting. This can take from 12–17 days.

Judging when fermentation has finished

a) Air locks

If you have fitted an air lock, bubbles of carbon dioxide gas pass up through the water or sulphite solution in the air lock while your cider is fermenting. As fermentation slows the bubbles become less frequent and eventually stop altogether. This is an indication that fermentation has ceased.

b) Cotton wool or covering square of polythene

Watch the surface of your cider. When bubbling has ceased and your cider is beginning to fall clear from the top downwards, your cider has probably finished fermenting.

Checks

Pour or syphon a little cider into a glass and take a sip to see if your cider tastes dry (non-sweet). If there is no hint of sweetness; no bubbles of carbon dioxide gas and the cider is not fizzy on your tongue, it has finished fermenting.

When you are satisfied your cider has finished fermenting:

a) Sterilise and rinse your plastic (food grade) bucket or brewing bin and syphon the cider from the 1 gallon (4½ litre) narrow-necked vessel into your bucket or bin. Cover.

b) Rinse the sediment from your 1 gallon (4½ litre) vessel. Sterilise and rinse the vessel and then pour the cider from your bucket or bin back into the 1 gallon (4½ litre) vessel through a sterilised, rinsed polythene funnel.

c) Top up to the neck with cold water or cider from a previously made batch.

d) Plug the neck with a sterilised, rinsed cork or rubber bung. Occasionally, a small fermentation of residual natural sugar (fructose and glucose) or granulated sugar (sucrose) in the cider takes place and forces up the cork or rubber bung. To guard against this possibility, cover the bung with a 7 inch (178 mm) square of sterilised, rinsed polythene; smoothed tightly over the bung and secured around the vessel's neck with two elastic bands (two in case one perishes and snaps). If a small fermentation does occur, the bung rises to release the carbon dioxide gas but does not fly off, exposing your cider to possible bacterial infection. Check bungs periodically and re-fasten where necessary. Store somewhere cool to clear and mature, about 10°C (50°F) to 13°C (55°F) is ideal.

Your golden cider should be clear and ready for bottling or barrelling (see page 95) about 3 months after it has finished fermenting and been stored to clear and mature.

After being bottled or barrelled, your golden still or sparkling cider should be allowed a further 8 weeks to develop and condition before being served.

Golden still cider remains in excellent condition in bottles for up to 6 months. It is not suitable for barrelling.

Golden sparkling cider remains in excellent condition in bottles for up to 10 months. When stored in a plastic pressure barrel it should stay in good condition for about 7 months, although its quality may begin a slow decline once the first few pints have been drawn off.

Scrumpy

For lovers of strong, rough cider. Meant to be drunk while young and cloudy, though it will clear and mellow if left to mature for 3 months after it has finished fermenting, before being bottled or barrelled.

Ready to drink as scrumpy 5 weeks after being bottled or barrelled (about 10 weeks after it has finished fermenting).

HANGOVER WARNING

Sip scrumpy by the wine glass full. It has a true scrumpy's west country kick. You have been warned!

Alcohol content about 8% alcohol by volume (14% proof).

*Use pure apple juice bought from your health food stockist.

Ingredients: To make 1 gallon (4½ litres)

Pure apple juice – 3½ pints (2 litres)

Mixed sweet and bitter apples – 3¼ lbs (1½ kgs)

Pure honey – 1 lb (454 gms)

   or granulated sugar – 14 oz (397 gms)

Brewed tea, strong – 1 level tablespoon

Pure lemon juice – 1 level tablespoon

All-purpose wine yeast starter bottle (see page 93)

   or all-purpose dried wine yeast

   or all-purpose liquid natural wine yeast

and

Water to 1 gallon (4½ litres)

Method

a) Pour the pure apple juice bought from your health food stockist into a sterilised, rinsed plastic (food grade) bucket or brewing bin. Cover.

b) Wash apples in warm water. Cut out and discard diseased parts. Chop the apples into chunks. Do not remove skins, cores or pips as these contain much goodness and contribute considerably to this scrumpy's full flavour.

c) Mince apple chunks with your kitchen mincer. Let the juice and minced apple pulp run into your bucket or bin. Cover.

d) Simmer 1 pint (½ litre) of water in a saucepan and dissolve the pure honey OR granulated sugar. Cover and allow to cool. When cool, add to apple juice and pulp in bucket or bin. Cover.

e) Make tea, strain and allow to cool, or use strained cold tea from an earlier brew. Discard leaves or bag. Then add to bucket or bin. Cover.

f) Extract juice from lemon and pour into bucket or bin.

g) Add the activated wine yeast from your starter bottle, or the quantity recommended by the manufacturer of the dried wine yeast, or liquid natural wine yeast.

h) Top up with cold water to the total quantity of scrumpy you require.

i) Check you have allowed at least 2 inches (51 mm)–4 inches (102 mm) at the top of your bucket or bin for frothing and foaming.

j) Cover and keep somewhere warm for 5 days, about 18°C (64°F) is ideal.

k) Stir juice and pulp twice daily.

After 5 days

a) Strain into a sterilised, rinsed 1 gallon (4½ litre) narrow-necked glass or plastic vessel. If necessary, top up to the neck with cold water.

b) Fit a sterilised, rinsed bored cork or rubber bung and an air lock filled with water, or preferably sulphite solution (sodium metabisulphite mixed with water, see page 32) OR plug the neck with cotton wool OR cover the mouth with a 7 inch (178 mm) square of sterilised, rinsed polythene; smoothed tightly over the top of the vessel and secured around the neck with an elastic band, string or strong thread.

Keep the scrumpy in a warm place until it has finished fermenting. This can take from 14–19 days.

Judging when fermentation has finished

a) Air locks

If you have fitted an air lock, bubbles of carbon dioxide gas pass up through the water or sulphite solution in the air lock while your scrumpy is fermenting. As fermentation slows the bubbles become less frequent and eventually stop altogether. This is an indication that fermentation has ceased.

b) Cotton wool or covering square of polythene

Watch the surface of your scrumpy. When bubbling has ceased

and your scrumpy is beginning to fall clear from the top downwards, your scrumpy has probably finished fermenting.

Checks

Pour or syphon a little scrumpy into a glass and take a sip to see if your scrumpy tastes dry (non-sweet). If there is no hint of sweetness; no bubbles of carbon dioxide gas and the scrumpy is not fizzy on your tongue, it has finished fermenting.

When you are satisfied your scrumpy has finished fermenting:

a) Sterilise and rinse your plastic (food grade) bucket or brewing bin and syphon the scrumpy from the 1 gallon (4½ litre) narrow-necked vessel into your bucket or bin. Cover.

b) Rinse the sediment from your 1 gallon (4½ litre) vessel. Sterilise and rinse the vessel and then pour the scrumpy from your bucket or bin back into the 1 gallon (4½ litre) vessel through a sterilised, rinsed polythene funnel.

c) Top up to the neck with cold water or scrumpy from a previously made batch.

d) Plug the neck with a sterilised, rinsed cork or rubber bung. Occasionally, a small fermentation of residual natural sugar (fructose and glucose) or granulated sugar (sucrose) in the scrumpy takes place and forces up the cork or rubber bung. To guard against this possibility, cover the bung with a 7 inch (178 mm) square of sterilised, rinsed polythene; smoothed tightly over the bung and secured around the vessel's neck with two elastic bands (two in case one perishes and snaps). If a small fermentation does occur, the bung rises to release the carbon dioxide gas but does not fly off, exposing your scrumpy to possible bacterial infection. Check bungs periodically and re-fasten where necessary. Store somewhere cool to clear and mature, about 10°C (50°F) to 13°C (55°F) is ideal.

Your scrumpy is ready for bottling or barrelling (see page 95) 5 weeks after it has finished fermenting and been stored to clear and mature.

After being bottled or barrelled, your still or sparkling scrumpy should be allowed a further 5 weeks to develop and condition before being served.

Still scrumpy ought really be drunk young but remains in excellent condition in bottles for up to 7 months. It is not suitable for barrelling.

Sparkling scrumpy ought really be drunk young but remains in excellent condition in bottles for up to 12 months. When stored in a plastic pressure barrel it should stay in good condition for about 8 months, although its quality may begin a slow decline once the first few pints have been drawn off.

WINE MAKING THE NATURAL WAY

Step-by-step natural methods can produce a splendid array of country-style wines for an outlay of only pence per bottle. A wine to complement every repast can be spread evenly throughout the year using his planner; a special chapter on quick-maturing recipes can put very drinkable wine on your table in a few weeks.

These simple recipes minimise the need for special equipment. Wholesome fruits, flowers, vegetables, etc., are free for gathering or can be bought in season while prices are low. Using them as close to their original form as possible safeguards healing properties and retains valuable oils and scents while maximum flavour, vitamins and goodness are extracted. Making the craft easy to learn and fun, Ian Ball ensures your year-round supply of refreshing wines.

Many wine makers desire sugar-free recipes for enhanced health and enjoyment. Pure honey and grape juice feature as a natural alternative in all recipes

Uniform with this book

ELLIOT RIGHT WAY BOOKS
Brighton Road, Lower Kingswood, Surrey, U.K.

OUR PUBLISHING POLICY

HOW WE CHOOSE

Our policy is to consider every deserving manuscript and we can give special editorial help where an author is an authority on his subject but an inexperienced writer. We are rigorously selective in the choice of books we publish. We set the highest standards of editorial quality and accuracy. This means that a *Paperfront* is easy to understand and delightful to read. Where illustrations are necessary to convey points of detail, these are drawn up by a subject specialist artist from our panel.

HOW WE KEEP PRICES LOW

We aim for the big seller. This enables us to order enormous print runs and achieve the lowest price for you. Unfortunately, this means that you will not find in the *Paperfront* list any titles on obscure subjects of minority interest only. These could not be printed in large enough quantities to be sold for the low price at which we offer this series. We sell almost all our *Paperfronts* at the same unit price. This saves a lot of fiddling about in our clerical departments and helps us to give you world-beating value. Under this system, the longer titles are offered at a price which we believe to be unmatched by any publisher in the world.

OUR DISTRIBUTION SYSTEM

Because of the competitive price, and the rapid turnover, *Paperfronts* are possibly the most profitable line a bookseller can handle. They are stocked by the best bookshops all over the world. It may be that your bookseller has run out of stock of a particular title. If so, he can order more from us at any time—we have a fine reputation for "same day" despatch. and we supply any order, however small (even a single copy), to any bookseller who has an account with us. We prefer you to buy from your bookseller, as this reminds him of the strong underlying public demand for *Paperfronts*. Members of the public who live in remote places, or who are housebound, or whose local bookseller is unco-operative, can order direct from us by post.

FREE

If you would like an up-to-date list of all paperfront titles currently available, send a stamped self-addressed envelope to
ELLIOT RIGHT WAY BOOKS, BRIGHTON RD.,
LOWER KINGSWOOD, SURREY, U.K.